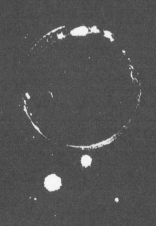

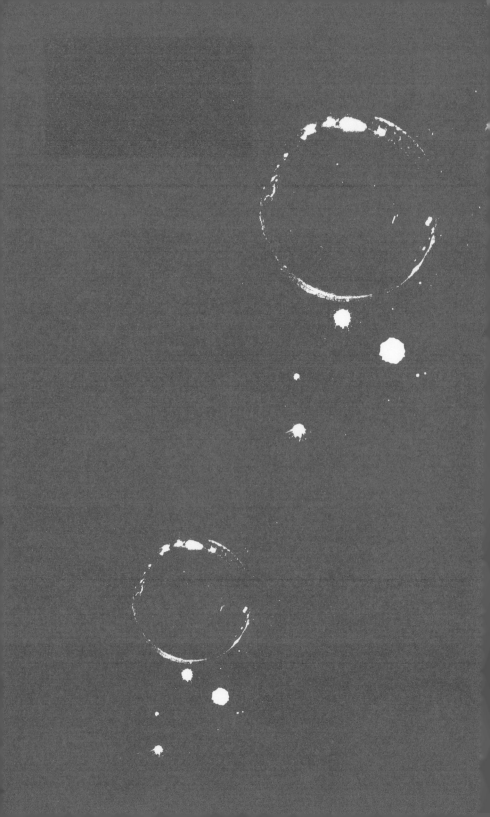

literary

activism

literary
activism

PERSPECTIVES

edited by
AMIT CHAUDHURI

OXFORD
UNIVERSITY PRESS

OXFORD
UNIVERSITY PRESS

Oxford University Press is a department of the University of Oxford.
It furthers the University's objective of excellence in research, scholarship,
and education by publishing worldwide. Oxford is a registered trademark of
Oxford University Press in the UK and in certain other countries.

Published in India by
Oxford University Press
2/11 Ground Floor, Ansari Road, Daryaganj, New Delhi 110 002, India

First Edition published in 2017
This edition published in arrangement with UEA Consulting Ltd
This edition not for sale in the United Kingdom

ISBN-13: 978-0-19-947498-1
ISBN-10: 0-19-947498-2

Printed in India by Replika Press Pvt. Ltd

On Literary Activism

From the mid-1990s onwards, we witnessed a convergence between literary language and the language of publishing, for it was publishers, increasingly, who told us about the 'masterpieces' they were publishing (the word, like the literary itself, had by then been disowned by most literature departments). We also became spectators, in the sphere of literary publishing, of a species of activity that added a fresh – and what soon became an indispensable – dimension to the publishing of novels and, indeed, how the novel would be thought of: a mode of intervention that can only be approximated by the term 'market activism'. The bolder agents and publishers abandoned the traditional forms of valuation by which novelists were estimated, published, and feted, and embraced a dramatic, frontiersman style of functioning that involved the expectation of a reward more literal than any form of cultural capital. Writers too made a pioneering contribution to this scenario. Andrew Wylie's acquisition of Salman Rushdie's novel *The Satanic Verses* and Rushdie's defection from his erstwhile agent is one example of the radical break effected by market activism. Vikram Seth interviewing a selection of London agents before finally choosing Giles Gordon to represent his novel *A Suitable Boy* is another. Then there are Martin Amis's moves to a new agent and publisher for *The Information* and the trajectory of Arundhati Roy's *The God of Small Things*, from its discovery by Pankaj Mishra (then the chief editor at HarperCollins India) to the flight taken by the agent David Godwin to India to meet Roy: all events in this landscape. Market activism was not, as many of these examples remind us, unconnected to the idea of the discovery of new literatures. Certain instances that form this narrative might have started out as straightforward acts of literary valuation (such as Mishra's excitement over Roy's novel), and then, as they developed inexorably, become full-blown instances of market activism.

Against roughly two decades of publishing, disseminating, and reading fiction and literature shaped by such exemplary actions, one might now ask about the place today of *literary* activism. What is 'literary activism'? The question has various implications, since we presently live in an epoch succeeding the financial crash of 2008, when publishing houses and bookshop chains – even the book itself – and all the other paraphernalia of market activism (some of which intersects, significantly, with the paraphernalia of the literary) are in disarray, or passing into extinction. Nevertheless, we continue to speak of the literary, and the habits of reading and writing, in the curious, inadvertent, but potent mix of urgent market-speak and superannuated literary criticism characteristic of the past two decades. No robust new critical discourse has emerged. What values, then, in the present context, is literary activism drawing our attention to, and what are its ends? Is literary activism a response both to the successes and, lately, the failures of market activism, or does it argue for a view of writing, writers, publishing, and the literary notwithstanding the market? Does it differ from market activism? For instance, how do we distinguish the journey that David Godwin made to India from the one Naveen Kishore (founder of the Calcutta-based independent publishing house Seagull, which came into its own internationally in the mid-2000s) made to Germany to acquire world rights from Suhrkamp's Petra Hardt for the works of writers including Thomas Bernhard? Godwin's entrepreneurship resulted in fanfare, and a substantial reputation – for the author and agent certainly, but also for the viability of the literary novel; Kishore acquired rights on 'trust' from some of the leading German authors of the twentieth century, and often for small sums of money.

Is literary activism similar to what was earlier known as 'championing'? If so, in what manner do the

4

writers being championed participate in the fashioning of a context for championing? (This question arises from the matter of 'trust' to which Kishore alludes.) What is literary activism's relation to the emergence of 'new literatures', and in what way is that relation reminiscent of, or divergent from, the relations created in the past in this regard by market activism?

Maybe these questions can be set against two relatively recent events that would qualify as literary activism. The first is the South African critic and academic Derek Attridge's contribution to the rise in the reputation of the South African novelist and short story writer Zoë Wicomb. Attridge's criticism has argued for a revaluation of Wicomb's writing in a way that has led to a genuine upsurge of interest in her work in the past five years; but this interest cannot be simply connected to a fresh narrative of 'new literature'. Also, Attridge's work on Wicomb is part of a project neither just for a national (in this case, South African) literature, nor a postcolonial one. Both Attridge and Wicomb are migrants who live in the United Kingdom; yet the interest in Wicomb as a result of Attridge's advocacy is not entirely reducible to an interest in the literature of migration. Wicomb, situated as she is at the crossroads of longstanding obscurity, artistic achievement, Attridge's preoccupations, South African literary history, and migrancy, reflects all these concerns in the shifting way that the 'literary' does. It's this shifting quality that, in the end, the context of literary activism in Wicomb's case foregrounds.

The second example makes it necessary for me to make an autobiographical interjection. In 2008, I proposed to Peter D. McDonald of St. Hugh's College, Oxford, that we nominate the poet, critic, and essayist Arvind Krishna Mehrotra for the post of Oxford Professor of Poetry in 2009. My reason for thinking of Mehrotra was that he defeated almost every prevalent

5

convention of what a postcolonial or Indian writer might be, and that his criticism reflected the anomalousness of his literary practice. I know that Prof. McDonald was in agreement with me in this assessment. The point of the nomination was not simply to create a comic disruption, as when Benjamin Zephaniah became a contender in 1989, and a competitor to Seamus Heaney. But neither was the point to win the elections. We intended to fashion an event; but, in retrospect, it seems that the irrelevance of winning was in some ways a feature of its conception – not because of some quietism, but because the tertiary status of winning gave us the freedom to make the maximum possible impact from revisiting, in Mehrotra, the notion of the cosmopolitan writer. So there may well be in literary activism a strangeness that echoes the strangeness of the literary. Unlike market activism, whose effect on us depends on a certain *randomness* which reflects the randomness of the free market, literary activism may be desultory, in that its aims and value aren't immediately explicable.

Amit Chaudhuri
Novelist and Professor of Contemporary Literature,
University of East Anglia

A Brief Background to the Symposium,
and Some Acknowledgements

Something unprecedented happened to the teaching of creative writing at the University of East Anglia (UEA) in 2013. It extended itself beyond the location with which it had been identified with for forty years – Norwich – and took on an abbreviated but periodic incarnation in Calcutta. The idea that this might be something worth pursuing wasn't mine; it was my colleague Jon Cook's. But once I agreed to take on the responsibility of leading the India workshop, I decided to design and experiment with the form. It was, after all, a plunge into the unknown. No British university, let alone UEA, had gone down this route before in India. If they'd done so in another country, I was unaware of it. One thing was clear to me from the start: the workshop should be an international one, open to applicants from anywhere. Since Calcutta, for decades in industrial decline, was one of the great cities of modernity, it seemed right that we should begin by allowing the city to redefine what an 'international workshop' might be. As it happens, each intensive eight-day workshop (there are two a year) in fiction and sometimes non-fiction has brought successful applicants from various parts of India and of the world to Calcutta. Unlike writers' retreats, which annul everything besides the immediate environment, and provide a kind of oasis for creative practice, these workshops are situated in the centre of the city, and it's part of the experiment they represent that they should be, on some level, in conversation with it.

Let me be frank here. I'm not an advocate of – or evangelist for – creative writing pedagogy. Nor am I one of its products. As with all pedagogies, though, you learn a great deal as you teach, or (in workshop parlance) lead. It's astonishing to follow the evolution of students' writing, whether it's over six months or eight days. One is also reminded that, especially today – when the radical, unstable metamorphoses that both writing and publishing have undergone have basically left them

9

unrecognizable – it's essential that writers do not stop thinking about what they are and do. This is beholden upon academics and professional thinkers too: that they do not allow themselves to be wholly demarcated by the conventional and disciplinary parameters of scholarship and enquiry.

The idea for the symposium arose around the same time as the establishment of the India workshop – and from several associated impulses and unsettlements: first, that it's no longer enough for writers simply to devote themselves to 'creative' practice and to teach or study creative writing and have nothing to do with the conceptual underpinnings of their writing and their lives, any more than it is for academics in literature departments simply to produce monographs and shut out the problem of *writing* itself. Second, there's been a feeling among many that there's an urgent need for a conversation, and a forum, that goes beyond what you hear or encounter either at a literary festival or an academic conference. To achieve this one has to, on the one hand, eschew celebrity and book signings in favour of dialogue and response; on the other hand, steer clear of the closed professionalism of the conference and open out the conversation to people from a variety of disciplinary backgrounds who have a stake in the discussion.

In April 2014, I wrote the mission statement on 'literary activism' that appears at the beginning of this volume and sent it out to people who might, I felt, have something valuable to say, given the attempts they'd made in their own work to widen the scope of what could be talked about. I contacted academics, novelists, poets, translators, and publishers. Each one would be given an opportunity to speak on the subject in a way that they wouldn't – I invoke that interdependent dichotomy once more – at an academic conference or literary festival. Not everyone invited could come to the first symposium, held in December 2014 at Jadavpur and Presidency universities, but many did – again, from different regions of the world, like the students who attend the workshops. Some of those who couldn't travel to Calcutta in December, such as the novelists Tim Parks and Kirsty Gunn, participated in a one-day event organized in partnership with St. Hugh's College in Oxford in October 2015.

In describing the drama of invitations, I should add a brief note here on David Graham, formerly managing director of Canongate and Granta Books. I had actually invited his wife, Kirsty Gunn, to the symposium. But Kirsty, who'd only recently taught the workshop with me in Calcutta, recommended her husband with a specific aim in mind. 'He will be able to tell you the story of Canongate,' she said, 'and its alarming transition to "market activism" from "literary activism" once it acquired Yann Martel's *Life of Pi*.' As it happened, Graham told us that story (as well as other, related ones) with a different emphasis in Calcutta. He argued for what I'd called 'market activism' being a robust and indispensable enabler of the literary novel in the 1990s. For those of us gathered that day in order to critique the terms the market had set us, it was instructive to listen to his argument. Graham is the only one in this volume who makes a case for the past achievements of the market in energizing the literary.

A few other things. Given that the symposium took place in Calcutta, we were fortunate to have papers on the role of literary activism in that city's historic past. The second event, in October 2015, led later to an email exchange among some of us who'd been present there. These emails are of interest, I think: I've included them in Appendix I and am grateful to the participants in that exchange for giving me permission to do so. Two short pieces emerged as a result of discussions that took place in that Oxford event, both of them by Tim Parks, and both written by him for his *NYRB* blog. These have gone into Appendices II and III. In December 2014, I had asked Jon Cook to give the closing address, so that we might have an overview of the proceedings. This has, in this volume, become the afterword.

One or two people with whom I'd shared the theme were misled by the word 'activism' – until they read the mission statement. They thought I meant to organize a meeting for those who undertook some form of activism through literature. They soon realized that, though this would have been an excellent idea, the symposium was going to excavate other meanings and possibilities from that word.

A final word to thank those who made the first symposium, the ongoing symposia and events – and this collection of essays – possible. There is UEA, of course, and Jon Cook; and Jadavpur and Presidency universities in Calcutta. The project has now been amplified in India with the setting up of the UEA Centre for the Creative and the Critical at Presidency University, which acted as a host to the 2016 symposium, and will host the one in 2017 in the university's bicentenary year. Other UEA colleagues should be mentioned: Peter Womack, Stephen Benson, and Claire Connors. Peter D. McDonald at St. Hugh's College, Oxford, for making the autumn 2015 event possible. Philip Langeskov and Nathan Hamilton of UEA and Boiler House Press, who have put invaluable work into this book, which has been carried forward by their energy. The team at Oxford University Press for responding to this project with enthusiasm and alacrity. The Infosys Science Foundation for funding Derek Attridge's keynote talk and supporting ongoing symposia. The *New York Review of Books* for generously giving us permission to reprint the two blog pieces by Tim Parks. The British Council and Seagull Books. *Open Letter* for generously giving us permission to reprint Dubravka Ugrešić's essay, which first appeared, in slightly different

12

form, in Europe in *Sepia*. Finally, I'd like to thank all the participants in the discussion and the contributors to this volume.

AC   15.9.2016

Translation as Literary Activism:
On Invisibility and Exposure, Arun Kolatkar
and the Little Magazine 'Conspiracy'
LAETITIA ZECCHINI

I would like to evoke the extraordinary work, life, and career of the bilingual English-Marathi poet Arun Kolatkar (1931-2004) and of his generation of poets, writers, publishers, and artists who started producing their work in the 1950s and 1960s, mostly in Bombay, and which I designate here as the little magazine 'conspiracy'.[1] This conspiracy raises important questions about the ways in which literature finds its readers and travels, is valuated, publicized, and mediated; on how writers themselves are perhaps the best literary activists of each other's work; and on the contradictions in which many writers – especially postcolonial writers who are supposed to aim at breaking into 'World Lit' or at being 'consecrated' by the centre – find themselves. This discussion may also highlight a certain tension between the extreme visibility required of writers-performers and writers-as-communicators today, and the anonymity where poetry – perhaps more than the novel, which has become the marketable flagship genre of world literature – can sustain itself.

Kolatkar and the little magazine 'conspiracy' of which he was part reveal that chance encounters, a craft that is patiently honed, and resolutely anti-commercial, underground creativity can still lie at the heart of literature and of its discovery and valuation. They also show that eccentricity or marginality is not just a predicament of literary production. These can become conditions of creativity, and even worldliness when minority is articulated 'across and alongside communities of difference', in acts of affiliation and activism that transcend boundaries of space, time, and language.[2]

Arun Kolatkar chose, in a sense, to remain a 'missing person', shunning publishers and publicity, disappearing completely behind – and in the interest of – the poems he wrote, to the point that the publication and thereby also the sale and appreciation of his work did not seem to be important to him.[3] Like other poets of this generation, he was also an extraordinary translator, especially of the Marathi devotional *bhakti* repertoire, and of poet-composers such as Tukaram, Janabai, or Namdev, whom he said he found fantastic and wanted other people to know about. It is this connection between the desire to give voice to others or not dissociate one's own words from the words of other writers, and the cultivation of a certain invisibility that I would like to explore here, bearing in mind that, as A.K. Ramanujan suggested, drawing on Bakhtin, 'without the other, there is no language for the self'.[4] Literary activism, and translation *as* literary activism, may be understood along these lines. That is also what prompted me to work on Kolatkar and translate him into French. It seemed imperative to make visible and audible this poetry, not as a specimen of a literature that was identifiably 'Indian', but simply as *fantastic* world poetry, far less spectacularly different than Indian literatures are often made out to be outside India: a voice of the other which is also a voice for the self.

Arun Kolatkar studied fine arts in Bombay, then turned unapologetically to commercial art to become an advertising legend. 'I'm god's gift to advertising' is a line that appears in his mock-picaresque poem 'today i feel i do not belong'. He worked as a graphic artist, visualizer, and art and creative director for different agencies, including MCM (Mass Communication and Marketing), the company that is said to have revolutionized Indian advertising during the 1960s. MCM was set up by Kersy Katrak, creative maverick, close friend, and fellow poet of Kolatkar, who is described by Katrak as 'a one-man agency' suffering from an 'acute case of awarditis'. Kolatkar was obviously acutely aware of the importance of visuals and visibility, of profit-making and image-making, and of the whole *business* of selling and promoting goods, including books.

And yet, in spite of a long career in advertising, Kolatkar was exceptionally wary of public attention. In his unpublished papers, he expresses horror at having to stand up in a crowd or make speeches, and recalls the sleepless nights he spent trying to think of ways of getting out of the few public situations he found himself in, 'with his speechlessness intact'. He shunned interviews, conferences, and festivals, and was invariably described as reclusive, secretive, or inscrutable by critics, journalists, and acquaintances. His absolute reluctance to stand in the spotlight was matched by a stubborn cultivation of the same elementary, and in part private, space. He hated travelling, lived the last thirty years of his life in a one-room apartment in Bombay without telephone or television, and most of the money he had earned from advertising or awards was spent on books. He was stubbornly pacing and probing the one same spot: his little corner of South Bombay around which his 2004 collection, *Kala Ghoda Poems*, revolves and where the Wayside Inn (a café he frequented most days of the week) was situated; the space of his poems and of the translations he wrote and re-wrote for years; and the space of friendship, with a tight circle of close friends, many of whom were instrumental in the writing and the publishing of his poetry.[5]

When Kolatkar died in 2004, Arvind Krishna Mehrotra called him India's best-kept literary secret and its unseen genius. Kolatkar published little; until the last year of his life, most of his poems appeared in journals, short-lived little magazines in English and Marathi, and anthologies. His work has long been very difficult to find, and a lot of it remains in boxes. 'A poet is under no obligation to stop writing just because he is buried,' warns Kolatkar in a mischievous, Pessoa-like comment: 'my

19

best is yet to come / I've laid by enough supply of writing materials / in my burial chamber / to last me an eternity.' In an unpublished version of the same text, which takes the form of a mock speech Kolatkar wrote, but never gave, for the Bank of India award he won in 1999, he adds ironically: 'i still can't get over the fact / that a bank is honouring a poet / this evening / aren't they supposed to be irreconcilable opposites / if not traditional enemies.'[6] If the poet acknowledged that he never sought a publisher or signed a publishing contract in his life, he also declined several offers from Oxford University Press and Penguin Books. But he was less averse to publishing per se than to publishing as business – that is, to mixing literature with uniform, undifferentiated mass-market considerations, and to confusing particular readers and familiar listeners with a mass audience.

If some collections did appear, it is largely thanks to his close friends, such as his publisher Ashok Shahane, who pioneered the little magazine movement in Marathi and started the small press Pras Prakashan to publish Kolatkar's first Marathi collection *Arun Kolatkarchya Kavita* in 1977, but also Arvind Krishna Mehrotra and Adil Jussawalla, who set up the independent publishing co-operative Clearing House with the poet Gieve Patel and Kolatkar. In 1976, Clearing House brought out *Jejuri*, Kolatkar's first collection in English. 'I waited twenty years to publish,' Kolatkar once declared. 'Without Clearing House, I could probably have waited for another ten or twenty years'.[7] In fact, he did not publish another collection for almost thirty years, until the last year of his life, when his friends who knew that he was dying from cancer persuaded him to do so. Probably no other modern Indian writer has benefited from the activism of fellow writers who believed unconditionally in the value of his work and continue to make sure that it is read and travels.[8]

20

Yet Kolatkar's apparent carelessness towards the publication of his poetry (some of his manuscripts were given away, lost, then rewritten), and seemingly total indifference to recognition, fame, or visibility is more ambivalent than may seem at first glance, and partly deceptive.

Again and again, in the few interviews he gave reluctantly during his lifetime, Kolatkar expressed his aversion to talking about himself or to discussing his work, suggesting that the only personal statement he knew how to make was to write a poem. As some of the following declarations reveal, there is something of Bartleby the scrivener in the poet. 'I can leave a whole lot of questions about life in a sort of suspended animation'; 'my specialty is not having opinions, to be vacuous, inane, opinion-free!'; 'I don't disagree or vehemently agree with personal reactions'; 'Indecisiveness is my nature, lots of things I can't make up my mind about, whether politics, economics or poetry'. Asked if he believed in God in the course of an interview, he gives a characteristic answer: 'Oh, I cannot say. I leave the question alone. I don't think I have to take a position about God one way or the other.' And in his unpublished papers, he writes: 'I'm sure there's a place for / need of someone like me / in any forum seminar / that a vacancy exists / for someone who refuses to make a statement.'[9]

Kolatkar undoubtedly preferred the listener-observer position of withdrawal, the wayside and oblique angle, to the position of speaker who takes centre stage, imposes a point of view, or provides definite answers. This is also perceptible in his poetry. Kolatkar writes in an anti-spectacular, anti-style idiom that stretches poetry to the limit. He also writes anti-discursive poems that do not demonstrate anything, but constantly invite us to look or watch out for the seemingly worthless and unspectacular. Things or people are never labelled or defined once and for all. The poet gives them space and time to surface from the unknown. 'I keep my ideas and attitudes in a limbo, in suspension, without firming them up, so that when I write, I feel free,' he acknowledged in a 2004 interview with Gowri Ramnarayan. Poems seemed to require that kind of suspension, both to write and to receive. And I would suggest that at the root of Kolatkar's ambivalence towards publication and publicity is his aversion to all the *middlemen* of literature, the professional publishers, critics, and academics. This may also explain why he was ferociously opposed to disclosing any kind of biographical details and never suffered notes or introductions for his collections. Nothing was to stand in the way of his poems, not even the poet. They had to speak for themselves.

And yet, in spite of his Salinger-like reputation for remaining in hiding (the expression was the poet Dilip Chitre's), Kolatkar did not hide. Anyone who wanted to talk to him could come to the Wayside Inn café in Kala Ghoda. You could in fact consider that he remained exceptionally accessible and visible throughout his life. What's more, Arun Kolatkar was certainly *not* careless about his poems. In fact, if he published so little, it's also because his poems had a huge gestation period. The poet worked on them continuously, going back to each piece again and again, not satisfied until he had been able to 'breathe life' into them, and probably seldom satisfied. In an unpublished passage from his papers, Kolatkar reflects on the practice of writing and translating, suggesting that a poem may disintegrate or come apart in your hands as soon as you start translating it, leaving you with a corpse, a dead poem. 'I like a poem / sturdy / that can take my full weight / give me / a poem i can stand on / a poem i can jump on'.[10] The publications of the two small publishing collectives in which he was involved, Pras Prakashan and Clearing House, were designed by him

22

and his friends with a stubborn attention to the minutest detail, from cover and paper to layout and typescript. Each book, especially those printed by Pras Prakashan, was worked out individually from the content itself and did not conform to standardized editorial or publishing constraints (the bindings were without titles, the text remained unjustified, the height and width of the page was calculated according to the number and length of the lines, etc.). Publishing was meant to be a craft and a collective experiment.

If the word 'conspiracy' to describe Kolatkar and friends seems appropriate, it's because poets worked collectively to form underground and dissenting enterprises. After the great pitched battles of Romanticism, 'poetry retreated underground: clandestine war, conspiracy in the catacombs', wrote Octavio Paz.[11] And in the short preface he wrote for an anthology of three poets published in 1978 by a small new publishing press modelled on Clearing House called Newground, Adil Jussawalla makes the following illuminating comments:

> The poet is the most conspiratorial of artists. No other artist is privileged to enter another person's mind so invisibly. Poems... do without publishers for years, as novels can't... Spoken or read, they require merely our confidence to receive them... It is perhaps for this reason that neither readers of poetry nor poets are unduly discouraged when the expected intermediary between them fails to materialize. I mean the publisher. 'Poetry doesn't sell'... We have heard it before and are not impressed. We simply re-strengthen the traditional link between poet and reader and listener: the direct, the conspiratorial link... The extent to which they [the poets] have relied on themselves to find their readers has gone unremarked... My intention is really to show that

23

the phenomenon of poets publishing themselves
and other poets is not a secondary feature of Indian
publishing, but the chief one. We are not and never
have been the poor cousins of big publishers. We have
been the only means by which poetry has been kept
alive while the big publishers slept... Welcome to the
conspiracy.[12]

Most of the poets who started writing during
the 1950s, 1960s, and 1970s have spoken of their hostile
anti-literary surroundings and of their fierce despair
in a culture of shortages: shortage of critical space and
recognition, shortage of critics, readers, and historians
of literature, shortage of publishers and editors.
'Nobody wants to see you', a line initially taken from a
song composed by Arun Kolatkar, was the name given
by Adil Jussawalla and Eunice de Souza to a poetry-
reading they had organized at St. Xavier's College in
the early 1970s with Kolatkar, Gieve Patel, Dilip Chitre,
and Kersy Katrak. This feeling of neglect was no doubt
heightened by the fact that many of these poets wrote
in English. In a 1972 article published in the student
periodical *The Campus Times*, Adil Jussawalla talks about
Indian writers in English as being the 'living acid' that
can eat the 'purdah' of English away; but he also likens
them to missing persons and invisible men.[13] And when
Arvind Krishna Mehrotra started writing poetry and
editing little magazines in English from Allahabad and
Bombay in the 1960s (*damn you: a magazine of the arts,
ezra: an imagist magazine*, and *fakir*), 'anything in the
colonial language was a red rag to a bull'.[14] It is crucial
here to keep in mind that although English is commonly
understood to be the language of prestige, privilege, or
'World Lit', it can also be considered to be the language
of marginality and 'outsidedness' whose practitioners
are constantly criticized in India for writing in an
'inauthentic' or alien tongue, for being illegitimate,

24

un-Indian, if not anti-national.[15] In 1977, the title 'The
Poet as an Outcast' was given to an interview with Adil
Jussawalla on the subject of Clearing House. Forty years
later, the metaphor has been updated, but the diagnosis
remains the same, and Arvind Krishna Mehrotra, with
characteristic irony, talks about Indian poets in English
as the 'LGBT community of Indian Literature'.[16]

As Raymond Williams has shown in an altogether
different context, modern writers who had broken from
mainstream institutions and inherited communities
to practise their art in the metropolis found the only
community available to them was 'a community of the
medium, of their own practices'.[17] That is precisely the
community that poets of Kolatkar's generation created
and cultivated. Ignored by mainstream publishers and
forced to practise their art in a hostile or indifferent
environment, they depended only on themselves
and on each other. As a long and frantic sequence
from Kolatkar's unpublished diary of the early 1960s
reveals, the poet was acutely aware of the logic of
competition, which is the logic of both the marketplace
and advertising, but is also the logic which governs
mainstream publishing:[18] 'COMPETITION BETWEEN
two dogs for a bitch, / two dâdâs for the title ... two artists
for a commission, / two prostitutes for customers,...
two contractors for a construction / ... Two poets for an
encore / Two taxi boys for the tip / Two undertakers for
a corpse / Two inventors for a patent / Two doctors for a
patient / ... Two banks for more clients / Two ad agencies
for an account ... Two builders for a brick / two whores
for a prick / two churches for a soul / two actors for a
role / two climbers for a peak / two showmen for a freak.'
In contrast, the dedications of some of these collections
demonstrate that poets conspicuously turned their back
on the logic of competition (which condemned them to
invisibility) to work and publish together.[19]

They created small presses and short-lived, often unpriced, cyclostyled or mimeographed little magazines where they cleared a space for themselves collectively. Putting their own resources, contacts or talents, and often their own personal money, into these publishing ventures, they became the editors, critics, anthologists, designers, and basically the promoters or activists of each other's work. In her entry for an anthology of Indian women poets, Eunice de Souza reveals the extraordinary network of solidarities that made the publication of her first collection possible. The inherited – and hostile – community in which the poet was born (a community as filiation) is replaced by a close-knit conspiracy of poets (a community as affiliation).

> Several poets co-operated in the publication of *Fix*, Eunice de Souza's first book. Newground, the co-operative started by Melanie Silgardo, Raul d' Gama Rose and Santan Rodrigues published it, Arun Kolatkar designed the cover, A. D. Hope and Adil Jussawalla provided the blurbs, and Arvind Krishna Mehrotra, Saleem Peeradina, Kersey Katrak and Jussawalla reviewed it. Several members of de Souza's community saw *Fix* as a betrayal. Some of de Souza's students told her that the book had been denounced from the pulpit at St Peter's in Bandra. Adil Jussawalla assured her that if she continued the same way, she would be denounced at St Peter's in Rome.[20]

By passing all middlemen and gatekeepers of literature, writers were also able to exert total control over the production of their books, and often worked with visual artists. The eight Clearing House collections, with their distinctly square format and extraordinary covers, all designed by Arun Kolatkar, bear witness to this impeccable design. If many little magazines of the period had a rough, handmade, sometimes handwritten

and 'DIY' appearance, some of them are also real
works of art, such as *Vrishchik*, a little magazine started
from Baroda in 1969 by the two celebrated visual artists
Gulammohammed Sheikh and Bhupen Khakhar, and in
the pages of which poets such as Adil Jussawalla, Gieve
Patel, Eunice de Souza, Arvind Krishna Mehrotra, or
Arun Kolatkar were published.

Little magazines abolished the frontiers between
'high' and 'low', art and non-art, art and the 'street',
and they expressed the art of a subculture. Explicitly
directed against dominant trends and institutions, they
also fashioned what the art critic Geeta Kapur has called
'signatures of dissent'.[21] In that sense, these poets were
not simply marginalized from the linguistic, cultural,
and publishing mainstream. They also *chose* to write
from the margin and from the 'outside', challenging the
elitism, academism, and apathy of the art and literary
worlds. 'Who were we saying *Damn you* (or Fuck you) to?
To the World at large, but perhaps more specifically, if
unconsciously to the Angrezi Hatao Hindi Mob,' writes
Mehrotra.[22] On the cover of *damn you* 5, the magazine
is described as: 'the only platform offered by a bitched-
up society from where you can really howl.' On another
cover of *damn you*, the following words are scribbled:
'despite discouragement, uneven sales, opposition,
financial catastrophes, frond, etcetera, the ezra-fakir
press continues & joins Vachel Lindsay in saying: if I
cannot beat the system, I can die protesting.' The cover
of the first issue of *Contra 66*, an art magazine edited by
artist J. Swaminathan from Delhi in 1966-67, boasted
the following quotation: 'art and liberty like the fire of
Prometheus are things that one must steal, to be used
against the established order,' and the cover of its last
issue quote the words of dissident Russian writer Yevgeny
Zamyatin: 'there can be no real literature only when it is
created not by executives and reliable civil servants but

by madmen, hermits, heretics, dreamers and sceptics.'
This signature of defiant 'outsidedness' is, as I have
shown elsewhere, a dominant feature of this literary
conspiracy.[23]

Yet it is crucial to observe that the conspiracy
was both created locally, through small publishing
ventures in Bombay (but also Baroda, Delhi, Calcutta,
Allahabad, and other Indian cities), and internationally,
since many Indian poets felt they belonged to the
international small press movement and to the counter-
culture of the times. If the little magazines served as
forums or platforms for a lot of artists to clear a space
for themselves and connect with each other across
the regional and linguistic boundaries of India, they
also served to stage, through the publication of letters,
reviews, and translations, their affiliations across time
and space, 'East' and 'West'. Indian little magazines
were exchanged with similar anti-establishment
publications in the West, especially with American little
magazines. New Directions and City Lights publications
were widely read. In *damn you* 4, the readers are asked
to 'smuggle' the journal into all the countries of the
world! In the course of a personal conversation in
Bombay, Ashok Shahane also remembered how the only
available copy of Burroughs' *Naked Lunch*, which Sham
Lal, the *Times of India* editor had in his possession, was
circulated clandestinely among Bombay writers in the
1960s. In the pages of *Vrishchik*, *damn you*, *ezra*, *Contra
66*, *Dionysus*, *Tornado*, and the many little magazines in
Hindi, Bengali, Gujarati, and other regional languages,
such as *Aso* and *Shabda* in Marathi with which Arun
Kolatkar and Ashok Shahane were deeply involved, you
find texts by Allen Ginsberg, John Cage, Apollinaire,
Hans Arp, André Breton, Octavio Paz, Howard
McCord, but also letters by American GIs protesting
the war in Vietnam, or excerpts from letters written

28

by Eric Oatman, the editor of *Manhattan Review*. The eccentricity of this little magazine Indian conspiracy was *everything but* provincial.[24] Although most of these writers were anonymous and marginalized figures, and although many are still, to a large extent, part of what Margaret Cohen and Franco Moretti after her call 'The Great Unread', these poets were *worldly* from the very start.[25] In fact, as I suggested at the beginning of this essay, their marginality also accounts for their creativity and their worldliness. It gave them the freedom to invent themselves, unburdened by many of the national conditionings and anxieties, to align themselves with other subcultures across the world and with each other. Homi Bhabha makes a similar kind of diagnosis in a conversation with Susan S. Bean about the art world in South Bombay during the 1960s and 1970s which he remembers as very small but also, precisely for that reason, as extraordinarily intense and interactive: 'I have a pet theory that one reason for such intellectual freedom and energy is that there was no art market worth speaking of. Artists didn't have to keep on claiming their authenticity, originality or marketability; they could explore what they wanted to explore.'[26]

As the cool and brash statements made by Arvind Krishna Mehrotra in the pages of his little magazines demonstrate, these poets also seemed absolutely confident on the value of their work: 'You like it or lump it.' (*ezra* 1) This spirit lives on today in Ashok Shahane. During the course of a personal conversation in Bombay, he shared his experience in dealing with American universities, when he was asked to send several copies of Kolatkar's *Kala Ghoda Poems* to the United States. Shahane was first made to fill out a ten- or fifteen-page contract. Never again, he said: 'Americans have to qualify to read Kolatkar!' – and it's certainly not Kolatkar who needs to qualify to be read by Americans.

These poets seemed to be creating a world of their own, with their own standards and audience, however limited.[27] They did not need the market or the public to know that their work was outstanding. If Kolatkar certainly bore a resemblance to the description that the New Directions founder James Laughlin drew of Pound: 'He seemed quite content if something he had written and given to some obscure magazine reached the eyes and beans of twenty-seven readers, if they were the right readers,' it's also because he had all the recognition he really cared for.[28] Literary value was bestowed to him by his close friends in Bombay, to whom he would often read out his poems, but also by a larger community and fraternity of deceased poets. The conspiracy extends beyond spatial and temporal boundaries. 'Orpheus exploded and broke up the nationalities so wide that they now include all nations, the dead and the living' is a line by Marina Tsvetaeva which Kolatkar quoted in the text 'Making Love to a Poem'. And in a moving passage from his unpublished papers, Kolatkar writes: 'All good poets when they die / go to heaven ... and from wherever they are / it may be / they are watching over me / i feel they are right here now / listening to every word i say / i feel their collective presence in the air / ... i write for their combined eye / for the collective ear / heine blake mandelstam appolinaire baudelaire vallejo catullus villon tufu kabir tukaram they're all there.'

Translation became a way for Kolatkar and for poets of his generation, so many of whom are translators of precolonial and especially devotional traditions in the vernaculars, to recreate a *collective*. In fact, the little magazines of the 1960s and 1970s were, at the same time, publishing the most modernist and contemporary texts, and their translations of *bhakti* compositions. But many poets took as much time to publish their own collections of poems as they did to publish their translations in

book form. A.K. Ramanujan began his translations
of the Kannada *vacanas* in 1952 and published them in
1973 (*Speaking of Shiva*); Dilip Chitre started translating
Tukaram in the 1960s and published *Says Tuka* in 1991;
Mehrotra started his Kabir translations in the early 1970s
and published them in 2011 (*Songs of Kabir*); Gieve Patel
started translating the seventeenth-century Gujarati
poet Akho in the late 1960s and his translations have yet
to be published. That also means that their practice of
writing their 'own' poems and of translating other poets'/
composers' texts was absolutely simultaneous, that their
words were enabled by the words of others, and that their
poetry was, to a large extent, *born in translation*.

Translation also became a means to engage in
a conversation with poets of the past, to make them
present, and given the 'culture of shortages' diagnosed by
so many Indian writers, to create literary value by placing
their own poetry in a literary genealogy which Arvind
Krishna Mehrotra likens to a 'tapestry' or an 'anthill'.[29]
Through translation, poets *choose* their neighbours in the
'heaven' where all good poets go and select the members
of their fraternity-conspiracy. Like the little magazines
and small presses, translation is meant to forge affiliations
and connections, to assert bonds of kinship, and to clear
a space, however minor or marginal, for themselves and
their predecessors – who are turned into contemporaries
by the process of translation itself. Kolatkar, who
read Tukaram, Namdeo, Dnyaneshwar, and Janabai
constantly, also knew hundreds of *abhangs* (devotional
songs) by heart, and would often say that he saw no point
in publishing his own poetry if Tukaram's remained
unpublished. 'To lose sight of another man's work is to
lose sight of one's own,' acknowledged Mehrotra.[30]

The only acceptable 'middleman', in a sense,
becomes translation. But as the translating practice of
some of these poets reveals, the distinction between 'self'

and 'other' disintegrates. Kolatkar in particular kept confusing the words of others with his own, and claimed that he wanted 'to create such confusion' that nobody could be sure about what Tukaram wrote, and what he did ('Making Love to a Poem'). He also mischievously inverses the habitual process of plagiarism, by taking up the challenge of passing off his own poems as Tukaram's: 'I'm not gonna pan off your poems as mine... I'll try to pass off mine as yours.' As a bilingual writer in English and in Marathi, Kolatkar often worked on the same poem in the two languages simultaneously. He also kept 'translating' himself from one language to the other, but revelled in covering his linguistic tracks and constantly blurred the line between what comes 'first' or 'second', between the 'original' text and its subsequent variations.

Bhakti poet-composers are reinterpreted as marginal and iconoclast figures, engaged in a countercultural movement of sorts. Bhakti seemed to appeal to the little magazine conspiracy because these poet-devotees addressed themselves directly to God and brushed aside all mediations and middlemen of the sacred (rituals, Brahmins, Scriptures, Sanskrit, etc.) and of their songs. Anyone can reach God, anyone can talk to him, anyone can become a poet, and any language is appropriate. Bhakti also represented the exteriorisation of a collective tradition. Images of bhakti are associated with acts of sharing, writes Christian Lee Novetzke, who suggests that bhakti can be translated as 'commensality'.[31] The signature line ('Says Tuka,' or 'Kabir says', for instance) that appears at the end of bhakti compositions that have been transmitted at different periods in time and by various disciples, served to federate a plurality of authors. These 'signatures of dissent' are also signatures of belonging. 'Tuka', in the contemporary translations of Indian poets, is both Tukaram and Kolatkar, and 'Kabir' is both Kabir and Mehrotra. Contemporary poets, using

32

forms that precede their poetry, *dissolve into the collective*, and into a socio-textual community whose repertoire doesn't belong to anybody and cannot be linked to a singular author or to an original Ur-text.

The anonymity cultivated by some Indian poets like Kolatkar may also be understood along those lines. 'I feel that the less of my personality comes into the poem, the better. So in that sense, doesn't one choose to be a missing person?... I am very attracted to the earlier concepts of the artist as craftsman in Hindu society ... You're anonymous and the work stays. And I really would be very happy if I saw someone reading a poem or reading it out loud in my presence; without knowing that I have written it,' Adil Jussawalla acknowledged in an interview.[32] Kolatkar also seemed to recognize himself in the figure of the craftsman and anonymous folk singer. He may even have had the secret dream of recycling his poems into common speech, like Tukaram, whose compositions have shaped Marathi language to the extent that some of his lines have been incorporated into everyday Marathi. The epigraph that opens his voluminous collection in Marathi, *Bhijki Vahi* (Mumbai: Pras Prakashan, 2003), reveals that Kolatkar might have aimed at such a dissolution, which is also an indication of dissemination: 'Let the paper dissolve, words dissolve in water. Let water be drunk by the cows, then when you milk the cows, poetry will be in it.'

By making these devotional voices in Hindi, Marathi, and other vernaculars into contemporary voices, by renewing them through the English language, through the *Zeitgeist* of the 1960s, through folk music, and through European or American writers such as William Carlos Williams, Allen Ginsberg, or André Breton, these poets also show that the possibility to 'resurrect' may be one of the defining characteristics of a work of literature. 'What distinguishes a literary work from a book that is merely entertaining or informative is the fact that the latter is meant literally to be consumed by its readers, whereas the former has the ability to come back to life. Poetry seeks not immortality but resurrection,' wrote Octavio Paz.[33] This is a wonderful definition of literature *and* of translation. More accurately still, it is a wonderful way to blur the line between both practices. Translation, which is potentially unlimited since literary texts can be translated over and over again, could be defined as the art of infinite variation, infinite resurrection, and infinite defamiliarisation. I would suggest that Kolatkar, who kept testing not only different patterns, voices, languages, angles of vision, but also different genres for everything he wrote, and whose poems had countless provisional variants, considered his poems like translations.[34] Marina Tsvetaeva's words, which Kolatkar copied in his diary, open on the following declaration: 'To create a poem means to translate from the mother tongue into another language' ('Making Love to a Poem'). And in an unpublished passage from his diary Kolatkar cites Tess Gallagher: 'poetry is the only second language I am ever likely to have.'

Poems can also be considered similar to translations because, like every literary text, they are transmutations and recreations of other poets' words. The inhabitants of Arvind Krishna Mehrotra's literary anthill 'make occasional stealing raids on their close neighbours'.[35] Namdeo transmuted in Tukaram is in turn recycled, defamiliarized, and reinvented by Kolatkar: 'Tuka has left me everything / everything he ever wrote / is mine by right ... / He certainly won't complain / he dare not / I can trace the ownership of some of his stuff / to namdeo' ('Making Love to a Poem'). The myth of the creative genius working in isolation to author and *inaugurate* an original masterpiece falls apart. Translation and/or recycling is the norm, as Kolatkar's poems, which are 'stolen / salvaged / plundered from rubbish

34

heap / junkyard / graveyard' ('Making Love to a Poem'),
demonstrate.[36] And as another wonderful passage from
Kolatkar's unpublished papers reveals, all literature
originates in a great 'food chain' of reading-translating-
recycling-(re)writing: 'i'm afraid i've been a glutton /
consumed poets of europe living and dead... / only after
they have first been eaten consumed / and regurgitated
by translators / the flourishing tribe into English... /
i've supplement my diet at various times with canned
catullus / smoked baudelaire reconstituted villon /
pickled appolinaire salted mashed mandelstam / and
cured thomas transtromer...'

A.K. Ramanujan used to say, after Valery, that
a poem is never finished, that it is only abandoned.[37]
To a certain extent, finishing a poem by committing
it to print might have been understood by Kolatkar as
putting it to death, at least provisionally, just like prizes
and awards which he compares to 'silver nails on the
poet's coffin' ('Making Love to a Poem'). Poems need
to be sung, spoken, and shared by a little conspiracy of
poets-readers-lovers. They also need to be retold and
recast, renewed and resurrected, just like *bhakti* which
relies on the 'logic of performance, not permanence'.[38]
If Kolatkar seemed reluctant to publish or publicize his
work, refused to draw attention to himself or to his poems,
did not court publishers or readers, it is also because he
knew that readers would come to him, that like Tukaram,
Namdeo, or Kabir before him, he would eventually and/
or posthumously be 'recycled' and brought back to life. In
an unpublished fragment from Kolatkar's papers, the poet
suggests that a poem is like a 'message in a bottle'. The
message is meant for anyone who may find it, on any shore,
whatever the time it takes to reach its destination. The
poem establishes a 'strange kind of dialogue... where what
you say may take a thousand years to reach me'. If a poem
is like a message in a bottle, translation helps make possible

this strange dialogue between poet and poet, or between poet and reader sometimes hundreds of kilometres, centuries and worlds apart. Poetry, its discovery and valuation then, relies on chance encounters, on the *longue durée* of genealogies, unpredictable connections and discoveries, exhumations, and resurrections.[39]

You can stumble upon a poem or a work of literature by chance, the same way that you fall in love. In my case, the impulse for translating Kolatkar was born from the conviction of having indeed stumbled upon a treasure of sorts, a 'secret' that had to be shared with as many people as possible. The discovery happened in 2004 at the Sahitya Akademi library in Delhi, as I was leafing through anthologies of modern Indian poetry. One day, I came across the poem 'The Butterfly' from Kolatkar's first (and only, at the time) collection in English, *Jejuri*. Suddenly a voice sounded right, and it was speaking to me.

Adil Jussawalla recalls that when he was studying in Oxford he tried to convince a fellow undergraduate that there was more to Indian literature than Tagore. But he failed because as the undergraduate put it: 'If there was much more, we'd have heard about it.' What you see just doesn't exist, adds Adil Jussawalla, commenting on this staggering blindness.[40] Translating Kolatkar seemed the only way to ensure that this poet – and not only Rabindranath Tagore or Salman Rushdie, as extraordinary writers as they may be – would be *seen* by the French and register on the map of world literature.

If Kolatkar is still, to a certain extent, a marginal writer in India – at least that was the case at the time of his death in 2004 – he was totally unknown in France. That Gallimard, the most prestigious French publishing house, also notorious for stealing many of the national or international awards (from the Prix Goncourt or the Prix Médicis to the Nobel Prize), agreed to publish Kolatkar in a bilingual edition seemed like a miracle. With a print run of 5,000 copies and paperbacks at an average price of eight euros, these volumes are perhaps the only poetry books that sell relatively well in France. What's more, the majority of the 250 published writers in the Gallimard poetry series are French or Francophone twentieth-century poets, and the few British or American titles represent canonical figures or fairly celebrated classics (Keats, Milton, Coleridge, Melville, Poe, Whitman, etc.).[41] It also meant that Kolatkar's work was almost overnight considered a masterpiece.[42] There are today four titles of Indian poetry published in the Poésie/Gallimard series, and apart from Kolatkar, it is telling to note that they are all related to Tagore, with two collections (including André Gide's translation of *Gitanjali*) by the Bengali poet, and a third collection of Kabir's verse translated into French from Tagore's own English recreations of Kabir.

It also seemed miraculous because as the number of Indian titles in the collection makes clear, the interest for Indian poetry in France is, to say the least, limited. Of course, Poésie/Gallimard is not the only Gallimard series in which Indian poets could be published. There is, for instance, a UNESCO/'Connaissance de l'Orient' series, with a specific Indian section, that includes the devotional compositions of Namdev and Tukaram, exquisitely rendered into French by Guy Deleury, whom Kolatkar greatly admired. What makes the publication of Kolatkar particularly significant, however, apart from the much-needed representation of a *contemporary* Indian voice is that he is not being published in a foreign, Oriental, postcolonial, or South Asian literature series, but as a poet among other poets.

And I imagine that Kolatkar would have liked that idea. For if the poetry and publishing collectives of this little magazine conspiracy represent a distrust of the marketability and publicity of literature and a form of secession from the mainstream, it's also because the 'clandestine war' to which Octavio Paz was referring is waged against ideas of Indianness, of what 'Indian literature' is, of what an Indian writer should be, or of the compact national identity he may be committed to embrace, fashion, and promote. In fact, the reactions of Kolatkar's first French readers corroborate that claim: Kolatkar did not correspond to what they had expected or fantasized Indian poetry to be.[43]

Many of these poets positioned themselves as defiant and triumphant 'traitors' to what the nativist Marathi novelist Bhalchandra Nemade has called a writer's 'filial relations' (towards a national language, a national culture, or a national literature). Against filial and national assignations, they display their staunch integrity towards their artistic practices, towards their reinvented affiliations, towards the members of their transnational conspiracy, and towards an idea of literature as inexhaustible process of translation where questions of origin, authorship, and property seem irrelevant. Against Hindutva attempts at constructing standardized, intangible, and national narratives of tradition whose ultra-sensitive frontiers have to be guarded from multiple, corrupt, or 'deviant' (mis)readings, they also claim the right to recycle, *estrange*, and rediscover both their own texts and their past through *other* languages and literatures. As Dilip Chitre, who relates *bhakti* composers to Bible translators in medieval Europe who were burned for heresy, remarks, translation is a sacrilege of sorts because it is linked to the plurality of messages, texts, and contexts, to the plurality of interpreters and interpretations.[44] This may help us to understand why writers *as* translators are increasingly targets of extreme violence in India today, and why writers *as* translators are, indeed, always activists. In the translating practice of so many of these poets, activism *on behalf of* literature and activism *through* literature become indistinguishable.

1. Here and in the following pages, I use the word 'Bombay' instead of Mumbai as the city was renamed in 1995 by the chauvinist Maharashtrian organisation, the Shiv Sena, since the little magazine 'conspiracy' which is the subject of this article coincides with the history of Bombay from the 1950s to the 1980s, and since the writers concerned still often intentionally retain the older name.

2. Homi Bhabha, *The Location of Culture* (New York: Routledge Classics, new edition, 2010), p. xxii.

3. Adil Jussawalla, *Missing Person* (Bombay: Clearing House, 1976).

4. A.K. Ramanujan, *The Collected Essays of A.K. Ramanujan*, ed. Vinay Dharwadker (Delhi: OUP, 1999), p. 26.

5. This tight circle of friends belonged to different linguistic, professional, and social worlds, which Kolatkar straddled with ease. The Marathi *bhajan* subculture was one of these worlds, to which Balwant Bua, an illiterate singer in the *varkari* tradition of *bhakti* singers, belonged. Balwant Bua and Kolatkar had weekly talking-singing sessions from which emerged several published and unpublished works.

6. The published version of 'Awards have many uses' appears in the appendices of Kolatkar's *Collected Poems in English*, ed. Arvind Krishna Mehrotra (Northumberland: Bloodaxe Books, 2010), p. 343.

7. *The Indian Literary Review*, August 1978, p. 9.

8. Amit Chaudhuri introduced a re-issue of *Jejuri* in 2005 (NYRB Classics); Ashok Shahane brought out some of Kolatkar's uncollected and unpublished texts in 2009 (*The Boatride and Other Poems*, Pras Prakashan) and keeps his Marathi and English collections in print in India; Arvind Krishna Mehrotra edited Kolatkar's *Collected Poems in English* (Bloodaxe Books, 2010).

9. These diverse statements appeared in a 1978 issue of *The Indian Literary*

39

Review, in an article from *Free Press Indore* on the Bhopal World Poetry Festival in 1989 for which the poet was interviewed, in a 2004 interview with Gowri Ramnarayan from *The Hindu*, and in an extensive and illuminating conversation with the poet Eunice de Souza. See: Eunice de Souza, *Talking Poems: Conversations with Poets* (New Delhi: Oxford University Press, 1999). A lot of the material used for this essay and all the quotations from Kolatkar's unpublished papers are taken from my book *Arun Kolatkar and Literary Modernism in India: Moving Lines* (London: Bloomsbury, 2014), which was published roughly at the time of the symposium on 'literary activism' in Calcutta.

10. A version of this text but without these particular lines is published under the title 'Making Love to a Poem' in Kolatkar, *Collected Poems in English*, pp. 345-355.

11. Octavio Paz, *The Other Voice: Essays on Modern Poetry* (New York: Harcourt Brace Jovanovitch, 1992).

12. *Three Poets, Melanie Silgardo, Raul d'Gama Rose, Santan Rodrigues* (Bombay: Newground, 1978).

13. 'Boys and Girls in Purdah', *The Campus Times*, Issue 1, Bombay, 1972.

14. Arvind Krishna Mehrotra, 'The Closing of the Bhasha Mind', *Biblio: A Review of Books*, May-June 2012, p. 27.

15. The nativist/nationalist bias against English in India is not the only bias against which Indian writers in English have to defend themselves. The romantic/modernist prejudice that no work was possible in a borrowed voice was shared by many Indian writers but also by Allen Ginsberg who, when he met the Bombay poets in 1962, asked them why they didn't write in their 'own' language (see my book on Kolatkar for more details on Ginsberg's and Orlovsky's stay in Bombay). But his declaration that Indian poets in English should go back to their language

('if we were gangster poets, we'd shoot you!') was made in response to the discovery of Nissim Ezekiel's and R. Parthasarathy's poetry (the first Indian poets in English he met when he arrived in Bombay), which he considered too established and too British, 'polite and genteel', compared to the 'starving poets in their mother tongue', or to the Bengali Hungryalists he met later in Calcutta. But had he met Arvind Krishna Mehrotra and Arun Kolatkar (he did meet Kolatkar in 1962, and both Kolatkar and Shahane were among the 'starving poets' with whom he roamed the streets of Bombay, but Kolatkar had only published a few poems in English by then), he might perhaps not have asked Indian poets why they did not write in their 'own' language.

16. Arvind Krishna Mehrotra, 'Toru Dutt and an Eurasian Poet', in ed. Rosinka Chaudhuri, *The Cambridge History of Indian Poetry in English*, (Cambridge: Cambridge University Press, 2016).

17. Raymond Williams, *The Politics of Modernism* (London/New York: Verso, 1989), p. 45.

18. Kiran Nagarkar, bilingual English-Marathi novelist and close friend of Kolatkar, with whom he worked at MCM and various other advertising agencies, remembers that MCM was notorious for breaking the rules: 'We were brash and we were shameless, we pitched for everything in sight' ('Arun Kolatkar: Some Memories', unpublished English version of an article initially published in Marathi).

19. Jayanta Mahapatra's *The False Start* (Clearing House, 1980) is dedicated to Dilip Chitre. Arvind Krishna Mehrotra's *Distance in Statute Miles* (Clearing House, 1982) is dedicated to Adil Jussawalla, and his next collection of poems, *Middle Earth* (1984) to Adil Jussawalla and to Arun Kolatkar; Kolatkar's last collections in English (*Sarpa Satra* and *Kala Ghoda Poems*,

2004) are also dedicated to Mehrotra and Jussawalla.

20. *Nine Indian Women Poets, An Anthology*, ed. Eunice de Souza (Delhi: Oxford University Press, 1997).

21. Geeta Kapur, 'Signatures of Dissent', *Art India Magazine*, Vol. 6, Issue 5, Mumbai, pp. 78-81.

22. Mehrotra, 'The Closing of the Bhasha Mind', *Biblio*, p. 27.

23. See 'By Way of Conclusion: The Trope of Outsidedeness and the Poet as Stranger' in Zecchini, *Arun Kolatkar and Literary Modernism in India*, pp. 196-206.

24. I use the word 'provincial' as Arvind Krishna Mehrotra does himself when he quotes Ezra Pound's famous essay *Provincialism the Enemy*. Provincialism consists of: 'a) an ignorance of the manners, customs and nature of people living outside one's own village, parish or nation; b) A desire to coerce others into uniformity', in *Partial Recall, Essays on Literature and Literary History* (Ranikhet: Permanent Black, 2012), p. 162.

25. Franco Moretti, 'Conjectures on World Literature', *New Left Review* 1, January-February 2000, pp. 54-68.

26. In Susan S. Bean, *Midnight to the Boom: Painting in India after Independence* (London: Thames & Hudson, 2013), p. 24.

27. The money for the Clearing House books was raised by pre-publication offers and by subscriptions at a discount. But the publishing co-operative never had more than 350 subscribers.

28. Quoted in Octavio Paz, *The Other Voice*, p. 124.

29. Mehrotra, *Partial Recall*, p. 152.

30. Mehrotra, *Partial Recall*, p. 157.

31. Christian Lee Novetzke, *Religion and Public Memory: A Cultural History of Saint Namdev in India* (New York: Columbia University Press, 2008), p. 19.

32. 'Before and After: An Interview with Adil Jussawalla' (with Vivek Narayanan and Sharmishta Mohanty), *Almost Island*, Monsoon 2012, pp. 29-30.

33. Paz, *The Other Voice*, p. 95.

34. *Jejuri*, for instance, exists both in English and in Marathi, but Kolatkar considered his first jottings as a script, there are musical partitions for some of the *Jejuri* poems, and the poet sung some of them on the guitar.

35. Mehrotra, *Partial Recall*, p. 153.

36. This is the case on a thematic level as well. *Kala Ghoda Poems*, for instance, is a collection filled with scrap, rubbish, and castaway objects which are transfigured into art. Kolatkar celebrates the regenerating capacity of a reality that is never definitely devitalised but can 'begin again' and breed new, unpredictable results.

37. A.K. Ramanujan, *Uncollected Poems and Prose*, ed. Molly Daniels-Ramanujan and Keith Harrison (Delhi: Oxford University Press, 2001), p. 45.

38. Novetzke, *Religion and Public Memory*, p. 245.

39. For more on the random and paradoxical circumstances by which the past is recovered and renewed, see Amit Chaudhuri's beautiful essay 'Poles of Recovery' in *Clearing a Space* (Oxford: Peter Lang, 2008), pp. 39-57.

40. Adil Jussawalla, *Maps for A Mortal Moon*, ed. Jerry Pinto (New Delhi: Aleph, 2014), p. 47.

41. The series was started in 1966 with Paul Eluard's *Capital of Pain*. The title is still one of its bestsellers, along with Apollinaire's *Alcools*, Baudelaire's *The Flowers of Evil*, Rimbaud's *Poésies*, and *The Nature of Things* by Francis Ponge.

42. If Kolatkar was published in France in a kind of vacuum, many reviews came out after the publication of the translation. And it was amazing to see the dissemination of the discourse on the poet, the ways in which words from the preface were reprinted and circulated, the agency of academics, publishers, and/ or translators in creating literary value and building a

literary reputation. Kolatkar had become, provisionally at least, one of the best, if not the best, contemporary Indian poet.

43. A.K. Ramanujan reflects on a similar experience for his translations of classical Tamil Love Poems (*The Interior Landscape*). When he first published these poems, a lot of his friends thought that this could not be Indian poetry, because it looked so different from anything they had seen, was not flamboyant or hyperbolic.

44. Dilip Chitre, 'Translation: Problems of a Paralysed Republic', *New Quest*, No. 154, 2003, pp. 45-49.

44

The Critic as Lover:
Literary Activism and the Academy
DEREK ATTRIDGE

Many years ago – in the days before email – I found myself engaged in correspondence with the postcolonial critic Benita Parry. She had visited Rutgers University, where I was teaching, and had given a paper on the fiction of J.M. Coetzee, in which I too had an interest. We had a friendly disagreement about the question of silence in Coetzee's novels: Parry argued that in representing oppressed and marginalised figures such as Friday in *Foe* or Vercueil in *Age of Iron* or K in *Life & Times of Michael K* as silent, or taciturn, or suffering from a speech impediment, Coetzee was perpetuating their oppression and marginalisation. (I am simplifying a much subtler argument, which Parry has developed in an important essay.)[1] My approach to Coetzee's fiction started from different basic principles: rather than scrutinising it for its ideological failures, I was attempting to do justice to what I saw as its remarkable achievements, registered as powerful effects upon me as a reader.

Parry summed up what she took to be my approach to Coetzee, and to literary works more generally, by saying – I'm quoting from memory – 'If I were to write a piece on your critical practice, I would call it "The Critic as Lover of the Text"'. She meant this as a gentle reproach, but I was happy to embrace the appellation.[2]

*

I start with this anecdote because I want to discuss the role of what we somewhat unfortunately call 'academic' literary studies within what Amit Chaudhuri has termed 'literary activism'. To begin with, it will be useful to distinguish between two ways of commenting on literary works in the academy, which we can call *literary criticism* and *literary scholarship*. (I leave aside

47

literary theory, which may draw on, or provide grounds for, commentary on specific works, but is in itself a philosophical discourse.) The two are not entirely separable, of course; the best examples of the former are informed by work in the latter mode, while the best examples of the latter evince skills in the former mode. But by and large one can say that the university study of literature (I'm referring to what is called 'research', not teaching) takes place today under the aegis of scholarship, at least in the Anglophone world. Such study is characterised by a preference for the empirical, the evidence-based, the data-driven, the historical, the archival; it conforms, or attempts to conform, to the 'science model' of research, which is where the bulk of funding is to be had. It is reflected as in a distorting mirror by the media frenzies occasioned by the 'discovery' of new ' facts' such as the diseases (preferably venereal) suffered by artists or – to take a recent example – the claim that the sketchy engraving on the title page of an Elizabethan study of botany is a portrait of Shakespeare. At its best, on the other hand, as dozens of examples in all periods testify, it is richly illuminating of literary history and biography.

Literary scholarship is not – at least explicitly – concerned with value (though there are some significant exceptions), whereas value is a central concern in literary criticism.[3] Such criticism involves a close engagement with works of literature *as literature*, not as historical documents, biographical evidence, or material objects. It is linked with the processes of canon-formation and the practice of reviewing. It is fundamental to the teaching of literature in schools and undergraduate literature courses, though much less evident at the level of graduate study.

For several decades, much of the literary criticism practised in the pages of academic literary journals and monographs has been carried out under the aegis of

what has been called 'the hermeneutics of suspicion'.
Critics working in this vein see their task as exposing
hidden faultlines that reveal ideological biases, showing
how literary works surreptitiously encode the ethical
and political iniquities of their time and place (or the
iniquities of the dominant classes of their time and
place), and reading 'against the grain' to counter the
explicit content and moral claims of the work.[4] Benita
Parry is an outstanding example of a critic in this mode:
to take the example of Coetzee, she argues that, although
his novels 'interrogate colonialism's discursive power',
they 'inadvertently repeat the exclusionary colonialist
gestures' they criticise.[5] Parry undertakes readings such as
this from a Marxist perspective; others read suspiciously
as advocates of the rights of women, oppressed racial
groups, non-human animals, or sexual minorities. Such
critical activity starts from the assumption that cultural
products are necessarily complicit to a greater or lesser
degree with the governing ideology of the social and
political formation within which they are produced, or,
at best, engage with it in complex ways that never achieve
complete autonomy.

I don't wish to dispute this picture of the
relationship between cultural production and the force
of ideology; artworks are separable neither from the
culture that produced them nor the one in which they
are received, and those cultures are in turn part of a set
of broader social, political, ethical, and economic forces.
Much work of this type is highly illuminating, both of the
works analysed and the context within which they were
written; it can be carried out (as in Parry's case) with great
sophistication and a clear sense of value. And it has been
a healthy antidote to easy claims about literary 'greatness',
'genius', and 'transcendence'. But one of the weaknesses
of this approach has been its tendency to relegate criticism
that tries to read *with* the grain to mere 'impressionism',

49

the product of a naïve and untheorised approach to literature. As for contemporary writing, it's often regarded as something that should be left to reviewers, the lack of historical distance rendering it less susceptible to ideological analysis. Hence Parry's characterisation of my approach: I'm not the steely, clear-eyed uncoverer of ideological bias but a 'lover of the text'.

The notion that the work of literature is something one might love has a long history, one which has been ably chronicled by Deidre Shauna Lynch in her recent book *Loving Literature: A Cultural History*. Lynch starts by asking how we reached a position in which the academic involved in literary studies finds herself caught up in a conflict between the rigorous study of literature as a mode of publicly acknowledged science and the private, intimate, affective, non-institutional relationship to literary works that we call the 'love of literature'. She tracks what she terms 'redefinitions of literary experience' from the mid-eighteenth to the mid-nineteenth century, but ends the story just as English literature emerges as a university subject.[6] This is the moment at which the tension between the two conceptions of literature becomes most marked; as Lynch notes, the campaigners for university English stressed its claims to be a serious, methodical, rigorous subject on a par with history or philology, yet in emphasising at the same time its usefulness in moral education and character-building they were appealing to a very different aspect of the activity of literary study. She continues:

> Given this dualistic setup, it is understandable
> that our pursuits of rigor or campaigns for a
> new professionalism have often been shadowed
> by expressions of nostalgia for a past ostensibly
> readier to acknowledge that the project of really
> understanding literature necessarily eludes the grasp
> of expert cultures – readier to acknowledge that

literature involves readers' hearts as well as minds, and their sensibility as well as training.[7]

In recent years these demands for rigour and professionalism have become ever stronger as universities find themselves having to justify their existence in economic terms and by measurable criteria, and the place of the more intimate dimension of literary engagement is more uncertain than ever – perhaps more so than it has been since those early decades when the subject had to be demonstrated to be worthy of legitimate university study.

In this context, and by contrast with ideological exposure and reading against the grain, I want to argue for what I would call an *affirmative* criticism, one that operates – with as much sophistication and care as any other approach – to understand, explore, respond to, and judge what is of value in works of literature. (I would rather avoid altogether the term 'criticism', with its connotations of a negative, fault-finding attitude, but no satisfactory alternative comes to mind; the word favoured in analytic philosophical circles, 'appreciation', seems to me too weak to capture the activity I am discussing.) This is a critical approach that has the potential to play an important part in academic literary activism, especially in relation to contemporary literary production, and it is this aspect that I wish to explore. It is worth quoting at some length a comment made by J.M. Coetzee in his critical collection *White Writing: On the Culture of Letters in South Africa*, which made a strong impression on me when I read it on publication in 1988:

> Our ears today are finely attuned to modes of silence... Our craft is all in reading *the other*: gaps, inverses, undersides; the veiled; the dark, the buried, the feminine; alterities.... Only part of the truth, such a reading asserts, resides in what writing says of the hitherto unsaid; for the rest, its truth lies in what it dare not say for the sake of its own safety, or in what

it does not know about itself: in its silences. It is a mode of reading which, subverting the dominant, is in peril, like all triumphant subversion, of becoming the dominant in turn. Is it a version of utopianism (or pastoralism) to look forward (or backward) to the day when the truth will be (or was) what is said, not what is not said, when we will hear (or heard) music as sound upon silence, not silence between sounds?[8]

Affirmative criticism is an engagement with the literary work which, while not ignoring the silences, pays most attention to the sounds, to what is actually being said.

A more recent comment by Coetzee shows that he is willing to use the word 'love' in talking about a powerful response to a work of art. In *The Good Story* he describes the experience of turning on the radio and hearing Bach's Goldberg Variations. He realised he was listening, in the company of unknown others, to a live performance (by Angela Hewitt, as it turned out):

> We were gathered to hear a pianist whom we knew and admired as she exposed herself to the music, and through her we were in turn exposing ourselves to it, letting it take us over. For the duration of the performance we were, so to speak, one soul, united in – I can't find a better word – love. From our communal body – and, bear it in mind, we were not all in the same physical space – there flowed a love directed through the priestly performer, bent over the keyboard, to Johann Sebastian, and beyond him to whoever or whatever directed his hand. And of course through the music we felt some sort of love flowing toward us (otherwise why would we have been there?).[9]

Two further points need to be made. The first is that the type of critical approach I have in mind can only be effective if it takes place in the context of dialogue and discussion. Reporting on one's own response to a literary work, even when doing all one can to take account of individual prejudices and predilections, is an act limited by a variety of factors to which one is unavoidably blind. The best way of overcoming this limitation is through an exchange with other readers of the same work, past and present. Reading earlier criticism helps to sharpen one's own response, and sharing that response with others will further sharpen – or perhaps correct – one's understanding, and quite possibly increase one's enjoyment, of the work in question. Being made to justify one's response to other readers is an excellent way of escaping impressionistic accounts that rely on stock reactions or irrelevant associations. No final, agreed account of the work is likely to emerge from this dialogue, but this is not something to be regretted: works continually remake themselves in new contexts. It is this continued affirmation by way of debate and adjustment that keeps literary works alive.[10]

The second point is that what I'm calling affirmative criticism isn't only a matter of celebrating literary successes; the critic shouldn't be afraid of making negative judgements where these seem appropriate (though – as I have just implied – he or she should always be ready to give serious consideration to opposing views). Such judgements, like positive judgements, are necessarily made in a particular time and place, and are not meant to be for all time; one is saying, in effect, 'For me, given my specific cultural and historical situation, this metaphor or this line or this characterisation, doesn't work – and I invite others to convince me that it does.'

*

If I may turn to the autobiographical mode, with apologies for repeated self-reference, I would like to

53

trace the route by which I came to this understanding of literary criticism: one which, in my published work, I have tried to justify both theoretically and in readings of writers I admire. In doing so, I hope to be able to specify more clearly what I take literary activism in the field of academic literary studies to be.

Growing up in South Africa during the epoch of apartheid's strongest hold on the country, I was sensitised early on to the impingement of politics on daily life, and I became aware at a young age of culture's capacity to reinforce the distortions and disparities of social and economic life for individuals and communities. I was, therefore, very open to the methods of ideological criticism. However, my training in literary studies at the University of Natal was strongly influenced by the critical practice and example of F.R. Leavis and the *Scrutiny* project, an influence that had both good and bad aspects. On the one hand, I was given a strong sense of literature's importance and encouraged to engage with literary works in detail, paying attention to form as much as to content, and I was taught that judging the quality of the works I read was a central part of literary criticism. On the other hand, the set of values to which I was trained to appeal was extremely limited and the range of works deemed valuable according to those values was worryingly narrow. There was, moreover, a suspicion of the popular that smacked of a certain elitism. And the critical procedure itself was mystified: it seemed to boil down in the end to the critic's possession of a certain type of sensitivity, without which proper judgements could not be made.

Partly as a reaction against this narrowness, I found myself drawn to the work of James Joyce – not a favourite of the Leavisites. And I wanted to celebrate Joyce, to share my enjoyment with others, and through Joyce make a claim for the value of literature. Teaching Joyce – which I began to do around 1980 – was

54

immensely satisfying, as I watched students discover for themselves the particular pleasures and insights offered by his work, and often carry this awareness over to their study of works by other authors. At about the same time as I started teaching Joyce I discovered the work of Jacques Derrida, which spoke to me directly: here was a philosopher who valued literature, seeing it as a gateway to understanding in ways to which philosophy was blind. However, Derrida's early reception in the Anglophone literary world was not consonant with this view of his work. He was seen, rather, as the inventor of something called 'deconstruction' (or sometimes 'deconstructionism', which sounded even worse), understood as the undermining of all certainties about language and the repeated demonstration that texts have hidden meanings that contradict their overt sense. In the toils of Derridean deconstruction, it was said, the critic reigned supreme, and the author was cut down to size as ignorant of his own meanings. In other words, Derrida was appropriated as a proponent of the hermeneutics of suspicion, and 'deconstructions' of literary texts along these lines filled the academic journals.

This view of Derrida involved a fundamental misconstrual. Derrida himself said at a round table in 1979: 'I love very much everything that I deconstruct in my own manner; the texts I want to read from a deconstructive point of view are texts I love, with the impulse of *identification* which is indispensable for reading.'[11] (The French word translated here as 'love' is *aimer,* which could imply a strong liking rather than a feeling with erotic overtones, but in any case the force of Derrida's approval of the works he analyses is clear. This passage came to my mind when Benita Parry categorised me as an example of the critic as 'lover'.) However, it's not hard to see why Derrida's readings of philosophical texts were misunderstood as evincing hostility towards

55

them rather than love or liking; he did, after all, show that Plato, Hegel, Saussure, Austin, and many others were not fully in control of the meanings of what they wrote – even though this analysis could be seen as a demonstration of the richness of their thought rather than of its poverty. His discussions of literary texts are quite different, however: they treat literature as an ally of deconstruction, because literary works (at least the ones Derrida valued) push thought and language to the limits of what is possible. There is something ironic about the widespread use, in the 1970s and 1980s, of Derrida's deconstructive readings of *philosophical* texts as models for the interpretation of literary works, and it was partly my dissatisfaction with this situation which led to my proposing to Derrida in 1984 a collection of his readings of *literary* works, a project which finally bore fruit in the volume I called *Acts of Literature*, published in 1992. One of the texts I wanted to include in full, since it is one of Derrida's most brilliant treatments of literature and deals with the author who was most important to me at the time, was his extended discussion of Joyce's *Ulysses*, given the English title 'Ulysses Gramophone: Hear Say Yes in Joyce'.[12]

Joyce was an extremely important author for Derrida: the young philosopher took advantage of his exchange year at Harvard University in 1956/7 to make a systematic study of *Ulysses* and *Finnegans Wake*, and often came back to Joyce later in his career when considering the importance of literature. So it is not surprising that I found my side-by-side engagements with Joyce and of Derrida enriching one another, and when I began to give conference papers and publish essays on Joyce it was with a strong Derridean slant. In other words, I wanted to demonstrate that Joyce, far from being an exhibit in a literary museum, was actually ahead of his readers in his testing of what language is capable of – and that there was much pleasure to be gained from opening ourselves to his experiments.

I'm not sure my championing of Joyce in this way can be called literary activism, however, except in a loose sense. Joyce's reputation in the United States was firmly established by this time, and although his reputation in the United Kingdom was shakier – the attacks of F.R. Leavis and his followers still resonated to some degree – he was by no means a marginal figure in need of activist support. And as post-structuralism became established as a major force in the academy, Joyce's star rose further (though this connection did him few favours outside the academy).

*

The term 'literary activism' becomes more appropriate for my critical practice in relation to a South African writer whose fiction I first encountered in 1979. When in that year a South African friend, then a student at Berkeley, lent me a book entitled *Dusklands* by one J.M. Coetzee, suggesting that I might find it interesting, I was struck by its originality and power; here was something quite unlike any South African fiction I had read. (Having grown up in South Africa, I had continued to read a certain amount of the country's literary output, though not with any idea that I might teach or write about it.) It was only later that I learned that the friend, Jonathan Crewe, in what was indisputably an example of literary activism, had been instrumental in getting the book accepted by Ravan Press, a small progressive publisher in South Africa.[13] I followed up my reading of *Dusklands* by reading *In the Heart of the Country*, which had been published in 1977, and thereafter read each of Coetzee's novels as they appeared. In 1985

57

I encouraged the Principal of Strathclyde University, where I had recently been appointed as a professor, to offer Coetzee an honorary degree; somewhat to our surprise, he accepted. (Our surprise was partly because Coetzee had very recently declined to travel to London for the award ceremony for the Booker Prize, which he won for *Life & Times of Michael K*.) Perhaps I can claim this acknowledgement of his stature as a writer as an instance of literary activism, as Coetzee was at that time only beginning to be known internationally (and since then has, of course, received a large number of honorary degrees).

The following year Coetzee published *Foe*, a novel that had an even more powerful and moving effect on me than his preceding works, and when I was invited to participate in a panel at the American Modern Language Association Convention on 'the literary canon' I decided to take it as my focus. Reflecting on this decision as the first move in what might be called a programme of literary activism with Coetzee as its object, I can see several factors leading to it. The operations of the market, together with my own personal interest in Coetzee's fiction, had brought the novel to my attention, and among the other operative factors were my South African background, a position in the academic world that led to the invitation, and the peculiar appropriateness of *Foe* for a discussion of canon-formation (since the novel revisits the originary scene of the English novel, the writing of *Robinson Crusoe*, in order to raise questions about the processes of inclusion and exclusion involved in the canon). However, it was the impact that the work had on me that most obviously led to my decision to write about it. The result was my first published essay on Coetzee, followed by a generous response from him, and a desire to continue writing about his work that led, after the publication of a number of further articles, to a monograph, published in 2004.[14] This study would not have come into being had each new book by Coetzee not stirred and impressed me with its originality, power, and remarkable use of language.

Coetzee now has as many readers as any serious novelist in the world, a Nobel Prize, and an unassailable position in the canon of English literature. It's not unusual to hear him called 'the greatest living writer of fiction in English'. Did my affirmative criticism of his work play a small part in this rise to literary fame? It's an unanswerable question, of course. However, the increasing academic attention paid to Coetzee in the 1990s by others as well as by myself, rising to a flood in the new millennium, must have had *some* effect on publishers' decisions, prize-awarding bodies, reviewers, and all the other agents in the literary marketplace.[15] When writing about Coetzee I was only dimly aware that I might be contributing to his escalating reputation; I certainly wanted to share my enthusiasm, but I also found his work fruitful in developing my own theoretical approach to literature. Indeed, the book I wrote on Coetzee started life as a combination of theoretical argument and critical analysis, a combination which proved unsustainable and eventually resulted in a division into two books. The other book, *The Singularity of Literature*, owes a great deal to Coetzee, who is referred to more than once in support of a theoretical position.[16]

*

My next venture in this vein was more self-consciously a case of literary activism. In 2007 I had a lunch date with a colleague, Kai Easton, at the School of African and Oriental Studies (SOAS) in London, and we found ourselves sharing our admiration for the fiction of the South African-Scottish writer Zoë Wicomb. In

59

1987 Wicomb, who grew up under the official racism of apartheid as a 'Coloured', had published a remarkable collection of linked stories, *You Can't Get Lost in Cape Town*. This was a considerable achievement in itself, and more so in the context of a literary establishment that was dominated by white male writers. In 2000 she published an even more remarkable work, the novel *David's Story*, a book that, for many who read South African fiction, stands among its most ambitious and accomplished literary productions. Two more novels, *Playing in the Light* (2006) and *October* (2015), and another collection of stories, *The One that Got Away* (2008), followed, and sustained the high level of her literary output. In spite of her then twenty-year record of remarkable work, Wicomb's international reputation, we agreed, was far less than it should have been. What was needed, clearly, was activism by others on her behalf. (I should mention that someone who encouraged us in this effort was Benita Parry.)

Being academics with no access to the world of marketing, we did what academics do: we planned a conference. This event took place at the University of London's SOAS in 2008, with contributions by critics and writers, and opened with a reading by Wicomb herself (something that took a good deal of persuasion on our part). It was a stimulating and rewarding two days. Emboldened by this success, we planned two more conferences: one in Stellenbosch in 2010 and one in York in 2012. These were equally successful, bringing together academics who write on questions of transnational and trans-local movements as well as more traditional literary critics and creative practitioners. As I write this, Kai and I are in the process of putting together a volume of essays, some of which started life at one of these conferences, together with photographs, an interview, and a contribution from Wicomb herself. We hope this volume will attract more readers to Wicomb's fiction, and help to correct the injustice of her relative obscurity as a writer.[17]

An opportunity to pursue the same goal by a different means arose in 2012 when I was invited to provide nominations in two categories for the first group of Windham-Campbell Prizes, administered by Yale University. These awards, created by Donald Windham in memory of Sandy M. Campbell, are presented every year in several categories, in each of which a grant of $150,000 is given to the selected writer. I was asked to nominate in two categories: a promising younger writer (I nominated Tom McCarthy) and a writer whose achievement hadn't been adequately recognised (I, of course, nominated Zoë Wicomb). Nominations are passed to a prize jury, who select five nominations in each category, and a nine-member selection committee then makes the final decisions. To my surprise, both my nominations were successful. Receiving the Windham-Campbell Prize undoubtedly boosted Wicomb's reputation, especially in the United States.

As with Coetzee, my efforts on Wicomb's behalf stem from admiration of the published work, from a belief that it is better than a great deal of writing that gets more attention and that many more readers would share in the pleasure it offers if it were better known. They are, in other words, premised squarely on a judgement of literary value. (The same, incidentally, is true of Tom McCarthy's fiction, though that has received much greater recognition.) But literary value alone is not enough to establish a literary reputation; apart from the factors I have already mentioned, there is also the question of the author's own willingness or unwillingness to be an activist on their own behalf. Coetzee, for all his famous reserve and unquestionable integrity, has always been an astute guardian and promoter of his own reputation. He has worked hard to find the right publisher, encouraged translations of his work, made careful decisions about award ceremonies (Booker, no – twice; Nobel, yes), participated in television programmes (sometimes uncomfortably) and published interviews, and has for a long time given brilliant readings of his work followed (at least in recent years) by book signings. Having been known as an extremely private person for most of his career, he has more recently shown a willingness to expose a large part of his personal life to the public: he co-operated with John Kannemeyer in the production of a large-scale biography, and made a vast quantity of archival materials – including a great deal of personal material – available at the Harry Ransom Research Center at the University of Texas in Austin. He has travelled widely to participate in events with other writers or attend conferences on his own or other writers' work.

Wicomb, by contrast, is reluctant to take part in the promotion of her writing. She doesn't use an agent to get the best out of publishers; she dislikes giving readings (though she is a superb reader of her own work); she is a reluctant interviewee. Her choice of publisher depends not on global visibility or marketing skills but on who she feels comfortable working with and whose values she endorses – hence The Feminist Press for *David's Story*, and The New Press (a not-for-profit public interest publisher) for *Playing in the Light*, *The One that Got Away*, and – although big-name publishers had shown an interest in her work after the Windham-Campbell Prize – her latest novel, *October*. Wicomb's own reluctance to go along with the market activists who hold the whip-hand in book promotion may in the end thwart the efforts of such literary activists as Kai Easton and myself.

Neel Mukherjee's enthusiastic review of *October* in the *New Statesman* (one of very few reviews, a paucity which is itself indicative) begins with one of those sentences that simultaneously offer praise and register pessimism: 'Last year the South African writer Zoë Wicomb won the inaugural Windham-Campbell Prize for fiction, along with James Salter and Tom McCarthy, leaving her $150,000 better off – and confirming her status as a major, if often overlooked, pillar of international writing.'[18] The contradiction implicit in the notion of an overlooked pillar of international writing is an interesting one; perhaps we can unpack it as meaning 'If Wicomb were given the attention she deserves she would become such a pillar, instead of what she is, an almost invisible presence on the global scene'. We have to recognise, too, that Wicomb's writing is demanding; for all its colour and verve it is replete with sly ironies and complex tones of voice that don't allow for rapid reading. As Eleanor Franzen remarks in her online review of the new novel,

> *October* is extremely thought-provoking, though on a first read, it will probably not satisfy. It is the sort of book that requires time to percolate, and perhaps needs to be read in several sittings over the course of a week. It is not long, but there is a great deal packed into it, a complexity belied by the straightforward, rational prose, pocked with 'surely', 'of course', 'must' and 'should'.[19]

All the more reason, perhaps, for academic critics to pursue literary activism to alert the reading public to the rewards of careful and repeated engagement with Wicomb's work.

*

In the past two or three years, I have started to pursue a new interest, one that also has a literary activist dimension. I have been struck by the quality of a number of recent fictional works by South African authors who write in Afrikaans – once the language of the ruling white minority, now one of the eleven official languages of the country, and the third most widely spoken as a mother tongue. (It holds this position, after isiZulu and isiXhosa, because of its several million Coloured speakers.) As with Coetzee and Wicomb (both of whom, interestingly, were the children of Afrikaans-speaking parents), it has been the impact of these writers' works on me that has spurred this academic study. There are three writers in particular who have produced a substantial body of work that, in my view, can stand comparison with any contemporary fictional oeuvre, though they are probably even less well known on the global scene than Wicomb. One is Etienne van Heerden, who has published eleven novels and many short stories. His most recent novels are *30 Nagte in Amsterdam* (2008), translated into English by Michiel Heyns as *30 Nights in Amsterdam* (2012); *In Stede van die Liefde* (2005), translated by Leon de Kock as *In Love's Place* (2013); and *Klimtol* (2013), as yet untranslated into English. Another is Ingrid Winterbach, who has published ten novels (the first five under the pen-name Lettie Viljoen), most recently *Die Benederyk* (2010), translated by de Kock as *The Road of Excess* (2014), and *Die Aanspraak van Lewende Wesens* (2012), translated by Heyns as *It Might Get Loud* (2015). The third, and the one most deserving of international attention in my view is Marlene van Niekerk, the author of three novels and several short stories, plays, and poetry collections. Her most substantial works are *Triomf* and *Agaat*, the first appearing in Afrikaans in 1994 and in an English translation by de Kock in 1999, and the latter appearing in 2004 and in Heyns's translation in 2006. Both these translations retained the original title, though a British edition of *Agaat* was published in 2007 as *The Way of the Women*.

With these writers a new issue in thinking about literary activism and its relation to critical practice arises, given that Afrikaans is a minor language with a very small readership and geographical spread and is therefore dependent on translation if it is to reach a global audience. In this situation, translators are among the most important of literary activists. My work has largely been focused on the English translations of this body of fiction, and my theoretical interest is in translation as the route to global dissemination. But a second aim is simply to spread the word about these fine literary achievements. It will have been evident from my short catalogue that only two translators were responsible for all the novels I have mentioned: Michiel Heyns and Leon de Kock. Both are outstanding translators, with an excellent understanding of the subtleties of Afrikaans and a good ear for what works in English (both, in fact, have published their own novels in English). The three writers I have mentioned are all themselves proficient in English, and so have been able to work closely with the translators in producing English versions of their work.[20]

I have started to publish academic essays on some of this fiction, but I am well aware that the challenge to the literary activist is especially acute when the work one is trying to promote was written in a minor language and can only achieve international attention through translation.[21] In Britain in particular, translated fiction is very little read. The organisation Literature across Frontiers launched a report at the 2015 London Book Fair on the number of translated literary works published in Britain, and showed that over the two decades up to 2012 only four per cent of the books to appear were translations.[22] If this prejudice is ever going to be overcome, literary activists will have to find ways of promoting literary value – rather than effective marketing or media fame – as the quality that determines reputation and gains readers.

To say this is not to suggest that literary value is an unproblematic concept, but it's precisely in conjunction with attentive, affirmative readings of specific literary works that debates about it can most profitably be pursued. This is a task that the university or college department of literature should be well fitted to undertake. After all, at the heart of *all* our endeavours as literary academics, whether as historians, bibliographers, hermeneuts, critics, demystifiers, or geneticists, is *the experience of the literary work*. Just as the vast edifice of sport – television channels, giant stadiums, megastores, and the rest of it – depends entirely on the intense experience of the individual spectator watching a particular game, so the almost equally vast edifice of literary education, publishing, and promotion would not exist if particular readers did not find from time to time that engaging with a novel, hearing a poem, or watching a play was a deeply felt, and highly valued, experience – an experience that it seems not inappropriate to term 'love'.

1.   Benita Parry, 'Speech and Silence in the Fictions of J.M. Coetzee', in *Writing South Africa: Literature, Apartheid, and Democracy, 1970-1995*, ed. Derek Attridge and Rosemary Jolly (Cambridge: Cambridge University Press, 1998), pp. 149-165.

2.   I should add that in spite of our differences, Benita Parry has been unfailingly generous to me over the decades in which we have known each other – the best kind of intellectual interlocutor one could imagine.

3.   An example of a study based on thorough archival work that presents important arguments about literary value is Peter D. McDonald's *The Literature Police: Apartheid Censorship and Its Cultural Consequences* (Oxford: Oxford University Press, 2009). Of course, the very act of choosing a particular work or author to whom to devote one's scholarly attention implies a value judgement.

4.   A wide-ranging critique of this approach has recently been presented by Rita Felski in *The Limits of Critique* (Chicago: University of Chicago Press, 2015).

5.   Parry, 'Speech and Silence', p. 150.

6.   Deidre Shauna Lynch, *Loving Literature: A Cultural History* (Chicago: University of Chicago Press, 2015), p. 5.

7.   Lynch, *Loving Literature*, p. 2.

8.   J.M. Coetzee, *White Writing: On the Culture of Letters in South Africa* (New Haven: Yale University Press, 1988), p. 81.

9.   Arabella Kurtz and J.M. Coetzee, *The Good Story: Exchanges on Truth, Fiction and Psychotherapy* (London: Harvill Secker, 2015), pp. 105-106.

10.   For an example of this kind of dialogue, see Derek Attridge and Henry Staten, *The Craft of Poetry: Dialogues on Minimal Interpretation*, (Abingdon: Routledge, 2015).

11.   Christie V. McDonald, ed., *The Ear of the Other: Otobiography, Transference, Translation*, trans. Peggy Kamuf (New York: Schocken Books, 1985), p. 87.

12. Jacques Derrida, *Acts of Literature*, ed. Derek Attridge (New York: Routledge, 1992), pp. 253-309.

13. The story is told in J.C. Kannemeyer, *J. M. Coetzee: A Life in Writing* (Johannesburg: Jonathan Ball, 2012), pp. 242-243, and by Crewe himself in *In the Middle of Nowhere: J. M. Coetzee in South Africa* (Lanham, MD: University Press of America, 2016), pp. 40-41.

14. The essay was 'Oppressive Silence: J.M. Coetzee's *Foe* and the Politics of the Canon', in *Decolonizing Tradition: New Views of 20th-Century 'British' Literature*, ed. Karen Lawrence (Urbana: University of Illinois Press, 1991), pp. 212-238, and the book was *J. M. Coetzee and the Ethics of Reading: Literature in the Event* (Chicago: University of Chicago Press and Pietermaritzburg: University of KwaZulu-Natal Press, 2004).

15. By 2000 there were eight volumes entirely devoted to his work, and in 1992 my colleague David Attwell's influential collection of interviews with Coetzee along with a selection of his essays, *Doubling the Point*, was published by Harvard University Press.

16. Derek Attridge, *The Singularity of Literature* (Abingdon: Routledge, 2004).

17. Kai Easton and Derek Attridge, eds, *Zoë Wicomb and the Translocal: Writing Scotland and South Africa* (London: Routledge, forthcoming).

18. Neel Mukherjee, 'Homing instinct: *October* by Zoë Wicomb', *New Statesman* 26 June, 2014, pp. 53-54.

19. Eleanor Franzen, 'October' in *Quadrapheme*, 7 May 2014, http://www. quadrapheme.com/ october-zoe-wicomb/

20. In a somewhat different position are those authors who produce two versions of their novels: one in English, one in Afrikaans. The leader in this field was André Brink, who wrote 19 of his novels in both languages, while exceptional recent examples are Dominique

Botha (*False River/Valsrivier*, 2014) and S.J. Naudé (*The Alphabet of Birds/Alfabet van die Voëls*, 2015).

21. See 'Contemporary Afrikaans Fiction in the World: The Englishing of Marlene van Niekerk', *Journal of Commonwealth Studies* 49.3 (2014), pp. 395-409, and 'Contemporary Afrikaans Fiction and English Translation: Singularity and the Question of Minor Languages', *Singularity and Transnational Poetics*, ed. Birgit M. Kaiser (London: Routledge, 2014), pp. 61-78.

22. Alexandra Büchler and Giulia Trentacosti, 'Publishing Translated Literature in the United Kingdom and Ireland 1990-2012 Statistical Report', Literature across Frontiers, 2015, http://www.lit-across-frontiers.org/wp-content/uploads/2013/03/Translation-Statistics-Study_Update_May2015.pdf. The figure for all types of book was three per cent.

'Market Activism':
A Publisher's Perspective
DAVID GRAHAM

I am a market activist. I make no apology for that – though I may apologise for some of the unintended consequences of my activity. I've worked in publishing all my adult life and, for the past fifteen years or so, have managed independent publishing companies that have – to a greater or lesser extent – been engaged in the pursuit of trying to make a business out of literary activity.

In this respect, I think, I am perhaps an outsider at this symposium. In fact, I feel a little like Michael Douglas's character Gordon Gecko in the movie *Wall Street*. And I can tell you that: 'Market Activism is Good.'

So, I am not an artist, or a writer, or an academic. I am not even a publisher or an editor – at the cultured end of the commercial transaction that exists between the artist and the market – whose role is that of supporting and nurturing creative talent. *The Guardian* newspaper once described me as (I paraphrase from memory) 'A sophisticated number-cruncher with literary nous' – a comment I still regard as something of a compliment.

I am a businessman whose business has been making literary works sell, acting as something like a midwife to literary talent: getting great books talked about, read, appreciated, and widely known so that they might go on to influence and shape our contemporary cultural landscape. Part of that remit, of course, includes making money from those books – both for the artist and, just as importantly, for the businesses that produce them, so enabling those businesses to continue to publish books of cultural and commercial value. And so the cycle continues – or at least, that's the idea.

Amit Chaudhuri's mission statement, 'On Literary Activism,' sets the terms of this debate. He describes the rise of market activism from the mid-1990s onwards, a time in which a literary agenda that used to be set by the academy or by artists themselves fell under the control of the publisher and the agent. Much of what he says is true and, while in many respects I defend this change, as I note later, one of the unintended consequences of this 'market activism' has been a significant reduction in the influence of the expert professional – by which I mean someone seriously engaged in the craft of publishing literature. In this respect, then, I would like to challenge Chaudhuri's terminology: what Amit describes as 'market activism,' I would prefer to call 'publisher activism' or, better still, 'expert activism'. After all, the market activism he describes was in the hands of people like me and my colleagues: the agents from whom we bought the books, the critics who commanded the attention of the market, and the bookseller, the critical final point of contact who brought the book to the reader's attention.

All the players in this chain were experts and their motivation, while not purely literary, was first and foremost their love of books, often deriving from a firm belief in the cultural capital held by books in modern society. Yes, revenue, status, and profits were important, but really no one but a fool would enter this industry in order just to make money – as the old joke goes: 'How do you become a publishing millionaire? Start as a billionaire.'[1] No, those who contributed to the chain of expertise were motivated by another, purer ambition: to bring the work of the originating artist to as wide a readership as possible. But things have changed. Today, I believe that our contemporary literary world is now *truly* – and almost exclusively – determined by market forces and we are all impoverished by this change.

*

When we look back, it is often hard to remember precisely how we felt at a given time. When I reflect now on that period in the late 1990s and early 2000s, it strikes me that I never really considered whether the professional

74

activity I was engaged in – what Amit calls 'market activism' – was new or, in adopted modern parlance, 'disruptive', but I know that I participated in it. I also know that – in comparison with the publishing industry as it exists today – that market activism was a positive force. Indeed, I would go further and say that, from the perspective of a professional publisher, in the early 2000s the market for interesting and challenging literature was about as good as you could hope for from what is, after all, a complex and imperfect collision between the worlds of art and commerce.[2] The diversity of the marketplace, coupled with the market activism that served it, created a much more polyphonic book culture than the one we have today. Many different voices were discovered by readers through different market channels, while different champions across publishing, media, and retail helped to get those voices heard. For me, certainly, it was an exciting time and one that I still truly believe made a positive impact on capital, both cultural and commercial.

Between 2000 and 2006 I was managing director of Canongate Books and my business partner was Jamie Byng, arguably one of the great market activists of our times. Together, we published several great books, two of which will, I hope, serve as examples not only of the commercial power of market activism, but also of its cultural value.

Canongate, when I joined, was a loss-making, Edinburgh-based publisher that the literary world thought interesting but not important; a maverick upstart that promised more than it delivered. But we had growing literary capital: a reputation for introducing new talent and taking risks on unlikely or unproven writers – writers our bigger and more established competitors chose not to publish. We introduced authors of undeniable talent – Michel Faber and Anne Donovan, for example, both of whom were shortlisted for several awards. Nevertheless, it was quite clear that we were not at the centre of the literary world – this was (and remains) resolutely rooted in London. Indeed, we fought hard and endlessly to emerge from our Scottish ghetto. In addition, like every other small independent, we lived off the scraps left behind by our bigger, better-resourced, and more valued competitors.

About a year after I joined Canongate, an agent offered us a book that had been turned down by every one of those big, prestigious London publishers. They had looked at this book and decided it was not a novel they could invest in. They had good reason; after all, it was a narrative that took a long time to get going, had a middle phase that was pretty engaging, but crucially it had an ending I thought would leave many readers confused and dissatisfied. Furthermore, this was no debutant untainted by the cruel reality of a sales history. The author in question had previously been published not once, but twice by Faber and Faber, that peerless arbiter of literary taste, and both these books had been commercial failures. So, rationally and correctly, the big publishers passed on the new book. All except Faber, which, as if to affirm my earlier point about the motivation of people in publishing, ignored the stark reality of the author's commercial track record and – to the house's credit and for the record – made a generous offer. However, given the sales history of his previous books, the author was reluctant to accept, knowing that especially with this house it would be a near-impossible task to revive his fortunes.

However, at Canongate we thought we knew better – arrogant young upstarts that we were and hungry for anything that approached really good literary writing. We loved the book, and while we couldn't afford to outbid Faber and Faber, we matched their offer. Our enthusiasm – and the promise of highly geared market activism – won the day and we secured the contract.

76

Even if I say so myself, we delivered on our promise in spades. We worked with tireless energy and consummate skill to promote this book that we loved and thought important, pushing this failing writer's third – and potentially last – work out into the world, employing all our skills in market activism to gain attention from critics, writers, and booksellers. Fabulous proofs were created and our retail and distribution partners were bombarded with copies and urged to read what we felt was a great book. Literary critics were targeted and sent copies with handwritten notes from the publisher imploring them to read the book and give it space in their publications. A carefully selected list of suitable writers and artists were also sent copies, part of what the publishers sometimes call a 'Big Mouth list' – people who will influence others with their opinions and who are not shy of sharing their views. I have somewhere an email (to which was attached the manuscript) dated a full year before publication to the sales director of Penguin Books, our distributor in Australia and New Zealand, urging her to read it, with the confident endorsement that 'this book will win the Booker next year'. Now, this was a bold assertion of a kind I have used very sparingly in my career. Nonetheless, it reveals something about the level of our belief in the book. Penguin responded to our confidence with an initial order of 4,000 copies, a significant number for a book by an author with a questionable track record. Above any individual activity, Canongate applied a focus, energy, and enthusiasm that generated a tremendous buzz around the book ahead of publication in spring 2002.

So what was this book? It was *Life of Pi* by Yann Martel – and it did indeed go on to win the 2002 Man Booker prize. Even on the night of the ceremony, I had our printers poised to press 'go' on a pre-ordered 30,000-copy reprint should we win. Minutes after

the announcement, I called them and the presses
were rolling. This massive – for a company the size of
Canongate – reprint was in the shops within three days
of the prize ceremony, helping to ensure the momentum
kept escalating. Indeed, at the time *Life of Pi* was the
fastest-selling Booker winner ever. Since then, the book
has gone on to sell many, many millions of copies in
more than thirty languages around the world. In so
doing, it changed the fortunes of Canongate and made
Martel a celebrated and respected literary author. Most
importantly, it was read and enjoyed by many, many
people.

Now, I am sure there is a broad spectrum of
opinion about that book among the readers of this essay –
as there would be about any novel – but that doesn't really
matter. It is a serious piece of writing and deserved not
just to be published but also to find an audience. While
one cannot be certain, I am confident that without the
full attention of Canongate's extremely energetic market
activism, this book, like Martel's previous works, would
most likely have sunk without trace. It's an example of
the kind of market activism Chaudhuri doesn't mention;
the kind that isn't about the size of the advance, or the
media-friendliness of the author, or confected advertising
hype; it's the kind of activism that tells a story about the
story itself.

Moreover, the book also broke the cosy hegemony
of the Booker Prize. In the ten years prior to 2002, the
prize had been passed around between only six publishers
– five of them international conglomerates that controlled
about seventy per cent of the English-language fiction
market. Canongate was the first independent, non-
London based publisher to win. In so doing, it introduced
a new voice to a global audience and announced the
arrival of a publisher whose defining point of difference
was a willingness to take risks on unheralded writers in

the belief that a willing readership existed. And none of it would have happened without market activism.

Following this success, Canongate went on to use its enhanced position to bring new voices to the fore, voices that otherwise might never have been heard in the UK – Jen Christian Grøndahl's beautiful, quiet, and deeply moving *Silence in October*, Nicollò Ammaniti's gripping debut *I'm Not Scared*, and Steven Sherrill's tender and moving *The Minotaur Takes a Cigarette Break*, as well as many others.

Beyond *Pi* and those celebrated writers, a Canongate achievement that seems particularly pertinent to this discussion was with a book many readers of this essay may not know: Sylvia Smith's *Misadventures*. It is a memoir of an entirely unremarkable life. The biographical note to the book reads as follows: *Born in East London to working-class parents as the Second World War was drawing to a close, SYLVIA SMITH ducked out of a career in hairdressing at the last minute to begin a life of office work. She is unmarried with no children. A driving licence and a school swimming certificate are her only qualifications, although she is also quite good at dressmaking.* Misadventures *is her first book. She lives in London.*

Like *Life of Pi*, *Misadventures* was a book that had been passed over by every one of our competitors. Again, at Canongate, we saw things a little differently. Where our competitors might have seen something dull and unremarkable, we saw a curious and powerfully moving memoir. And, like *The Life of Pi*, it was the power of market activism that brought *Misadventures* to a wide audience, selling about 30,000 copies in the UK.

Writing for the *Daily Telegraph*, Mick Brown described it in these terms: 'What was banal becomes weirdly compelling – a life of utter normality (whatever that means) drawn in the way literature seldom, if ever, describes it: funny, poignant, tragic and, in the end, curiously hopeful.'[3] In *Misadventures* Sylvia Smith somehow found her way to expressing the dilemma contained in the closing lines of Beckett's *The Unnameable* – 'you must go on, I can't go on, I'll go on.'

On a personal level, I love this book and think it makes a real and original contribution to existential thinking. From a professional point of view, I love it because it was our 'Pygmalion' project. While the book is a testament to the indomitable strength of the human spirit, it has nothing that would make a publisher feel it could work commercially. It is a monotone account of unconnected events in an uneventful life, written by a woman with no literary profile or connected to any kind of group of influential literati. (Nor was the author an idiot savant, the kind of damaged outsider the literary establishment likes to adopt from time to time. As far as I could see, Smith wasn't even particularly excited about being published. As a business, then, all we had was a text that we thought rare and good and our market-activist skills.)

What I hope I have described with these examples was how we employed market – or, as I prefer to call it, 'expert' – activism to bring new, fresh, and important voices to readers around the world and how, without that expert activist intervention, those voices would not have been heard.

Even as we achieved these successes, the commercial landscape continued to change. It became increasingly evident that applying our renowned market-activism skills to bring forward unlikely artistic talent from outside the establishment would no longer be enough to maintain and grow a flourishing business. This was in part due to the company's own publishing lifecycle, but the demands of the marketplace were also making it increasingly difficult to uphold not only our literary standards but also our bank balance. Our success had grown the business and inevitably increased our overheads, which placed additional demands on the revenue streams of the books that supported the business. As the retail market narrowed – and in the absence of the Net Book Agreement – the increasingly dominant big retailers demanded an ever-increasing share of revenue, putting pressure on our margins. In a period of less than ten years, an average trade publisher's gross margins declined by nearly one-third, as a direct consequence of the escalation in trade discounts.[4] Authors' income from royalties was – and continues to be – similarly squeezed.

Traditionally, publishing reinvested the profits from its successes into new or yet-to-be-successful work, or into keeping faith with writers yet to deliver a commercially viable return on investment. There are many stories – mainly set in an increasingly distant past – of publishers keeping faith with authors who had yet to break out and make money. For example, Ian Rankin was not dropped by his publisher Anthony Cheetham despite disappointing sales on – as I understand it – his first six books. Today, cumulative sales of Rankin's novels stand at well over twenty million copies.

So the slightly skewed economics of publishing have always advocated employing revenue from the hits to pay for losses on the misses. But when the profits from the books that *do* sell are so depleted, the inevitable consequence is that the publisher becomes much more risk-averse and less adventurous. In such a context, the new, challenging (or just different) title becomes harder and harder to publish and therefore a much more rare commodity.

In the face of these changes, publishers had to adapt to the new market realities. At Canongate, we began to engage in producing some books for money and some books for love. Indeed, if you look at the business profiles of most literary houses now, you will find they have changed significantly from the days I have just described – and changed for reasons I understand very well and respect.

For my part, I tried another tack. I moved on to run Granta and Portobello Books, which had been acquired in 2006 by Swedish philanthropist and billionaire Sigrid Rausing. In my three years there, it would be fair to say that the quality of literary output was unimpeachable. *Granta*, the long-standing magazine of new writing, remained the journal of record – in the UK at least – for the short story and long-form non-fiction, while the two imprints published many great books: Robert MacFarlane's seminal *The Wild Places*; *Somewhere Towards the End* by Diana Athill, which won the Costa Award for biography in 2008; and *Nothing to Envy* by Barbara Demick, which won the Samuel Johnson Prize in 2010. We also acquired two books by an astonishingly young and amazingly gifted New Zealand writer Eleanor Catton, whose debut *The Rehearsal* won many admirers and whose second, *The Luminaries*, won the 2013 Man Booker prize.

Despite these successes in terms of literary capital, other agenda came with the largely benign and well-intentioned patronage of our wealthy owner: agendas that constrained and compromised the necessary market activism that would make Granta successful in terms of commerce. While that freedom may seem appealing to those sceptical about the pressing commercial demands of market activism, I can only tell you that I think the future of our culture is questionable if it must rely on the patronage of the very rich. Granted, that model seemed to work pretty well in Renaissance Italy, but from my experience it doesn't seem to be a paradigm for publishing in the twenty-first century. Writers want readers for their work and that desire is better served if the publisher employs the full range of market activist strategies to help those works reach the widest possible audience.

As I experienced this shift of emphasis in ethos and business practices from Canongate to Granta, the market was becoming even harder for those trying to pursue the twin ambitions of literary excellence and financial success. On top of the increased pressures on margins and profits, which constrained publishers' ambition and adventurousness, another factor was introduced: the internet. This, more than anything else, broke the chain of expertise that led from the author to the reader.

So, although Chaudhuri is correct to draw attention to the way in which the setting of the literary agenda has changed in the last two or three decades, it is this break in the chain of expertise that has had – and promises to continue having – the most significant and, I think, damaging effects on the place of the 'literary'. I would go so far as to strongly suggest that art and culture should remain in – or somehow be returned to – the hands of expertly informed, seriously engaged, and culturally serious and committed individuals, rather than the world wide web.

While it might seem like an act of yearning for an irrecoverable past, it is worth briefly setting out the way in which things worked when the chain of expertise was intact. It was the agent or publisher who set the chain in motion, effectively becoming activists on behalf of manuscripts or authors that had caught their expert eye. In the first instance, they would do this by sharing their enthusiasms with colleagues in other departments – sales, marketing, publicity, and design – before moving out into the wider world of critics and commentators, many of them experts in their field, too, and, finally, booksellers – often the best and most widely read of the whole lot. It was then the bookseller's job to lead the reader, overwhelmed by the choice the book industry presented to them, to 'the good stuff'. It might sound like I'm describing a utopian paradise but, while not without its flaws, the system worked after its own fashion.

This chain has all but ceased to exist, and where it does it exists in a severely weakened form. Decision-making within publishing houses is increasingly concentrated in the hands of sales directors (who always want something that looks like the last thing that sold well). In the wider world, the role of critics and commentators has immeasurably diminished. Not only is print media circulation in freefall decline, but the amount of space and resource devoted to literary reviews has shrunk to an alarming degree: I know the books editor of a large regional newspaper whose budget for putting together the books pages is now £150 per week. And, while high street booksellers continue to exist, to a large degree the market is dominated by the giant bazaar of Amazon, employing algorithms to tell you that if you liked X you'll probably like Y.

With everything seemingly available to everyone all the time, in order to gain the attention of potential readers, publishers are – perhaps unsurprisingly – relying on two things: the tried and the tested. It is no coincidence that in the last ten years the market share of the bestseller has steadily increased. And if a publisher is to introduce something new, it must be a book with a hook – and that almost inevitably means relying on something outside the literary merit of the work itself: the book's topical reference points or the backstory of the author.

Indicative of this shift is the increasing use of the term 'promotable' as a guiding principle for publishers seeking to attract the attention of an audience overwhelmed by data and choice. And this, I would argue, is the new and darker version of what Chaudhuri calls market activism.

84

There are, of course, many examples of this form of market activism in action. I can think of several extremely successful and mightily praised novels that seem to me to be little more than consciously constructed confections that instrumentally - if not cynically - tap into the concerns of modern Western society: multiculturalism, the growing gap between rich and poor, Islamic radicalism, money, power, and bankers. And while there is nothing wrong with novels that hold a mirror up to society, when these real-world concerns become the driving force of the work, the danger is that the art is lost.

This is also true of the many high-profile works that choose as their subject the personality of the author. The works trade on the fact that they are, overtly or covertly, a biography, satisfying the audience's prurient curiosity by providing some - usually dark - insight into the maker's real life. Despite this, these works are regularly regarded as literary endeavours of high merit and follow the most reliable route to commercial success. And all rely on agendas that lie outside the work itself, in order to provide the publicity that will drive them to a large market. But the risk is that we will move towards a monoculture in which only books with an external agenda are read, or indeed written, and, moreover, that writers are becoming increasingly aware of this necessary requirement and tailor their work in order to achieve this essentially commercial goal.

This leaves the artist no longer standing behind his work 'paring his nails' but right out front engaged in a personal or political debate with his or her audience.

And this is where the new aspect of market activism - which has nothing to do with the work, or with expert opinion, or with a professional commitment to the promotion of the work - threatens to replace the literary agenda with its own strictly commercial one, and furthermore threaten the role and activity of the artist themselves.

The process inevitably leads us increasingly to consider the content of the story and its relevance to the outside world while increasingly ignoring how the story is being told. I am regularly shocked by friends and colleagues – successful, influential, and sophisticated readers who fulfil roles as publishers, critics, and judges of high-profile literary prizes – who not only do not concern themselves with the issue of the integrity of the authorial voice and how the tale is being told (who is telling the story, why, and how) but also *actively* disregard it. It seems they do not view these literary concerns as having any place in consideration of a piece's literary merit. The contemporary critical world is focused almost exclusively on the what, to the near exclusion of all other factors. And in so doing, it is risking the pleasure of reading and degrading the pleasure of literature to that of watching the latest box-set.

In this maelstrom of noise, publishers are intimidated out of taking risks on stories without an outside agenda because of the spectacular lack of traction those books achieve in the vast, anonymised world of book retail. And, as I suggested earlier, the even greater risk is that writers are turning ever more to the personal or topical simply in order to stay relevant in the new set of terms adopted by the market.

But while these challenges threaten the state and future of literary publishing, there remains hope; there remains a future for great books. With the disruptive force of new technology comes opportunity. Access to a global reading audience lies in everyone's hands at the touch of a button. The cost of effective marketing has never been lower and the digital revolution brings the means of production down to virtually zero – dismantling

86

the barriers to entry so that individuals can publish their own works.

Now, I do not advocate self-publishing – I passionately believe in the curative power of the publisher – but the key benefit to these changes in the means of production and distribution is that it enables the very small expert publisher to flourish. The future of true literary publishing lies in the hands of the micro-publisher. To my mind – certainly in the UK – the most interesting literary works today are being published by houses that employ fewer than 10 people with an annual turnover of less than about £2million: Hesperus, Alma Books, Persephone, Arcadia, And Other Stories, Pushkin. This growing group of very small independent houses is producing challenging and innovative work with flair and élan.

Eimear McBride's astonishing *A Girl Is a Half-formed Thing* is the perfect example of what I mean. It is an uncompromising literary work that is all about how it was made, a work that doesn't seek references outside the narrative. It was originally published by Galley Beggar Press, a tiny publishing house in Norwich, England. McBride had spent nine years trying to get the book published – ironically, that was the story that helped the book get noticed.[5] It is rightly celebrated as a significant work by a talented new author with a highly distinctive voice and has been recognised by four major literary prizes, including the Goldsmith (which brought the work to wider attention) and the Baileys Women's Prize for Fiction.

It is quite astonishing to me that *A Girl Is a Half-formed Thing* took so long to be published, and it is equally alarming how many people I know – who really should know better – describe it as being a very 'difficult' novel. Its long journey and eventual success at a micro-publisher is the story of our times.

In conclusion, I think the future of literary publishing lies with the micro-publisher. Through them we are seeing a return to the values of 'expert activism' I described at the beginning of this piece. Unquestionably, we operate in a more competitive, more hostile, more anti-intellectual environment than hitherto. But that environment creates an even greater need for expert activism to support and bring forward great writing. There is an indomitable spirit in publishing that keeps believing that quality will rise to the top... and still, sometimes, I believe it does.

1. Actually it's pretty easy to make money publishing books with no other merit than their commercial appeal. It's also pretty easy to publish great books if making money is not an ambition (or a requirement). The hard thing – and therefore the thing that is endlessly engaging – is making money out of good or even great books.

2. It is worth remembering that at the turn of the century book retail was booming: the UK had three confident and expanding bookselling chains (Waterstones, Borders, and Ottakars), a plethora of vibrant regional bookstores, and more than 4,000 bookshops on the high street (more than double the number we have today).

3. Mick Brown, 'Woke up, got out of bed, had a fag... and wrote a bestseller,' *Daily Telegraph*, 17 February 2001, http://www.telegraph.co.uk/culture/4721776/Woke-up-got-out-of-bed-had-a-fag...-and-wrote-a-bestseller.html

4. John B. Thompson, writing about the collapse of the Net Book Agreement and the rise of Amazon and the chains, has the following to say: 'The overall impact has been an upward drift in the average discount that publishers offer to the retail sector: roughly ten per cent of margin has been transferred from publishers to retailers in a period of less than ten years.' See John B. Thompson, *Merchants of Culture: The Publishing Business in the Twenty-First Century*, Second Edition (Cambridge: Polity Press, 2012), p. 312.

5. 'I finished the third draft of girl in the summer of 2004 so between then and publication in the summer of 2013, she had quite a bumpy ride. There was the glitzy agency who said they "might" offer representation if I re-wrote it to their exact specifications and the publisher who said he was only interested if he could sell it as a memoir. Then all the major publishing houses turned it down with glowing refusals – although it was nearly taken up by two, who shall remain nameless, only to be vetoed

later on the grounds of being unmarketable. A small press in Dublin showed interest for a while and then also backed off as they couldn't "afford to take any risks". When I pulled them up on this they said they'd reconsider, were just waiting to hear about their Arts Council funding and would be in touch. They never were. So eventually girl was consigned to the drawer and over time I made some embittered peace with that.' See David Collard, 'Interview with Eimear McBride,' *The White Review*, May 2014, http://www.thewhitereview.org/interviews/interview-with-eimear-mcbride/

'What about Criticism?'
Blanchot's Giant-Windmill
PETER D. MCDONALD

In the prefatory note to this collection of essays, Amit Chaudhuri identifies what he calls 'market activism' primarily with publishers and literary agents, or, perhaps more specifically, with the large publishing corporations and 'super-agents' who began to reshape the literary world during the early 1990s.[1] But he also looks briefly askance at universities in order to point out an implicitly fatal coincidence. By the time publishers and agents were turning the language of critical evaluation into a marketing tool, creating among other things a new mass-market genre called 'literary fiction', 'most literature departments' had, he comments, 'disowned' that language altogether, shying away from a word such as 'masterpieces' and even withdrawing from 'the literary itself'. I am assuming he is, in the latter case, thinking about the rise of cultural studies, which in some of its more militant formulations did discard Shakespeare for supermarkets. In the former case, I imagine he is referring to the 'hermeneutics of suspicion', which became something of a critical orthodoxy during the 1980s and 1990s.[2] On this last issue he has the support of the fictional author-figure in J.M. Coetzee's *Diary of a Bad Year* (2007). At one point, JC, as this figure is called, observes that students of the 'humanities in its postmodernist phase' were 'taught that in criticism suspiciousness is the chief virtue, that the critic must accept nothing whatsoever at face value'.[3] Unlike the more militant forms of cultural studies, this left room for Shakespeare but only as an object of wary scrutiny, not as a canonical master of his medium.

As I take it, then, the question of 'literary activism' – What is it? What are its goals? And so on – can be posed not only against the background of 'market activism' but against what Coetzee's author-figure also calls 'the *trahison des clercs* of our time';[4] or what Chaudhuri calls, no less forcefully, the betrayal of 'the literary itself' by 'most literature departments' – JC is invoking Julien Benda's attack on party intellectuals of the left and the right in *La Trahison des Clercs* (1927).[5] As I am a salaried academic – perhaps even a latter-day *clerc* in JC's sense – I'll focus on this last issue in the context of contemporary debates about the university.

I should make it clear from the outset that while I recognise and deplore the betrayal Chaudhuri identifies, I was not unsympathetic to the cultural turn in the 1990s, a position I still maintain. True, it had many crudely anti-literary advocates – the New Zealand-born academic Simon During was among the most prominent – but there were others, such as the American professor of English and comparative literature Bruce Robbins, who had a more nuanced sense of the stakes involved.[6] As Robbins recognised, the problem was not so much literature per se, but what he called 'traditional literariness', a notion he understood primarily in relation to American New Criticism – he served his academic apprenticeship at Harvard in the late 1960s and through the 1970s, when this was still very much in its heyday.[7] At the heart of this critical enterprise, as Robbins saw it, was a 'non-pragmatic, non-instrumental' formalism, which all too often reduced the experience of literature to a matter of 'inconsequential privacy'.[8] Under the aegis of New Criticism, 'traditional literariness', he argued, put 'a safe distance between itself and officialdom, or the public', thereby justifying the turn to cultural studies, which he saw as a more ethically and politically engaged form of enquiry.[9] So, for some advocates of cultural studies, the issue was not so much 'the literary itself' but versions of literariness associated with some influential but questionable styles of criticism.

Two examples of what might count as 'literary activism' are highlighted in Chaudhuri's prefatory note and elsewhere in this collection of essays:

94

Derek Attridge's critical championing of Zoë Wicomb, and Arvind Krishna Mehrotra's nomination as Oxford Professor of Poetry in 2009 in which Chaudhuri and I both played a part. My understanding is that Chaudhuri drew attention to these cases because both were clearly acts of critical evaluation, albeit of a very particular kind. If they expressed a firm commitment, even endorsement, they did so without laying claim to the megalomaniacal hype with which such endorsements are too often associated. While Attridge was not interested in holding up Wicomb as an exemplar of some or other 'new literature', we in Oxford were not concerned about winning the election. The point in both cases was to 'fashion an event', to shift the terms of critical debate, and – most importantly – to do so in a way that was in keeping with the 'desultory' character of the literary itself.[10] I take this last point to be central. It suggests that what might be most interesting about literature, as a mode of public intervention, is that it is itself, or at least in its most compelling forms, indifferent to power. Even when it takes on other more potent forms of public discourse, whether political, religious, journalistic, or whatever, it does so without claiming rival authority for itself – without, that is, getting caught up in the game of 'market activism'. What it does is open up a space in which all kinds of authority and definitive forms of language are put in question, including its own – hence Chaudhuri's claim about 'the strangeness of the literary'.

So for me the question is: how do we fashion a critical language equal to this strangeness? Clearly neither the 'hermeneutics of suspicion', nor 'traditional literariness' are going to be much help. If the former is too preoccupied with its own claims to power, the latter is too keen to see literature as a safely sanitized aesthetic zone, above or at least protected from the public fray. I'd like to suggest that a largely forgotten short essay by the twentieth-century French critic and writer Maurice Blanchot offers an alternative way forward. Before I turn to the details of the essay itself, however, I should say something briefly about its provenance.

It first appeared in French in the journal *Arguments* in early 1959 under the title 'Qu'en est-il de la critique?' (or 'What about criticism?').[11] *Arguments* was a relatively short-lived forum for a dissident group of Marxists and fellow travellers who broke with the still strongly Stalinist French Communist party (PCF), following Khrushchev's denunciation of Stalin in 1956, and with the orthodoxies of Marxist criticism. The editors angered György Lukács, for instance, by insisting on translating and publishing his early work, which did not observe strictures of dialectical materialism. They also published Roland Barthes, Gilles Deleuze, and Blanchot, among others. Some forty years later the essay resurfaced in English, translated by Leslie Hill, in the *Oxford Literary Review* under the rather more forbidding, and less interrogative, title 'The Task of Criticism Today'.[12] Though very different to *Arguments*, the *Oxford Literary Review* is not quite what it seems: the title was intended as a joke. It has only a tenuous connection to Oxford University, and it does not publish or review original literature. Founded in 1977, it has during the past three decades made a name for itself as the primary platform for French deconstructive thought in the English-speaking world.

Why dwell on these details? If there is one lesson from cultural studies worth reaffirming, it is that we cannot talk about fashioning a critical language without considering the media and institutions through which that language might find its way into the public domain. In this regard, these changing forums tell their own story. At one level, they reflect the ongoing structural transformation of the public sphere and suggest something about the increasing dependency of criticism on the university. *Arguments*, which served as a model for the British *New Left Review* (founded in 1960), was a little magazine of sorts, though it had at its peak around 4,000 subscribers. Published by Editions de Minuit, the French resistance imprint, it created a forum for autonomous debate 'situated in the space between political activity and intellectual work, Marxism and that which escapes it', as the founding editor Edgar Morin put it.[13] Like Blanchot, many of its contributors were what we might now call public intellectuals with no direct links to universities. By contrast, the *Oxford Literary Review*, for all its own doubts about the modern university, is run by salaried academics essentially for salaried academics and published by Edinburgh University Press. It has never had more than 420 subscribers.[14] At another level, these changing forums also track the various moments and contexts through which Blanchot's question 'What about criticism?' has moved in the past half century or so. Here I am thinking not only of the move from intellectual arguments within Parisian journals to academic debates within the university, but from dissident French Marxism in the late 1950s to what came to be called 'Theory' during the 1980s and 1990s, and, of course, to our own debates about 'literary activism' today.

There is one further thing I need to do before I turn to the details of the essay. For reasons that will, I hope, become clear, I am at this point going to have to dispense with the fiction of writing in only one voice. I know that the essayistic monologue is *de rigueur* for academics generally, but, given my own conflicted thoughts about the issues under discussion, I'm going to have split myself in two. For ease of identification, I'll call the first voice Don Q, and the second Sancho P.

DON Q: To my mind one of the most compelling things about Blanchot's essay is its bracingly sardonic tone. After describing the critic as 'this mediocre

97

hybrid, half-writer, half-reader, this bizarre person who specialises in reading yet can read only by writing', he remarks that when 'we subject criticism to serious scrutiny, we get the impression that there is nothing serious about the object of our scrutiny'.[15] In part, this is because criticism, at least as he saw it in France in the late 1950s, depends for its very existence on 'two weighty institutions': 'journalism' and the 'academy' (i.e., the university).[16] Though often accused of being high-mindedly philosophical, Blanchot was in fact always alert to the real-world dynamics of institutional power and, in this case, to its many ironies. Criticism's dependency on 'journalism' and the 'academy' was particularly hapless, he felt, because neither really shares its concerns, 'each having a firm direction and organization of their own.'[17]

This unfortunate institutional predicament had the further consequence of exposing the fragility of criticism's authority. Since it produces neither the 'scholarly knowledge' of the university, which Blanchot believed has the virtue of being 'solid and permanent', nor the 'day-to-day knowledge' of journalism, which may be 'trivial and short-term' but is at least 'expeditious', it is, like a perpetual teenager, never quite sure about its status or function. Perhaps, Blanchot wondered, it might find a place for itself as a somewhat needy mediator between these institutions and kinds of knowledge, an 'honest broker' linking scholarship to the everyday concerns of journalism and the wider public?[18] Or maybe it could take on a role as an advocate of 'higher values'?[19] In this last scenario, he envisaged the critic achieving some status as 'a spokesman applying general policy'.[20] It is difficult not to think he had party *clercs* like the later Lukács in mind here – though, if we read this in more self-critical terms, then he could well have been thinking of his own earlier incarnation as a French nationalist *clerc* of the 1930s. Yet, if this is the 'task of criticism', he

98

wrote, it 'hardly amounts to much' – 'it could even be said to amount to nothing at all', since all *clercs* require is 'a degree of competence, a talent for writing, a willingness to please and a measure of goodwill'.[21] Again, read not just as a jibe at party intellectuals of all kinds but as the profession of an *ex-clerc*, this carries some additional weight.

Having sketched the unpromising institutional conditions of criticism in general terms, Blanchot then paused briefly to reflect on what we might too succinctly call the orthodoxies of 1950s French Marxism, although he never named them as such, according to which literature had to be read and critiqued as a symptom of history, specifically history as understood in French Marxist terms. With what is perhaps too much politesse – he was well aware of how this would play outside the pages of a dissident journal such as *Arguments* – he acknowledged the force of this dominant critical tradition, but claimed that criticism 'has no authority to speak seriously in the name of history', which has 'taken shape within disciplines that are more rigorous, more ambitious too'.[22] The task of showing 'how a literary work relates to history at large or to its own evolution' could be left, he suggested, to 'the science of historical interplay', to which he added wryly and in parenthesis '(if it existed)'.[23] Again, it is difficult not to think he had not just the *clercs* of the PCF but the later Lukács in mind.

So if criticism cannot achieve any distinction as a mediator between journalism and the university, as an advocate of 'higher values' serving one or another set of political interests, or as a branch of the 'historical sciences', then what is left for it to do?[24] Characteristically, in working his way towards his own more affirmative answer to this question, Blanchot turned what he had just identified as criticism's weakness into its strength. 'A derogatory view like this is not offensive to criticism,' he insisted, 'for criticism readily welcomes it, as though, on the contrary, the very nullity of criticism were its most essential truth'.[25]

In one of many attempts to characterise this 'nullity', and to make a virtue of it, he observed: 'Criticism is nothing, but this nothing is precisely that in which the work, silent, invisible, lets itself be what it is'.[26] Or, in a more extended formulation:

> Criticism is no longer a form of external judgement which confers value on the literary work and, after the event, pronounces on its value. It has become inseparable from the inner workings of the text itself, it belongs to the movement by which the work comes to itself, searches for itself, and experiences its own possibility.[27]

Crucially, for Blanchot, this kind of criticism, which follows no prescribed protocols, effectively inventing itself anew in the face of every new work, or act of reading, is equal to what Chaudhuri calls the 'strangeness of the literary'. As Blanchot put it: 'precisely because, modestly, obstinately, it claims to be nothing, criticism ceases to distinguish itself from its object, and takes on the mantle of creative language itself, of which it is, so to speak, both the necessary actualisation and, more figuratively, the epiphany'.[28] It is difficult – and don't forget I'm still speaking as Don Q – to imagine a more compelling antidote to the 'hermeneutics of suspicion', which knowingly stands apart from the work assured of its own mastery, and to the 'traditional literariness' Robbins identified with American New Criticism, which is no less confident about its own formalist aesthetics and capacity to separate literary from political interests, or vice versa.

SANCHO P: This is all well and good but the world has moved on since 1959. For one thing, criticism, no less than creative writing, is now almost wholly dependent on the university for its survival. We no longer live in a world in which a critic such as Roland Barthes, or indeed Blanchot, could make his name in a newspaper. When it is not preoccupied with anxieties about its own potential extinction in the digital age, journalism today is at best a forum for reviewing and celebrity author gossip, at worst an instrument of 'market activism'. And, when it comes to criticism, it is not too far-fetched to argue that it has become an almost wholly self-enclosed professional discourse, the kind of writing produced solely for the advancement of academic careers. The fact that Blanchot's essay moved from *Arguments* in 1959 to the *Oxford Literary Review* in 2000 is just one small instance of this larger trend. In the face of this significant reality, as even the most rudimentary sociological analysis of the academic world would show, treating 'the very nullity of criticism' as its 'most essential truth' is unlikely to get much traction. Contemporary *clercs*, in JC's sense, even those who eschew the easy exaltations of suspicion or the onanistic joys of aesthetic pleasure, are under too much pressure to build professional networks, perhaps even empires, founded on transferable methodologies and generalisable styles of reading, and to champion 'new literatures', or new categories such as 'World Literature', in short, to chase the next professionally saleable and reifiable (or is it REFable?) idea.

Yet professionalisation is perhaps the least of the difficulties a Blanchot-style critic would face today. If we consider the vulnerability of the contemporary university itself as a sponsor of humanistic study, let alone criticism, then the situation appears even more unpromising. As the American scholar Jim Collins has noted, the 'massive infrastructural changes in literary culture', which, like Chaudhuri, he associates primarily with the 'conglomeration of the publishing industry' since the 1990s, coincided with a significant shift in 'taste hierarchies', among which he includes 'the radical devaluation of the academy and the New York literary scene as taste brokers who maintained the gold standard of literary currency' and 'the transformation of taste acquisition into an industry with taste arbiters becoming media celebrities.'[29] He had in mind ventures such as Oprah Winfrey's enormously influential book club. To this I would add the rise of online communities and social media as forums for literary discussion, which bypass traditional reviewing and more or less ignore, if they are not actively hostile to, academic criticism. In this context, it is difficult to see what weight criticism, defined in Blanchot's terms, can possibly carry. At best, it would generate just one more opinion in an ocean of digital opinions, at worst it would be discredited in advance as the opinion of a professor nostalgic for the producer-centred age of print and a time when the university was looked upon as a custodian of one or another great tradition.

To the seismic effects of these broader changes in the media environment we have to add the simultaneous reconfiguration of the university itself at the hands of various governmental authorities in thrall to the orthodoxies of statist neoliberalism (Stalinist Thatcherism?) and its forms of 'market activism'. For a pithy summary of this history, we can return to JC, Coetzee's author-figure in *Diary of a Bad Year*.

> What universities suffered during the 1980s and 1990s was pretty shameful, as under the threat of having their funding cut they allowed themselves to be turned into business enterprises, in which professors who had previously carried on their enquiries in sovereign freedom were transformed into harried employees required to fulfil quotas under scrutiny of professional managers. Whether the old powers

of the professoriat will ever be restored is much to
be doubted.[30]

With the future of humanistic enquiry in mind,
JC then suggests that, if the 'spirit of the university
is to survive,' professors may have to become like the
'dissidents who conducted night classes in their homes'
in the 'days when Poland was under Communist rule'.[31]
This was not just JC's rather pessimistic opinion in a
work of fiction. For those interested in 'the strangeness of
the literary', particularly as it pertains to the question of
authority, Coetzee said much the same thing in his own
person in the foreword to a recent collection of essays
on *Academic Freedom* (2013).[32] For all these reasons –
and of course I'm still speaking as Sancho P – I suspect
criticism, as Blanchot understands it, is going to have to
become a subject for 'night classes', given off campus,
and published in dissident blogs or the online equivalent
of *Arguments*.[33]

DON Q: This is all far too gloomy.

Professionalisation is a fact of modern life and,
besides, in any impartial comparisons with bankers or
politicians, the professoriat comes out rather well. And
no matter how the media environment changes, or what
governments do to universities, you can always rely on
younger people not to accept reality as the previous
generation attempted to define it, and, in my experience,
they do not seem to have lost the desire to ask serious
questions about themselves and the cultures they inhabit.

Moreover, your pessimism rests on a false
assumption about Blanchot's contemporary relevance.
Far from being a hopelessly dated anachronism, he speaks
directly to many of our own concerns. In the conclusion to
the essay I have been discussing, for instance, he addresses
Chaudhuri's observation about literature departments
disowning the language of evaluation. 'The complaint is
sometimes made that criticism is no longer capable of

judging,' he says.[34] Yet, reinforcing his underlying case for a self-effacing style of criticism without protocol, he insists: 'It is not criticism which lazily resists evaluation.' Rather it is the literary work that 'withdraws from evaluation because it seeks to affirm itself in isolation from all value'; that is, from all established protocols of value, which too many guardians of the literary devote themselves to upholding, or, for that matter, any pre-given political values of the kind Benda's overly compliant *clercs* championed.[35] Again, once criticism opens itself up to the demands of the work, once it 'belongs more intimately to the life of the work', then 'it experiences the work as something that cannot be evaluated'.[36] For Blanchot, this is not a matter of 'inconsequential privacy', to recall Robbins's phrase, nor is it simply about literature or criticism. It is 'closely related to one of the most difficult, but most important tasks of our time': 'The task both of preserving and of releasing thought from the notion of value, and consequently opening history up to that which, within history, is already moving beyond all forms of value and is preparing for a wholly different – and still unpredictable – kind of affirmation'.[37] In the first, untranslated version of the essay, he spelt out what this affirmation might mean in more detail, linking it via a series of provocative questions to 'a neutral and impersonal power, beyond any distinct interest, any definitive word (*parole déterminée*)' and to a 'profoundly indeterminate movement' expressing the 'future of communication and communication as the future.'[38]

Such comments about disinterestedness, the unpredictability of history, the transvaluation of values, and the possibility of a radical openness to the future clearly had a special resonance in the pages of a dissident French Marxist journal in the late 1950s and another kind of resonance in an academic journal devoted to French deconstructive thought in 2000. I think they have as much to say to our own concerns about 'literary activism' today.

SANCHO P: You sound like someone I have read about who believed, madly and incorrigibly, 'that, by the will of heaven, I was born in this age of iron, to revive in it that of gold, or, as people usually express it, "the golden age"'.[39]

DON Q: I read that story myself and couldn't help noticing that a certain Sancho Panza plays a curiously double role in it. Yes, he mocks the engaging but easily deluded Alonso Quixano, pointing out that the giants he claims to see are in fact windmills. Yet he also helps him along in his amazing adventures and so keeps the story, and Alonso's efforts to revive the 'golden age', going.

1. For an informative academic study of these new circumstances, see John B. Thompson, *Merchants of Culture* (2010; Cambridge: Polity Press, 2012).

2. For my own further take on this, see Peter D. McDonald, 'Ideas of the Book and Histories of Literature: After Theory?', *PMLA* (January 2006), pp. 214-228; for a recent account, see Rita Felski, *The Limits of Critique* (Chicago: Chicago University Press, 2015).

3. J.M. Coetzee, *Diary of a Bad Year* (London: Harvill Secker, 2007), p. 33.

4. Coetzee, *Diary of a Bad Year*, p. 33.

5. Coetzee, *Diary of a Bad Year*, p. 33, and see Chaudhuri's prefatory note to this collection, p. 3.

6. For During's views as one of the chief proponents of cultural studies, see his introduction to *The Cultural Studies Reader* (London: Routledge, 1993), and 'Teaching Culture', *Australian Humanities Review*, August 1997, pp. 1-7. For his return to the literary, see *Against Democracy: Literary Experience in the Era of Emancipations* (New York: Fordham University Press, 2012).

7. Bruce Robbins, *Secular Vocations* (London: Verso, 1993), p. 110.

8. Robbins, *Secular Vocations*, p. 110.

9. Robbins, *Secular Vocations*, p. 116.

10. Chaudhuri, prefatory note, pp. 5-6.

11. Maurice Blanchot, 'Qu'en est-il de la critique?', *Arguments*, Jan-Feb 1959, pp. 34-37. A revised version subsequently appeared in Maurice Blanchot, *Lautréamount et Sade* (Paris: Minuit, 1963), pp. 9-14.

12. Maurice Blanchot, 'The Task of Criticism Today', trans. Leslie Hill, *Oxford Literary Review*, 22.1 (2000), pp. 19-24. Hill based his translation on the revised 1963 version of the essay.

13. Edgar Morin, et al., *Arguments 1 : La bureaucratie* (Paris, Union Générale d'Editions, 1976), p. 11.

14. I am grateful to Professor Nicholas Royle, the current editor of *OLR*,

for giving me these details. Personal correspondence, 17 October 2014.

15. Blanchot, 'Task', pp. 19-20.

16. Blanchot, 'Task', p. 19.

17. Blanchot, 'Task'.

18. Blanchot, 'Task'.

19. Blanchot, 'Task'.

20. Blanchot, 'Task'.

21. Blanchot, 'Task'.

22. Blanchot, 'Task', p. 21.

23. Blanchot, 'Task'.

24. Blanchot, 'Task', pp. 19, 21.

25. Blanchot, 'Task', p. 20.

26. Blanchot, 'Task', p. 21.

27. Blanchot, 'Task', p. 23.

28. Blanchot, 'Task', p. 22.

29. Jim Collins, *Bring on the Books for Everybody* (Durham: Duke University Press, 2010), pp. 7-8.

30. Coetzee, *Diary*, p. 35.

31. Coetzee, *Diary*, p. 36.

32. See John Higgins, ed., *Academic Freedom* (Johannesburg: Wits University Press, 2013), pp. xi-xv.

33. Coetzee, *Diary*, p. 36.

34. Blanchot, 'Task', p. 23.

35. Blanchot, 'Task'.

36. Blanchot, 'Task'.

37. Blanchot, 'Task', p. 24.

38. Blanchot, 'Qu'en est-il de la critique?', *Arguments*, p. 37.

39. Miguel de Cervantes, *Don Quixote*, trans. E.C. Riley (Oxford: World's Classics, 2008), p. 142.

The Amatory Activist
SAIKAT MAJUMDAR

Throughout their history, the humanities have been haunted by a question that has threatened their legitimacy as academic fields. Is the humanist thinker a professional or an amateur? If philosophy, literature, music, and the visual arts are 'soft' subjects, naturally moored in our daily hopes and fears, pain and pleasure, our quotidian language and emotions, our private, social, and communal relationships, how badly do they need the 'hardness' of academic discipline? In early twentieth-century England, for instance, literary studies fought and finally overpowered this very scepticism in order to entrench itself as an academic discipline, but that did very little to seal the amateur-versus-professional debate. The assumption of academic identity has, quite naturally, arrived with attempts to dismiss this nagging question, but it has never done so with definitive success. The amateur has never quite withered away. Unlike merely recreational – and perhaps just a little ridiculous – figures such as the amateur engineer or the amateur scientist, when we talk about literature, history, or even philosophy, the amateur even becomes an empowered figure of sorts, occasionally cheating the fully credentialled academic specialist of her authority.

Marjorie Garber reminds us that the respective prestige of the amateur and the professional have been historically variable in the humanities more than anywhere else. She accounts for the changing prestige of the amateur and the professional in the Anglo-American world of letters by returning to the term 'virtuosi' as it was used in seventeenth-century England as a prestigious antecedent of the intellectual amateur. The term embodied a unique intersection of power, privilege, and cultural literacy: 'Virtuosi were connoisseurs and collectors, gentlemen of wealth and leisure, identified with the aristocracy.'[1] Intellectual, social, and economic privilege came together to turn the virtuoso into a gentleman-scholar and distinguished him not only from those who did not have money, but also the newly rich who could not claim an ancient family name. Throughout the eighteenth century, while the dilettante sat in a position of humility next to the 'better-informed' virtuoso, neither of them had the trivial or derogatory cast that they were quickly to earn with the increasing professionalisation of the humanities. It was through the nineteenth century that the virtuoso, the dilettante, and the belletrist gradually came to be devalued, to the point where an Oxford don could measure academic success with the claim that: 'We have risen above the mere belletristic treatment of classical literature.'[2] And by the 1920s, John Middleton Murray was articulating what had become a decisive dismissal of the amateur: 'No amount of sedulous apery or word-mosaic will make a writer of the dilettante belletrist.'[3]

The 1920s and 1930s were crucial decades for the institutionalisation of the discipline of English literary studies on both sides of the Atlantic. At the University of Cambridge, the entrenchment of English as an academic discipline through the intellectual and entrepreneurial energy of canonical figures such as F.R. and Q.D. Leavis and I.A. Richards was, to a great extent, dependent on its emergence as a specialised subject of definite academic rigour, as opposed to a domain of dilettantish debates about aesthetic taste. If the journal *Scrutiny*, launched in 1932, was the celebrated platform for the Leavisite championship of this disciplinary rigour, a comparable stance was taken by the American poet and critic John Crowe Ransom, who likewise made a powerful case for literary criticism as a serious, significant, and specialised activity, and founded *The Kenyon Review* in 1939 as a platform for it. Ransom's famous 1938 essay 'Criticism, Inc.' argues, much like F.R. Leavis had done, for a rigorous and scientific model of criticism, an endeavour that requires a level of sustained collaboration that is only possible at the university: 'Criticism must become more scientific, or precise and systematic, and this means that it must be developed by the collective and sustained effort of learned persons - which means that its proper seat is in the universities.'[4] This scientific instinct continued to thrive in the academic development of criticism and reached its peak with structuralism in the mid-twentieth century, a methodological approach that drew its primary inspiration from the disciplines of linguistics and anthropology.

The aspiration to a scientific model waned somewhat from that point but it seems to be back in full swing today, with the ascendancy of computational methods of criticism and the prosperity of digital humanities. But whether we use quantitative or qualitative methods, criticism today has fully severed any umbilical link with amateur practice as outlined by Garber above. This is not to say that this has happened without dissent - often productive dissent as criticism, and especially criticism in the arts, has always contained a powerful anti-professional strain within itself that has militated against the institutionalisation of critical activity as an academic discipline. During the past couple of decades, Bruce Robbins has persuasively and repeatedly reminded us of this contradiction, pointing out the narrative of regret - of the 'sad fall of the man of letters into professionalisation' that has often accompanied accounts of the academisation of literary study.[5] Not that this has actually deterred academic professionalisation of critical discourse, nor has it made it compromised or deficient in any way. Rather, Robbins argues, this scepticism or sense of loss has been health-giving, instilling a permanent critique of professionalism within the academic study of literature.

For Robbins, therefore, the scepticism about the academic institutionalisation of criticism is both the sign of its peculiar inner conscience and a periodic jolt of rude good health that routinely works through a clever strategy of self-denigration. Many of the attacks on professionalism in the humanistic disciplines come from professionals themselves – insiders rather than outsiders – and end up as clever celebrations of the discipline concerned. One such self-affirming attack is Richard Rorty's disavowal of philosophy as a professional discourse. 'Richard Rorty's effort to end professional philosophy can keep professional philosophy going for years,' says Robbins, quoting the journalist T.S. Klepp, who is likewise unconvinced by Rorty's disavowal: 'He has reinvigorated philosophy by writing its epitaph.'[6]

Maverick and idiosyncratic as he might be – and certainly in this particular claim – Rorty ends up affirming disciplinary professionalism, which approximates a responsible intellectual socialism, one of the chief virtues of a properly institutionalised discipline. To bring a mode of thought together as an academic discipline is, before anything else, to make it a team game; push it past the idiosyncratic interiority of the maverick mind and turn it into a system in which others can participate on clear and legible terms. Ransom said as much when he called for criticism to be housed in the university, for it to be: '...developed by the collective and sustained effort of learned persons – which means that its proper seat is in the universities.'[7] For Robbins, it is academic criticism that is more likely to be open to the public, even though such criticism has been blamed for the disappearance of public voices such as the New York intellectuals. The reason behind this public access to academic criticism is simple – it is the collective that goes into the making of the profession, unlike the mystique of the individual thinker.

The two modes of thought and reading – the individual and the collective – I would suggest, approximate two kinds of relationship to the literary text as they might be understood today – that of the critic and that of the scholar. They remain ontologically entwined – scholarship must be critical in spirit, and there is much criticism that is deeply scholarly. But I would argue that they are epistemologically separable. The scholar is defined by her commitment to her archive of study. Her subjective self is subordinated to (though not effaced by) this commitment. The critic, on the other hand, celebrates and foregrounds her subjective self; the archive, in her case, is subordinated to the self, through which it is processed, and presented, the very subjective colour of that refraction remaining the most cherished element of the process. In this the critic is more closely allied to the poet or the fiction writer than to the scholar. In fact, inasmuch as the creative is a celebration of the idiosyncratic self, one can go so far as to say that interpretation remains a creative act. Scholarship, on the other hand, seeks to move away from the idiosyncrasy of the personal self and use information that is agreed upon by an institutionalised community as objective – information that can variously ethnographic, historical, quantifiable, or verifiable through technology.

*

But what about the larger professional community, the university, within which criticism sought its institutional location?

It is clear that during these crucial mid-century decades, it wasn't just the humanities that were on a fast track of professionalisation The university on the whole was fast transforming itself into a venue of professional knowledge and advancement, moving farther and farther away from the liberal arts mission that had once been its core. It felt like a natural process – and the right

115

thing to do – as post-secondary education opened up beyond the privileged elite. In the US, for instance, this happened gradually under the dual impact of the post-World War II GI Bill of 1944, which sponsored university education for war veterans, and that of the creation of land-grant institutions, which emphasised vocational and professional training as opposed to a classical liberal education. In England, the so-called 'red brick' universities, initially established as science or engineering colleges, offered their new entrants to post-secondary education a more pragmatic track, as opposed to the liberal arts enshrined in Oxbridge. The physical layout of most university campuses in the Anglo-American world usually tells the story. The older architectural core of most universities is where the liberal arts are housed, while the professional schools, whenever they are present – medicine, business, law, and engineering – with their larger spatial appetite, are located outside, sometimes in separate campuses altogether.

It is hard to miss the historical irony. Just as the humanities were seeking increasingly to professionalise themselves, the institution of the university itself was professionalising on a far greater scale. As the twentieth century drew to a close, the traditional core of the university had essentially shifted outside to the professional schools. The shift is felt acutely at American universities where the collaboration between academic research and the forces of corporatisation has been felt to be particularly ominous for several decades now. But it is felt everywhere, and with a different intensity in the rising economies of Asia, where professional upward mobility is both the anxious goal of individual desire and the urgent public mission of the nation state, a culture reflected in the predominant focus on scientific and technological education in universities across Korea, China, Taiwan, Singapore, and India. Clearly, even as the trajectory of professionalisation pushed the humanities into exciting new terrain, something was also getting radically out of sync between the internal professionalisation of these disciplines and the larger professionalisation of the university itself. The former was absolutely of no interest to the latter and, one might say, only helped to push it further back from the terrain of relevance.

*

But let me step back in time and look at the long history of the institutionalisation of criticism in the discipline I know best: literary studies, especially literary studies in English.

In J.M. Coetzee's quasi-fictional piece, 'The Novel in Africa,' the African writer Emmanuel Egudu – novelist-turned-speaker/performer – makes the claim that reading is not a normal activity in Africa.[8] The essential solipsism of reading, and the abstracted nature of its rewards, makes it an alien activity in African culture, which is too deeply rooted in a robust and vital communality to care for the isolation of reading and far too attentive to the appeal of the sensory to privilege the essentially abstracted and intellectual 'pleasures' offered by the private consumption of books. No wonder, therefore, that African culture is one of orality, with oral storytelling its favourite mode of sharing stories.

The reader is left with little doubt that the claim is wholly ironised in the piece. Egudu comes across as quite the poseur, an aggressive marketing genius selling a delicious, essentialised idea of Africa to wealthy elderly white consumers, as with the passengers of the luxury cruise where he delivers his entertaining lectures. Even if Africa – and even this entails substituting an idea for a vast and heterogeneous continent – is characterised by a strong culture of storytelling, who is to say that original and powerful works of written literature could not be inspired by such a culture? Beginning with the early example of Amos Tutuola, we have seen successful and highly acclaimed instances of such literature come out of African countries in English alone, to say nothing of vernacular or other European languages.

There is no doubt that Egudu deserves the irony and the suspicion he gets in Coetzee's piece, not merely from its protagonist, his friend and fellow writer Elizabeth Costello, but also from us, the readers. And yet Egudu's claim was made with a force and confidence that gave me pause even if it was staged – the force and confidence being rooted in a certain culture of conceiving and perceiving Africa, not merely from outside but from within as well.

This niggling feeling never quite went away. And then suddenly, it took a large and formidable shape when I finished reading a brilliant essay on Thomas Babington Macaulay, the celebrated – and reviled – colonial administrator of British India in the nineteenth century. The writer Jonathan Arac reminds us that Macaulay achieved public standing as a significant literary intellectual in nineteenth-century England, one whom Matthew Arnold considered a worthy rival. Macaulay, who rose to fame with a key essay on John Milton in the *Edinburgh Review* in 1825, writes Arac: 'is still known, and condemned, as the great practitioner of "Whig" history writing, but he was also a pioneer of a new social history' who drew out alternative and non-mainstream sources in order to write history. In 1834, named 'legal member' of the Supreme Court of India, 'he became one of the five men responsible for ruling British India, at an annual salary of £ 10,000'.[9]

What gave me real pause, however, is the daily reading habit of this influential administrator. From five to nine in the morning every day, he read the classics, and finished a mindboggling range of key Greek and Latin texts – in some cases, entire oeuvres of authors – at least once, and often twice. In the evening, after his day's work was done, he read works in English, French, Italian, and a little in Spanish and Portuguese. One cannot even begin to imagine an administrator today with anything remotely resembling such reading habits, and so there is little irony in Arac's statement about Macaulay: 'I imagine that nowadays it would be grounds for impeachment to reveal that a public official spent so much time reading classics.'[10]

Suddenly, the fact that Macaulay is most significantly remembered today as an educational administrator took on a new urgency in my mind, and I'm sad to say, of a not entirely salutary kind. His most lasting legacy is the role he played in the establishment of a curriculum of European humanities as central to Indian post-secondary education. His now-infamous dream, to create 'a class of persons Indian in blood and colour, but English in tastes, in opinions, in morals and in intellect'[11] has long been considered the very essence of the administrative ideology of British colonialism, a well-thought out programme to instil English cultural values and norms to shape the superstructural dominance of empire over its economic and military components of its material base. It approximates the thoughts of the Kenyan writer Ngũgĩ wa Thiong'o, which he cast in an unforgettable metaphor of violence: 'The night of the sword was followed by the morning of the chalkboard.'[12]

Chris Baldick has demonstrated convincingly that the institutionalisation of English as an academic discipline in England was rooted in providing education to members of various subordinate social groups at home and overseas. The formative force was the figure of the English poet and critic Matthew Arnold; both Baldick and Terry Eagleton have argued that Arnold looked to literature and its pedagogic application as a means of social cohesion in a world where both religion and aristocracy were rapidly losing their authority and cohesive power. Arnold, who significantly used the term 'culture' as a translation of the German 'bildung' (more commonly translated as 'education' or 'training'), was a staunch champion of 'the idea of formative training, of contact with good literary models in particular, in the hope that a new trained body of teachers could be brought "into intellectual sympathy" with the educated of the upper classes'.[13] Arnold's bold claim on behalf of the civilising force of literary studies laid the ideological ground for the institutionalisation of the discipline, but larger social and educational developments eventually made this institutionalisation possible. Of these developments, Baldick lists three as most important: 'first, the specific needs of the British Empire expressed in the regulations for admission to the Indian Civil Service; second, the various movements for adult education including Mechanics Institutes, Working Men's Colleges, and extension lecturing; third, within this general movement, the specific provisions made for women's education.'[14] If English was to be a 'civilising subject', its civilising impact was to play the most crucial role in the education of women, the working classes and in the business of empire, in the training of its civil servants as well as of colonised subjects. 'Arnold's conceptions of the humanizing and socially healing power of literary culture,' writes Baldick, 'had in fact quickly taken root where Homer was unavailable: among women, artisans, Indians, and their respective teachers.'[15] Not that this implies that the colonised was wholly a passive subject in this process. In work on what she calls the 'Gentlemen poets in colonial Bengal,' Rosinka Chaudhuri, for instance, has warned us that the weight and force of the Macaulayian enterprise should not delude us into undermining the agency of colonised Indians, many of whom were active and vocal in their desire for an English education.[16]

But neither does this change the fact that the professionalisation of English studies had important ideological motivations and equally far-reaching ideological consequences. If the amateur signified an older world of aristocratic male privilege, professionalisation, while conferring on literary-critical discourse a clear disciplinary identity and distinct institutional status, it was also a pedagogic gesture towards attaining social cohesion in an increasingly unstable world, nowhere more so than in late-Victorian England. This was done most clearly in the form of providing an accessible and ideologically appropriate subject to new social groups – women, the working class, and colonised peoples – that needed to be trained and educated in a professional way. English literary study was felt to possess not only adequate intellectual value but also the correct ideological capital to be designed as a disciplinary condition of professionalisation for subjects key to imperial administration. Gauri Viswanathan has done pioneering work to reveal the symbiotic relation between the institutionalisation of English studies and the British imperial project in India. She has reminded us that 'English literature appeared as a subject in the curriculum of the colonies long before it was institutionalised in the home country.'[17] It was in fact as early as the 1820s; when the classics dominated the curriculum in England, English literature had already become a curricular subject in British India. If the institutionalisation of English literature was, in turn, to become a condition of 'bildung' of professional subjects, it had a two-fold goal: to train and qualify British civil servants for service in India and to educate a class of native Indians in English culture and values so that they became effectively English in their taste and sensibilities while Indian in flesh; a class of men who would be the intermediary between the British rulers and the native masses. English literature was to occupy the central place in this education. The professionalisation of English as a curricular discipline, in other words, got under way with definite goals of social and imperial cohesion in view.

*

The university, I would argue, must become a crucial site of 'literary activism', which is the name this symposium has given to the crucial work that seeks to restore the importance of the literary to the public sphere. One of the things it needs to do in order to achieve this is to allow the amateur to be retrieved from the academic discipline of literary study that is entrenched within the university. Even as we celebrate the riches harvested by the professionalisation of the study, teaching, and scholarship of literature throughout the twentieth century, we need to initiate an equally important strand of resistance, within the academy itself, against the professionalisation of the literary intellectual. This will involve redrawing attention to the dialectic of the individual and the collective that constitutes the practice and sensibility of such an intellectual, and that of the amateur and the professional that lingers around it. The epistemological forces of both criticism and scholarship, as driven, respectively, by individual and collective consciousness, deserve equal respect and appreciation, whether they appear in the sensibility of the same intellectual or are separately embodied in the practices of different academics. This glorious tension, sometimes articulated within individual intellectuals and often within the discipline on the whole, is neither meant to be abandoned nor resolved, but rather reinstated as an essential element of the practice of literary study. In the Indian context, it will also mean leaving behind the colonial-bureaucratic mode of the modern university set up by the British in the nineteenth century, and the instrumental use of literary study towards the certification of credentials through a standardised set of examinations.

The happy news is that well beyond the institutionalisation of a humanistic curriculum in the Anglophone world, the amateur critic of literature, culture, and social phenomena remains a striking figure. It is not surprising that such a figure is at its most provocative in its startling defection from the programme of institutionalisation of the humanities as part of the ideology of late-colonial Britain. My particular interest here is the intellectual self-fashioning of the provincial autodidact who hails from a background where the curricularisation of English literature – and, in a wider sense, of the European humanistic tradition – formed part of the administrative strategy of colonialism. In such a context, autodidacticism signifies – above and beyond the idiosyncratic imagination of the individual subject – a peripheral position in relation to the mainstream narrative of professional and intellectual development that this administrative strategy sought to design. I seek, therefore, to foreground the amateur intellectual who springs from the kind of autodidactic 'bildung' that has something in common with the literary self-tutelage of the English working class as chronicled by Jonathan Rose.[18]

The amateur and imperfect nature of autodidactic education, I believe, is central to this narrative of development. The colonial and postcolonial writer shaped by such an autodidactic 'bildung' offers a powerful model of the literary public intellectual whose flawed or deviant relation with curricular education significantly shapes their wide, often provocative appeal.

Such is the writer who grew up in the light – and perhaps more appropriately, the shadow – of the humanistic tradition of European modernity, with English literature occupying a central position within the colonial curriculum, upheld by the ideological enterprise of the British Empire. But at the same time, their engagement with this tradition, which shaped them to a great extent, strikingly disrupts the narrative of professionalisation this pedagogy sought to design in order to satisfy the administrative needs of the Empire. Such a provincial amateur, who charts his own relationship without access to community, institution, or essential archive, can only aspire to be a critic. Rarely, if ever, a scholar.

*

A key example of this, in my opinion, is Nirad C. Chaudhuri, one of modern India's most intriguing and controversial intellectuals. Chaudhuri, who was born in Kishorganj in 1897 and died in Oxford in 1999, is well known as one of the most provocative, insightful, and entertaining Indian memoirists and essayists of the twentieth century. His wide readership in both English and Bengali is only matched by the raging invectives he has inspired with his utterances on everything from colonial history to the place of Muslims in modern India. He sits at an uneasy angle with almost every narrative of postcolonial writing, most blatantly with the liberatory image of the Empire writing back. He has proved embarrassingly difficult to integrate into the progressivist politics of postcolonial criticism. His long life and his late start as a writer (aged 54) make him a strange sort of anachronism, not only in the historical but also in a political and aesthetic sense. His Anglophilia occasionally evokes an older model of the colonial mimic man; socially and intellectually, he shares biographical space with the Bengali liberal middle class but throughout his writing life, he seemed to survive on the prickly delight of disrupting almost every value and belief upheld by this social group. Tempted by the illusion of his pro-Hindu, Sanskritic sensibility, Hindu nationalist groups occasionally tried to court him, only to meet with the same frustration that he inspired in the liberal and progressive segment of the Indian middle class. At the heart of these infuriating anomalies, I would suggest, is a certain way of looking at the world. This is the way of the engaged amateur, of an eccentric talent who trained himself to ways to reading cultural phenomena through an act of inspired but eclectic self-fashioning. Such self-making kept him at some distance from the conventions of institutional knowledge, and hence from the recognisable markers of both reactionary and progressive political worldviews. But throughout his life, he flirted with both, and drew the wrong kind of attention from both at the same time.

Chaudhuri's relationship with the institutions of colonial education is more strikingly one of failure than of success. He is, in fact, the perfect example of the popular intellectual whose very scholarly and political 'flaws' and oddities win him a wide audience, but an audience that alternatively loves and hates him. Blame for such seductive flaws must fall to the polymath sensibility driven by a kind of cosmopolitanism that is paradoxically provincial in origin. Ian Almond's layered praise for Chaudhuri's erudition illustrates this intriguing mix. Admiring Chaudhuri's 'reference-peppered prose', Almond reminds us that Chaudhuri is 'the Bengali who has not simply read the biography of Napoleon, but also that of his valet; or who can describe the village communities and practices of Mymensingh in terms borrowed from classical Greek – polis, nomos, metoikoi'.[19] But this cosmopolitanism, Eurocentric as it might be, is made memorable by the accent of provincialism that undercuts it: 'hidden beneath all the references to Bernheim's *Lehrbuch* and Zola's *La terre* lies the subaltern voice of Chaudhuri's east Bengali, speaking the language almost completely excluded from the *Autobiography*, a language not even conceded the tradesman's entrance of a footnote or a parenthesis.'[20] The various dialects of east Bengali, associated with the eastern part of undivided Bengal (now Bangladesh) have often been imagined to be less urbane and sophisticated than the dialects spoken in the western districts (including Calcutta). Such a prejudice is doubtlessly one of the cultural consequences of the large-scale migration of homeless and uprooted peoples from the east to the west for religious and political reasons. The binary of the cosmopolitan and the provincial contained in the cultural assumption about the East Bengal accent is exactly the kind of response Chaudhuri invites seductively, if only to scatter and confuse it. Nobody, in fact, can deny Chaudhuri the self-mocking humour he retained about his east Bengali origins throughout his life; he would have certainly chuckled at the English Almond's playful detection of Bangalbhasha, or east Bengali in his analysis of Bernheim or Zola! At the same time, it is precisely this kind of unpredictable, utterly idiosyncratic cosmopolitanism that governs larger decisions, such as that to write in English when the predominant – indeed, cosmopolitan – trend among his generation would have been to write in Bengali.

'I never became a scholar,' Chaudhuri writes, 'But every true scholar will forgive me, for he knows as well as I do that the greater part of his métier is the capacity for experiencing the emotion of scholarship.'[21] Passionate and a little bit crazy, this emotion of scholarship is inspired by a desire to embrace the world. It reminds me of Apu in Bibhutibhushan Bandopadhyay's novel *Aparajito*, who moves back and forth whimsically between history, drama, astronomy, poetry, botany, and every subject he stumbles on. His friend Pranab, who is a far more organised scholar, reprimands him for his lack of discipline: 'Dur? O ki pora? Tomar to pora noy, porapora khela' ('Come on, you call that studying? What you do is not studying; it's just make-believe studies!').[22] Miraculously, around the same time, another young man, also from the provinces, also enrolled in a city college, was also playing a very similar 'poraporakhela.' They might have run into each other had Apu been a figure alive in real time, perhaps in the bookstores along the pavements of College Street or the sweetshops in Bowbazar.

Nirad C. Chaudhuri could perhaps be seen as the real-life version of this young man. He comes from a somewhat more privileged background than Apu, but they both arrive in Calcutta from rural or suburban places; Chaudhuri from the country town of Kishorganj, and Apu from Nischindipur, a village in the southern part of West Bengal. Both of them are students – Apu, at intermediate college (classes 11 and 12), and Chaudhuri at the undergraduate and later at the master's level. Both of them attend Ripon College, as did Apu's creator Bibhutibhushan, a close friend of Chaudhuri. Ripon (now Surendranath) was at some distance from Presidency College in College Street, the great seat of the marvel of modernity and cosmopolitanism in nineteenth-century India – the Bengal Renaissance, which rather intimidates the poor and rustic Apu. And both of them are students in a peripheral and precarious way. There are moments of interaction with memorable teachers, and occasionally there is a great lecture that grabs their attention, but both of them spend most of their time reading on their own, in an earnest but patchy way, sometimes trying to impose structure but failing more often than not, floating in a scholarly flanerie that stares in a kind of childlike defiance at the curricular grids of college education. The classic image of this defiance is that of the student lounging at the back of the lecture hall, reading a book of his choice while the tedious and uninspiring lecturer drones on. This exact image is captured in the novel *Aparajito* as well as in Chaudhuri's *Autobiography of an Unknown Indian*. Apu is caught in the back benches with a book that is not welcome in a class on Logic – Palgrave's *Golden Treasury*. The professor is not amused. After a moment of public humiliation, Apu slips out through the back door to head to the library, where he chats with the staff and loans a volume of Gibbon's history. And in his autobiography, Nirad C. Chaudhuri records a similar indifference to the lectures at Calcutta University, making exceptions for just a handful of professors. 'As for the rest,' he writes, 'I paid no attention whatever to what they said and sat on one of the back benches, either reading a book of my choice, or scribbling, or thinking my own thoughts.'[23] If the autodidact owes a debt to an institution, it is the library. 'It was another institution, the Imperial Library, to which I owe nearly all my higher education.'[24] The library offers an archive of knowledge that seems limitless; at the same time, it seems to promise unlimited freedom for the intellect.

By fleeing the classroom, both Apu and Chaudhuri try to escape the bureaucratised tedium of the colonial higher education system. They continue their quest for a wider, more exciting world in a European humanistic tradition, whether in the Roman history of Gibbon or the poetry anthology of Francis Turner Palgrave. But they do it as undisciplined interlopers, a habit that derives from their historic background as provincial aspirants to cosmopolitan knowledge. But this irregular engagement with humanities scholarship is not only the historical destiny of the colonial literary intellectual, but also essential to his 'bildung', to his development into a writer of a unique charm as opposed to the methodical rigour of a professional scholar.

At the very beginning of the chapter 'Initiation into Scholarship' in the *Autobiography*, Chaudhuri warns us that: 'This chapter has certainly been presumptuously titled, for I never became a scholar.' What prompts the presumption is the feeling that he has at least experienced 'the emotion of scholarship'.[25] The capacity to experience the emotion of scholarship, he knows, is in many ways the very life and breath of the pursuit. Everything Chaudhuri writes, in this book or elsewhere, trembles with this momentous emotion; it is his hallmark and appeal as a public intellectual. 'I hardly know,' he writes, 'what made me read Stubbs week after week, month after month, when I could not understand three-quarters of him.'[26] Even when he does not understand these books, he knows, they give him something else, something less tangible perhaps, but more valuable. 'I should have been,' he writes, 'driven away by Stubbs after breaking my teeth on him, and if I was not, even after breaking my teeth, it was to be explained only by the taste of the emotion of scholarship I found in the book.'[27]

There is something in Chaudhuri's amateur aspiration as a polymath that evokes an older worldview that was already on the wane during his student days. 'The compulsion of our humanistic culture of the nineteenth century was still strong.'[28] He recognizes, however, that students like he and his brother were among the last products of this culture. 'It was,' he writes, 'almost the last proddings of this compulsion which made my brother, when he had just entered the degree class of Calcutta University in 1914, buy Comte's *Positivism*, Mill's works, and some of Huxley's essays.'[29] Wistfully, he knew, as did some of his peers, that this interest was more utopian than real, as the great age of the polymath had passed. Frequently, they 'discussed the relative merits of the encyclopaedic or polymathic mind and the mind of the specialist', identifying Leibnitz and Goethe as the great encyclopaedic minds at the end of the seventeenth and the eighteenth centuries respectively.[30] They concluded that the polymath had disappeared by the end of the nineteenth century, due to emergence of the specialist. But it was the polymath they loved and wanted to become, even if they knew somewhere that it was not to be, not any more. For them, the magic word was 'synthesis.' The concept, they felt, epitomized the Hindu way of life. A more immediate representation of synthesis was someone they saw every day – Professor Brajendra Nath Seal, then holder of the George V Chair in Philosophy in Calcutta University. He was a figure who evoked in Chaudhuri and his fellow students the admiration inspired by the polymath, fast becoming an anachronism, and also a little jealousy.

Still he tried to become a polymath, with curious results. 'I could pass from physics to Sanksrit literature or from novels to astronomy with an agility which seemed like volatility to those who did not know me well.'[31] The mixed social response to his aspirations predicted pretty well both the immediate and long-term consequences of this mode of scholarship. Those who did not like him called him: 'Jack of all trades, master of none.'[32] To them, he knew that he 'appeared like a squid or octopus in the world of knowledge'.[33] Indeed, throughout his life, the idiosyncrasies that amused his friends also endeared him to the non-specialist reader looking for narrative gratification; at the same time, they put him at odds with conventions of scholarship. For all of his interest in large structures such as origins and histories of people, Chaudhuri retained, throughout his life, a mischievous interest in trivia. It is the kind of knowledge that might help one win a game show on TV rather than achieve scholarly citations. Knowledge of this kind delights both the writer and the man, and it gives a novelistic feel to his social analysis, sometimes (though not always) at the expense of real sociological rigour.

The odd angle between scholarship and trivia comes fully to life in Chaudhuri's encounter with the Indian literary academic Meenakshi Mukherjee. Mukherjee was at work on a monograph on Jane Austen when she visited Chaudhuri in Oxford in 1989. As part of her research, she had been spending time at the British Museum, reading eighteenth-century bestsellers mentioned or referred to in Austen's own novels. The idea was to get a sense of Austen's own reading. It is the kind of knowledge, most would agree, that is still valued in academic scholarship. Chaudhuri had no interest in this sort of thing. An avid reader of Austen all his life, he was busy with much more fascinating stuff, such as 'the details of Darcy's clothing on specific occasions, knowing the meaning of certain colours of British heraldry, the distance between Hunsford and Longbourne, the number of horses used for drawing different kinds of carriages...'.[34] Mukherjee faced a test in Austen trivia of the most exotic kind before the ninety-two-year-old Chaudhuri, and she confessed that she 'barely managed a B grade'.[35] The most exotic question was about 'the size of Fanny Price's room in the attic in Mansfield Park' which, Mukherjee recalled, 'had something to do with the space taken up by Fanny's bookshelf which he calculated by locating the original edition of each book mentioned and adding up their dimensions'.[36]

I will not deny that the collection of such arcane – sometimes absurd – details, on one level, reveals Chaudhuri's sense of humour. But the humour is not irreverence, and neither does the trivia trivialise the archive. On another level, it is also a genuine expression of Chaudhuri's preferred mode of reading cultural phenomena, which remains more anecdotal and novelistic than faithful to established models of scholarly research. If the amateur's work articulates a celebration of his subjectivity rather than a self-effacing dedication to the archive, then, ironically, the amateur cannot but be a celebrated figure in the history of literary criticism – one that exists in a more seamless continuity with the archive of literature itself than the relatively self-detached figure of the scholar. It is no surprise, on the other hand, that the successful academic Mukherjee scored a B in Chaudhuri's test. Perhaps it is itself a trivial hint as to why nearly seventy years ago, Chaudhuri himself had failed his MA examination. Chaudhuri writes: 'The great adventure came to nothing. I failed to pass my MA examination.'[37] Such a failure looks all the more spectacular after his great success at the preceding BA examination, where he had stood first with honours in history! The amateur's place in academia, if there is any at all, it seems, must be defined by an idiosyncratic and utterly unpredictable trajectory of absurd rise and fall, where his capacity of excellence is more than matched by his aptitude for failure.

It is a key failure, not only for Chaudhuri himself, but also importantly for the figure of the Bengali intellectual enrolled in the great colonial institution of higher education, the University of Calcutta. Such a failure, for instance, shows that as a Bengali subject of colonial education, he is very different from what is perhaps the most famous Bengali mimic man of English literature, Hurree Babu of Rudyard Kipling's *Kim*, who is keen to remind everybody that he is 'an MA of Calcutta University.'[38] Hurree Babu is awfully keen himself on institutional education and is very eager to convince Kim of its importance. He is absolutely certain that 'going to school' was the only way Kim could get an education founded on the best in classical European humanities.

In Chaudhuri's case, this is not only his own failure to professionalise himself as a scholar (and possibly as an academic, as he once wished to be), but also the failure of the institution to interpellate him into the ideological enterprise of the Empire. The more popular imagination of Chaudhuri as a lifelong Anglophile misses the significance of his failure at this important venue of colonial learning. There were points in his life when he aspired to the utopian intellectual ideals of European humanism and even Enlightenment science, and these ideals also definitely shaped him to an extent. But in the end, colonial pedagogy failed to produce him as a subject after its vision, one who might be a capable agent of the Empire, such as the Indian civil servant who was part of Thomas Macaulay's dream. Not only was Chaudhuri *not* a professional, he was, in every sense, an amateur – a very good one, but still an amateur who was as disruptive as he was incorporated as a colonial subject.[39]

There is nothing in Chaudhuri's autobiography that suggests a sense of betrayal or even surprise at his failure. Towards the end of the section titled 'Academic failure,' he makes it clear that he came to understand well why he failed: it was the very eclectic nature of his developing scholarly identity, which, no matter how striking it was, lacked consistency, and did not amount to any real command on any subject. 'Thus, although I came to acquire a deep knowledge in certain aspects of certain subjects very unusual in a student of my age, taking it all in all, I did not succeed in having an even grounding in any subject.'

But why, in the first place, did he try so hard to achieve something that could not really be achieved? To possess that remarkable anachronism, the encyclopaedic mind? Doubtless it was, as he says, the still-living compulsion of the 'humanistic culture of the nineteenth century' that pushed him towards this impossible goal.

133

But there was, I would suggest, another impulse more peculiar to his personal history. This is the passion for self-making that marks the scholar who makes the arduous and exciting trek from the province to the metropolis. The emergence of the critic of great subjective idiosyncrasy, in Chaudhuri's case, necessarily follows the failure of the emergence of the scholar. While this is the most striking and direct realisation of this failure, I would argue that the development of these (post)colonial amateurs as critics neeessarily involves their disavowal of – or failure at – scholarship, which remains welded to institution and community that remained far beyond their reach, at least, in their crucial formative years. The budding thinker who comes to the metropolitan centre of learning and culture from a small, peripheral place has in him a scale of ambition and a dreaminess of vision that necessarily pushes him towards a utopian goal. This is the dream of cosmopolitanism born in the provincial periphery, which awakens through the eclectic routes of amateur and autodidactic learning.

*

Mourning the absence of what he calls a 'literary landscape' in Indian English writing, the poet Arvind Krishna Mehrotra blames English departments in the country. By way of introducing his book *Partial Recall*, an exquisite hybrid of memoir, criticism, and literary history, he grieves their failure to sponsor exactly the phenomenon that we are calling literary activism:

> The great betrayal of our literature has been primarily by those who teach in the country's English departments, the academic community whose job it was to green the hillsides by planting them with biographies, scholarly editions, selections carrying

new introductions, histories, canon-shaping (or canon-breaking) anthologies, readable translations, revaluations, exhaustive bibliographies devoted to individual authors, and critical essays that, because of the excellence of their prose, become as much a part of the literature as any significant novel or poem. Little of this has happened.[40]

It is a sad reality, but one that will surprise no one who has studied literature, or more generally the humanities in India. If I may say so, Mehrotra provides the reason behind the failure of the universities to shape, and participate in, such a literary landscape. In the title essay of the book, a poignant account of his adolescent 'bildung' as a poet, he narrates stories of his days as a student at the University of Allahabad in 1964. He studied English as his main subject, along with history and economics, but his relationship with academic study, even in the subjects of his general liking, was far from what one might call inspiring. His choices of specific fields were shaped by instrumental criteria: 'because the subject was "scoring", which is to say the examiners were believed to be liberal, awarding high marks to every script they read.'[41] Though this brought in inevitable disappointments, 'scoring ancient history was easier said than done, for next thing we learnt was that the marks awarded depended on the length of the answers than what was written in them'.[42] This in return shaped a bizarre kind of instrumentalism, part clerical drudgery, part archival labour: 'Perhaps studying is the wrong word for what we did, for most of our time went in making "notes"'. He explains further: 'So making notes in fact meant copying at high speed whole chapters in longhand, the drudgery made worse by the condition of the books.'[43] Following such note-taking, studying simply implied committing vast swathes of this material to memory: 'Quite apart from the hundreds of pages to be crammed,

we had dates in history and quotations in English
(Graham Hough and Maurice Bowra on the Romantics,
A.C. Ward on Shaw) to commit to memory.' It wasn't, of
course, merely a brutal labour of rote-learning; there was
clever strategising involved, in the attempt to guess likely
exam questions based on the most crucial archive of all:
the compendium of test papers from the past:

> We studied selectively of course, like everyone else.
> There were parts of the syllabus we left out and others
> we mugged up, depending on the 'guess papers' in
> each subject. To make a guess paper we scrutinized
> the previous ten years questions, available in
> inexpensive booklets with flimsy pink or yellow covers
> on University Road, and after taking into account
> the hints dropped by teachers and the gossip among
> students, and after listening to our inner voices,
> we drew up a list of questions that were likely to be
> asked.[44]

Clearly, Mehrotra's literary education took
on a vibrant life exactly at the time this was going on;
and clearly most of it wasn't really happening at the
University of Allahabad, another venerable colonial
institution. In 1964, the heavily bureaucratised, rather
oddly instrumental nature of humanistic education
evoked in Mehrotra the same indifference the University
of Calcutta had evoked in Nirad C. Chaudhuri in 1919.
Clearly, both of these writers are exceptional, deeply
imaginative, and strongly idiosyncratic individuals who
would have perhaps felt at least a little out of place in any
academic institution. The paradox of institutionalising
the humanities probably comes alive in their relation with
the academy more than anywhere else. But is that all?
What about the particular nature of institutions we are
talking about here?

The issue of institutionalising the humanities
for the purposes of professionalisation takes on a whole

new meaning if we inquire into the establishment of the modern university in India. André Béteille reminds us that the colonial universities set up by the British in the nineteenth century could not be more different from the centres of higher learning that had existed in Western Europe for centuries before that. Specifically, the mission of the research university – which originated with Wilhelm von Humboldt's reformed University of Berlin in the early nineteenth century and was introduced later in the century in the US through the establishment of the Johns Hopkins University – had no relation whatsoever with the universities set up in India by the British, where Thomas Babington Macaulay institutionalised a curriculum of Western humanities and possibly pioneered the academic study of English literature. 'The first universities that came into being in 1857 in Calcutta, Bombay and Madras,' Béteille writes, 'were set up primarily for conducting examinations and awarding degrees, and not for undertaking research or even teaching.'[45] Venues for research included specialised institutions such as the Asiatic Society or the Indian Association for the Cultivation of Science, and teaching was left to the colleges.

The Acts of Incorporation passed by the Governor-General and Viceroy Lord Curzon in 1857 provided for the establishment of the three universities in the three presidencies: Calcutta, Bombay, and Madras. The preambles to the three Acts, Suresh Chandra Ghosh has pointed out, were identical. They all defined the objects of the universities as 'ascertaining by means of examination the persons who have acquired proficiency in different branches of Literature, Science and Art and rewarding them by Academic Degrees as evidence of their respective attainments'.[46] Indeed, as Ghosh also indicates, two of the major criticisms against the university system – as early as in the State Paper on

Education, which was issued as a Resolution of the Governor-General in Council on Indian Education on 11 March 1904 – were that 'higher education was pursued with too exclusive a view to entering government service, which unduly narrowed its scope, and those who failed to obtain employment under government were ill fitted for other pursuits' and that 'excessive importance was given to examinations'.[47]

Clearly, the British did not believe that the university as a place for higher learning and research – as those that thrived in Western Europe since the medieval period – could take root in India. This is not to imply, Béteille reminds us, that they had no salutary role in society. They were important venues of secular modernity, and played a distinctive role in the shaping and sustaining of a civil society in India. Moreover, a few universities had emerged as centres of intellectual and scholarly excellence, but by and large: 'Under colonial rule, the universities did mainly what they were set up to do, that is, produce increasing numbers of graduates of indifferent quality.'[48]

Even the Nehruvian vision for higher education, which shaped the birth of the University Education Commission in 1948 under the leadership of Sarvepalli Radhakrishnan, failed to change this fundamental character of Indian universities. Decades after independence, the expansion of higher education continued to respond to social and political pressures rather than the need for the advancement of knowledge. 'Despite the best efforts of the leaders of the community of scientists and scholars,' writes Béteille, 'the universities have failed to free themselves from their older legacy of having to produce more and more graduates.'[49]

This was the colonial institution that bored and distracted Nirad C. Chaudhuri, pushing him to a track of eclectic autodidactism. Half a century later, Mehrotra, at another colonially established university, was weighing subjects to choose based on how well one could score marks in them, because examinations, and examinations alone, mattered at the universities, and the degrees one obtained were the result of scoring well at them. Please allow me an autobiographical voice to give a sense of how things looked close to another half a century after Mehrotra had been a student.

It is a kind of sad revelation that reading Béteille and Viswanathan – several years after I graduated from college in Calcutta in 1996 – has enabled me to put my own undergraduate education in illuminating perspective. I had honours in English – the subject Viswanathan puts at the heart of the mission of the imperial educational enterprise. Even half a century after independence, the life of the subject, as lived in the university, revolved around the heavily bureaucratised system of mass-examination outlined so memorably by Béteille. This system had long since become safely archived in public memory, and the most visible form of this archive was easily available for purchase in the bookstalls of College Street, just as it was for Mehrotra in Allahabad in the 1960s – the famous anthologies of test question papers, from the last ten, twenty, or thirty years, depending on the resourcefulness of the publisher. The trick was to avoid the questions that the university had set the previous year, as we were assured that the authorities did not like to repeat questions in successive years. Questions from odd and even-numbered years, as such, did not mingle in the same question set – since our BA Part I was to be held in an even-numbered year, I zealously prepared the answer to a question on the tragic structure of J.M. Synge's *Riders to the Sea* that had first appeared, in more or less the same words, on the Calcutta University exam script in 1943. Who knows if Mehrotra also prepared the answer to that question? That would depend if he took the exam in 1966 or 1967.

Education in India, however, is nothing if not dazzlingly uneven; like Oxbridge, in Calcutta, it mattered far more which college you attended than the vast, sprawling university that conducted the examination and gave you the official degree. My institution, St. Xavier's, a private Jesuit college, gave me an excellent literary education, deepened with a genuine spirit of liberal humanism and sharpened with the attentive skills of close reading. Most of this was achieved by the intellect and charisma of individual professors, something the college, and, indeed, the city of Calcutta, has never lacked. Most of all, there was love, which made the subject special, which it remained, for many of us, for the rest of our lives.

But all this love was contained, in the end, within the larger pedagogic framework scaffolded by the colossal machinery of colonial bureaucracy – the University of Calcutta, the same institution from which Nirad C. Chaudhuri had ultimately defected through his magnificent failure in the MA examination in 1919. At the close of the twentieth century, just as much as at the beginning, everything was tested by the final yardstick of the university examination, made up of wagering on potential questions based on the test-paper chronicles. In short, even the liberal arts and sciences survived on a method of professional certification that essentially required a bureaucratic consumption of knowledge. English literature, from its inception, was the classic government service prep subject. Just as Macaulay had envisioned.

*

The universities have a much larger role to play in the phenomenon we are calling literary activism. Sometimes a sneaking worry irritates me: perhaps it isn't just 'English literature' that Macaulay left us with, but in fact the culture of reading itself, and especially the notion and praxis of literature as defined by the act of reading. This is the reality of literature that Egudu, Coetzee's consummate performer of African orality, mocks and dismisses. If the modern notion of literature – the notion deeply embedded in us – is doomed by this historical fragility – can any amount of activism really re-energise its declined importance in the contemporary public sphere?

But on the other hand, it is also clear the universities, where the systematic study of Anglophone literatures took clear disciplinary shape for the first time, continue to exponentially grow in importance, though in directions that could not be further removed from their traditional liberal arts mission, whose core was constituted by literary, historical, and philosophical study. There is a contradiction here that is loaded with historical irony: the gulf between these two stories of decline and prosperity that grows daily. It is this contradiction that makes Mehrotra's accusation of English departments pertinent and poignant at the same time. As the aspiration for upward mobility across the length and breadth of twenty-first century India translates into a keen and irreversible interest in university education, English departments at universities nationwide need to do all that Mehrotra says they have failed to do. Most importantly, in terms of training, they need to nurture the amateur humanist, one who undertakes her practice impelled by love, which lies at the root of amateurism, as it lies in the Latin root ('amō') of the word itself. Not all of them will become Chaudhuri or Mehrotra, nor do they need to be – they will translate their natural obligation to upward mobility through professional identities as doctors or lawyers or engineers. As the middle class continues to expand in the wake of economic energisation, this obligation is rightfully irrevocable across India. The lover, or the amateur humanist, is the best bet for the university's contribution to any activism that might enhance the importance of literature in the public sphere.

1. Marjorie Garber, *Academic Instincts* (Princeton: Princeton University Press, 2001), p. 12.

2. Garber, *Academic Instincts*, p. 15.

3. Garber, *Academic Instincts*, p. 15.

4. John Crowe Ransom, 'Criticism, Inc.', in *Selected Essays of John Crowe Ransom*, ed. Thomas Daniel Young and John Hindle (Baton Rouge, LA: Louisiana State University Press, 1984), p. 94.

5. Bruce Robbins, *Secular Vocations: Intellectuals, Professionalism, Culture* (London & New York: Verso, 1993), p. 18.

6. Robbins, *Secular Vocations*, p. 20.

7. Ransom, 'Criticism, Inc.', p. 94.

8. J.M. Coetzee, *Elizabeth Costello: Nine Lessons* (London: Secker and Warburg, 2003), pp. 35-59.

9. Jonathan Arac, 'Peculiarities of (the) English in the Metanarrative(s) of Knowledge and Power', in *Intellectuals: Aesthetics, Politics, Academics*, ed. Bruce Robbins (Minneapolis: University of Minnesota Press, 1990), p. 195.

10. Arac, 'Peculiarities of (the) English in the Metanarrative(s) of Knowledge and Power', in *Intellectuals*, p. 197.

11. Minute by the Hon'ble T.B. Macaulay, dated the 2nd February 1835, *Bureau of Education. Selections from Educational Records, Part I (1781-1839)*, ed. H. Sharp (Calcutta: Superintendent, Government Printing, 1920; Reprint: Delhi: National Archives of India, 1965), p. 117.

12. Ngũgĩ wa Thiong'o, 'The Language of African Literature', in *Colonial Discourse/Postcolonial Theory: A Reader*, eds. Patrick Williams and Laura Chrisman (New York: Columbia University Press, 1994), p. 436.

13. Chris Baldick, *The Social Mission of English Criticism, 1848-1932* (Oxford: Clarendon Press, 1983), p. 34.

14. Baldick, *The Social Mission of English Criticism*, p. 61.

15. Baldick, *The Social Mission of English Criticism*, p. 72.

16. Rosinka Chaudhuri, *Gentlemen Poets in Colonial Bengal: Emergent Nationalism and the Orientalist Project.* (Calcutta: Seagull, 2002).

17. Gauri Viswanathan, *Masks of Conquest: Literary Study and British Rule in India* (New York: Columbia University Press, 1989), p. 3.

18. Jonathan Rose, *The Intellectual Lives of the British Working Classes* (New Haven: Yale University Press, 2001).

19. Ian Almond. 'Four Ways of Reading Nirad C. Chaudhuri: A Case Study of a Postcolonial Conservative,' *Orbis Litterarum* 66.6 (2011) p. 2.

20. Almond, 'Four Ways of Reading Nirad C. Chaudhuri', *Orbis Litterarum*, p. 2.

21. Nirad C. Chaudhuri, *The Autobiography of an Unknown Indian* (London: Macmillan, 1951), p. 324.

22. Bibhutibhushan Bandopadhyay, *Aparajito. Upanyas Samagra* (Kolkata: Mitra, 2006), p. 50, my translation.

23. Chaudhuri, *The Autobiography of an Unknown Indian*, p. 333.

24. Chaudhuri, *The Autobiography of an Unknown Indian*, p. 333.

25. Chaudhuri, *The Autobiography of an Unknown Indian*, p. 324.

26. Chaudhuri, *The Autobiography of an Unknown Indian*, p. 327.

27. Chaudhuri, *The Autobiography of an Unknown Indian*, p. 327.

28. Chaudhuri, *The Autobiography of an Unknown Indian*, p. 329.

29. Chaudhuri, *The Autobiography of an Unknown Indian*, p. 329.

30. Chaudhuri, *The Autobiography of an Unknown Indian*, p. 329

31. Chaudhuri, *The Autobiography of an Unknown Indian*, p. 330.

32. Chaudhuri, *The Autobiography of an Unknown Indian*, p. 330.

33. Chaudhuri, *The Autobiography of an Unknown Indian*, p. 330.

34. Meenakshi Mukherjee. 'We Say Desh: The Other Nirad Babu', in ed. Swapan Dasgupta, *Nirad C. Chaudhuri, the First Hundred Years: A Celebration.* (Delhi:

HarperCollins India, 1998), p. 83.

35. Mukherjee. 'We Say Desh', p. 83.

36. Mukherjee. 'We Say Desh', p. 83.

37. Chaudhuri, *The Autobiography of an Unknown Indian*, p. 351.

38. Rudyard Kipling, *Kim* (Oxford: Oxford University Press, 1987), p. 162.

39. Chaudhuri, *The Autobiography of an Unknown Indian*, p. 352.

40. Arvind Krishna Mehrotra, *Partial Recall: Essays on Literature and Literary History* (Ranikhet: Permanent Black, 2012), p. 2.

41. Mehrotra, *Partial Recall*, p. 63.

42. Mehrotra, *Partial Recall*, p. 63.

43. Mehrotra, *Partial Recall*, p. 64.

44. Mehrotra, *Partial Recall*, p. 67.

45. André Béteille , 'Viable Universities', *The Telegraph*, Calcutta, April 22, 2010.

46. Suresh Chandra Ghosh, *The History of Education in Modern India: 1757-1998* (Hyderabad: Orient Longman, 2000), p. 110.

47. Ghosh, *The History of Education in Modern India*, p. 123.

48. Béteille, 'Viable Universities'.

49. Beteille, 'Viable Universities'.

Globalisation, Literary Activism, and the Death of Critical Discourse
TIM PARKS

In late 2015, I interviewed around thirty candidates for positions in my university's postgraduate course in translation. This in Milan, Italy. As always, I asked them what they were reading. 'Murakami,' says one. 'Isabel Allende,' says another. 'Harry Potter,' says a third. However, most of the students didn't mention names at all. 'Fantasy,' was the most common response. I read fantasy. And who writes this fantasy, I ask; where and when was it written? One of the students knew she was reading George Martin, but didn't know whether George was American, English, Australian, or even South African. Others had simply never thought about the author's name or nationality, though they did know the name of the series. *A Song of Ice and Fire. The Kingkiller Chronicle.* The stories in fantasy novels don't happen anywhere in particular, or not anywhere your satnav will take you; their characters move in imaginary, though generally quite familiar worlds, exploiting tropes now well-known around the globe: that curious mix of medieval garb and futuristic technology. So an author located in time and place is hardly necessary. The book is a product out there. Millions of Italians read Harry Potter, but few register the name J.K. Rowling.

However, what mattered to me was that not one of these aspiring translators was reading contemporary Italian fiction, nor was it immediately clear to them why an Italian translator should necessarily be reading Italian fiction. They had no sense of a continuing and specifically Italian literary world into which a foreign text might be introduced. Rather, a translation was simply an Italian version of an internationally available novel. A product.

I should stress here that I do not think these students are below average in any way. Nor do I wish to make fun of them. The fact is that over recent years the old connections that linked writer to community have been drastically weakened and in many cases altogether

severed. Young readers, who have grown up browsing
in bookshops where seventy per cent of the fiction
is translated, often do not think of a writer as being
radically housed or nurtured in a particular language or
culture. They do not assume that a writer writes to his
community about life in that community, thus earning
his livelihood from that community. I hope to show how
this state of affairs inevitably alters the way even the most
literary works are written, read, and promoted; it is this
accelerating globalisation of narrative and literary culture
that lies behind what Amit Chaudhuri has described
as market activism and, in reaction to that, a hoped-
for literary activism, the first deploying the language
of literary greatness to promote any and every product
in a crowded market, the second eager to recover some
genuine literary values in this market-driven environment.

But let us first consider some other manifestations
and implications of this phenomenon. Some years ago
I had the pleasure of meeting the director of a major
British literary festival, I think at a reading by the
excellent Swiss author Peter Stamm. I told the director
of my enthusiasm for Stamm's work and she spoke of her
determination to bring the best authors from around the
globe to her festival because, she said: 'If a work is good it
will reach out to everyone the world over.'

This is an extraordinary claim. There are
many thousands of languages around the world, many
thousands of idioms and narrative traditions. Yet of
course the festival director was doing no more than
repeating a contemporary orthodoxy, a common credo: a
great work of literature is great for everyone. That's that.

I somehow grew up with the spoilsport impulse.
I pointed out to the director that this faith in the
universal appeal of fine literature coincided perfectly
with commercial convenience: if a good book reaches
out to everyone, then every literate person on the planet

is a potential consumer. She was not deterred by this reflection; it sounded rather cynical, she thought. I also suggested that this presumably meant the end of any notion that expertise or special knowledge might be required to enjoy works coming out of radically different cultures: Japan, China, India, Nigeria. She told me that writers from all those countries had been present at the festival and had read to warm applause. Particularly the Chinese. I accepted that this must mean she was right. So what was cheering, I then observed, was that we need not fear that we were missing out on anything in any part of the globe, since if it were good it would inevitably have reached out to us, wouldn't it? And if it hadn't, it wasn't. She agreed, with the caveat that this was exactly where literary festivals and people like herself were important, to make sure the best work did indeed circulate. Clearly, there was a little equivocation here: the best works reach out to everybody, but only on the understanding that publishers and international literary festivals make sure that they are widely available. The intention here no doubt was literary activism – well-meaning promotion – but my suspicion remains that many festivals are concerned with their own success before that of the literature they promote.

Let us move swiftly to the reductio ad absurdum. The enthusiasm for 'World Literature' – an understandable enthusiasm, I should say, in a world that has opened up so dramatically in recent decades – has led to an explosion of new university courses and new anthologies complete with critical accounts not only of contemporary literature worldwide, but also literature from the past, even the very distant past, and from all narrative traditions. So alongside *The Longman Anthology of World Literature* and *The Norton Anthology of World Literature* ('still the most trusted', its blurb tells us, indicating again the importance of the mediator's role when no one has any idea who half the authors are), we have books such as Steven Moore's *The Novel: An Alternative History*. Across two enormous volumes (a third is promised), Moore repeatedly claims that all long narratives from the earliest times to the present day and in whatever culture can be approached the same way we approach a modern novel. Here he is talking about early Egyptian fiction:

> When fiction-writing resumed during the Ramesside period (c. 1292-1070 BCE), Egyptian writers invented a few more genres, like the war story, the ghost story and the fairy tale, but mostly pushed magic realism to bizarre lengths. In *The Tale of Two Brothers*, for example, an upright young man named Bata lives with his older brother Anubis, a landowner. One day, Anubis's wife makes a pass at Bata, but is rebuffed. The scorned woman tells her husband that Bata tried to assault her. Anubis then hides himself behind the stable door to kill his brother when he returns from the fields, but a talking cow warns Bata of Anubis's plan. He runs off but is pursued by his brother, so he prays to the sun-god for protection, who obliges by creating a wall of water between the two brothers, infested with crocodiles. Then things really get weird. To demonstrate his innocence, Bata cuts off his phallus and throws it into the water (where a catfish swallows it). It's a remarkable testament to the colourful imagination of one Egyptian fantasist.[1]

What is really 'weird' here is the way all this is presented with no context. Perhaps to the original audience it was not surprising at all that Bata cut off his phallus; perhaps it is exactly what they expected. Moore makes no reference to the translation process from hieroglyphics. There is no sense in his account that this story might stand in a totally different relationship to the community it was written for than, say, Marquez's

One Hundred Years of Solitude to the people of Colombia. But this elimination of context is entirely consistent with the underlying assumption that what matters is not the humus from which the work sprung, nor the response of readers who knew, so to speak, where their writer was coming from (if in fact there was an individual writer), but our response now. For the final implication of this approach to literature is that I, whoever I am, am the supreme arbiter of whether any work of literature produced in any time or clime is good or bad. If it reaches out to me (via literary festivals, World Literature anthologies, or aggressive publisher promotion), it is good. If not, not and it's just as well I didn't waste my time reading it. Interestingly, the covers of Moore's anthologies (published by Bloomsbury) show piquant paintings of naked girls stretched out on their bed coverlets reading, as if to say that literature is as universally appealing as the erotic nude, though these are very white, very Western nudes (with fashionable hairdos) in very bourgeois surroundings and both were painted long after the historic periods their respective volumes address.

Moore is an extreme case. The director of an international literary festival understandably has a personal investment in this universalist position. But we can begin to feel confident that what is being expressed here is a genuine manifestation of our zeitgeist when even the most serious minds and accomplished writers get on board. 'We must believe in poetry translation,' said Nobel Prize for Literature-winning poet Thomas Tranströmer, 'if we want to believe in World Literature.'[2] And the assumption here is that yes, we do want to believe in World Literature, indeed, the desire is non-negotiable, while at the same time we know perfectly well that translating poetry is a hazardous adventure that often prompts more questions than answers. In his discussion of his own versions of Tranströmer's work, Robert Robertson, having admitted that his Swedish is far from perfect, describes a process where his Swedish girlfriend gives him a literal line-by-line translation of each poem into English, then reads the Swedish to him to give him 'the cadences', after which he creates 'relatively free' versions in English so the work can reach out to everyone. Can we imagine offering a literal translation of, say, *The Waste Land*, into our second language and then reading it out to make sure our translator/partner gets the cadences? Our cadences? The way we hear it? Or those solemn beyond-the-grave cadences that Thomas Stearns used when he read his work for his contemporaries? What would the result be? It doesn't matter. The best literature reaches out to everyone. Every individual must be put in a position to experience the best that has been written, everywhere, every when.

Having mentioned Tranströmer, a word on the Nobel and the rapidly growing number of international literary prizes seems appropriate. Prizes are important for the construction of a body of world literature precisely because of the inevitable disorientation readers feel when they move outside their own culture. They also give us the welcome impression that the authors we are invited to read are winners. Awarding the Nobel to Tranströmer, a man who writes in Swedish and whose entire oeuvre can be printed in a single pocket book edition, must have amounted to a year off for the Swedish judges; in the normal way of things they would be sifting through work in tens if not scores of languages, often reading neither in the original – Indonesian? Khosa? Urdu? – nor in their own native Swedish, since many candidates for the prize will not have work available in Swedish translation. Then of course the judges, all members of the Swedish Academy (a lifetime appointment that does not allow for resignations), can hardly be expected to be familiar with the cultures from which these authors are writing. They read the texts in a linguistic and cultural limbo.

The Swedish Academy, it's worth mentioning in passing, was established in 1786 to promote the 'purity, strength, and sublimity of the Swedish language'.[3] Alfred Nobel instead invited the organisation to choose, year by year, the finest oeuvre of 'an idealistic tendency' from anywhere in the world.[4] These two tasks are quite different, if not incompatible, and doubtless the academy would have refused the offer were not huge sums of money involved. It is precisely the richness of the prize and the celebrity it brings that makes it a goal and instrument in the hands of activists, whether market- or literary-oriented. At a conference in Milan, Orhan Pamuk's translator Maureen Freely described how friends of the author would get together in Istanbul to plan his promotion for the Nobel and other international awards.[5]

Alfred Nobel's requirement that the winner's work should display 'idealistic tendencies' suggests an awareness that once we start taking books away from their culture of origin in order to compare them, we must find some universal measure of value, something outside the text or extractable from it that we can talk about, talk up, in order to explain why we gave the prize to this author rather than that. How can we praise the brilliance of the language and its special relationship to the general use of language in the novel's culture of origin, if we don't know that language? How can we talk about a novel's or poem's exciting take on a foreign culture if we know nothing about it aside from what we've learned through the novel or poem? We cannot. So we must talk about the dignity of man, the denunciation of evil, the tragic fragility of human relationships in the face of tumultuous circumstance, and so on. Aesthetics are so 'inaccessible', Borges observed, and require a sensitivity that comes from long experience; which was why most people resorted to the easier criteria of morals and politics.[6]

In a sense nothing could be more literary and activist than the Nobel, or international literary prizes in general. They want to champion the finest literary work. Yet they do so from absurd premises and in a manner that inevitably attracts the attention of the market activists who see prizes primarily as a vehicle for sales and promotion. Looking back over the years, many of the Nobel selections have been grotesque, so much so that it is hard to take it seriously. Yet no conversation is more frequent in literary circles than the Nobel conversation, no subject matter is easier when one finds oneself at some multi-racial dinner party in Delhi or Guadalajara. Who will win? Who deserves to win? Which country, which writer? Which kind of writing? Again and again I have insisted that the Nobel is nonsense and that I will not talk about it, and again and again I find myself talking about it, falling back on it, as it were, on the farce of the Nobel and this intense contemporary hunger for winners and losers, even when there is apparently no competition between them. It is the break between writer and community that makes such conversations possible.

This is not mere anecdote. Conversation is important. One of the rarely mentioned social uses of literature is to provide a complex subject of conversation, especially for people who perhaps don't know each other well enough to talk about more intimate or dangerous matters. What better way to understand who we are talking to than to see how he or she reacted to a novel such as Coetzee's *Disgrace* or Knausgaard's *My Struggle*? But in order for books to become a subject of conversation, we need to have read the same authors. This might be easy in London where some new novel by Mantel or McEwan or Amis will perhaps be on everyone's lips, but more difficult when we are travelling, when we are at those literary festivals, or perhaps in London, but not in the company of the local literary set. The Nobel and the Nobel winners provide a focus of conversation that brings the world together, in much the same way that international sports tournaments bring the world together, or the Olympic Games.

All this then to suggest that, quite beyond distinctions of market or literary activism, one of the functions of literature in the present time is to contribute to the global conversation, to the business of establishing a worldwide culture, at least among a certain class of educated, liberal-minded, relatively wealthy folk in every corner of the globe. It should hardly come as a surprise. It was only a couple of centuries ago that literature was called on to make a major contribution to the consolidation of national cultural identities in Europe; one thinks of Germany and Italy in particular. If this means that to keep the conversation going we have to talk about a kind of book that we might not otherwise have wanted to read, or at least to accept that the books most talked about will only be those that 'reach out to everybody', then so be it. The zeitgeist is so strong that there is really no point in resisting it. How pleasant, then, to convince oneself that what reaches out to everyone is also the best.

Amit Chaudhuri describes very well the self-promoting antics that over recent years have often risked transforming the literary world into a celebrity sport. Why has this come about and in what relation does it stand to the ongoing breakdown of local and national literary communities? Perhaps the easiest way to think about this is to reflect on the way a book might have stood in relation to context, culture, and language in the past. In particular, since achievement in literature used to be equated with the creation of a certain personal and recognisable style, we might want to ask ourselves what happens to literary style in a more international environment.

Of course style is hard to define. It is everywhere and nowhere. We cannot put our finger on it. We cannot quote it in its entirety or offer an exhaustive description of it, the way one might aspire to offer an exhaustive description of an object circumscribed in space. However, if we take an extreme case, it's easy enough to sense its presence, even in a paragraph or two. Here are the opening lines of Henry Green's masterpiece *Party Going* (1939).

> Fog was so dense, bird that had been disturbed went flat into a balustrade and slowly fell, dead at her feet. There it lay and Miss Fellowes looked up to where that pall of fog was twenty foot above and out of which it had fallen, turning over once. She bent down and took a wing then entered a tunnel in front of her, and this had DEPARTURES lit up over it, carrying her dead pigeon.[7]

This is not standard English. The deixis, in particular the combination of dropped articles and unnecessary demonstratives, is wayward. There's something unusual too in the syntax of the opening sentence of the second paragraph: 'Miss Fellowes looked up to where that pall of fog was twenty foot above and...' And what? 'And very thick,' you could say. Or, 'and decided to pick up the pigeon.' But you can't at this point say, 'and out of which...' It's as if two different syntactical structures had been imperfectly aligned around the word 'and', an effect not unlike the breaking up of visual planes in cubism. In general, there is an odd fragmenting of information, and a curious uncertainty about where sentences are going, 'turning over once'.

It's easy enough to see how this fragmentation links to what is being described: the loss of direction and orientation that a fog might provoke, the idea of departures, both from railway stations and in prose. But alongside the disorientation, the alliterative rhythms of the writing suggest purposefulness and solidity. Fog, flat, fell, feet, the first sentence offers, and again: dense, bird, disturbed, balustrade, dead. The acoustic effect is intensified by the prevalence of monosyllables and the elimination of unstressed articles, or their substitution with a stressed demonstrative. Then, as in nonsense poetry, while the sense seems wayward or uncertain, the forward movement of the phrasing is extremely confident. Here is another sentence playing the same tricks:

> Headlights of cars above turning into a road as they swept round hooting swept their light above where she walked, illuminating lower branches of trees.[8]

So many strategies interact in a pattern to create something homogeneous and distinct. You know immediately you are reading Henry Green. But this doesn't happen in a vacuum. Readers would not notice the text was 'special' if they were not expecting something different. There must be a shared understanding of standard language and syntax, a range of more common usages that generally prevails. English readers in particular (as opposed to American) will notice that some of the effects here recall the working-class dialects of northern England, in which articles are often dropped and one says 'foot' rather than 'feet' when indicating lengths. There's an irony here since the novel focuses on London's aristocratic rich, while the voice recalls a working-class north, distant and potentially critical. Yet the voice is not a straight imitation of dialect, since many other dialect elements are missing. In the end, it is not clear what Green's style 'means' or where exactly it's coming from, but it does begin to establish, as it were, a position, a new and unusual space, within the known cultural setting of the 1930s England.

Style, then, involves a meeting between arrangements inside the prose and expectations outside it. You cannot have a strong style without a community of readers able to recognise and appreciate its departures from the common usages they know. Much of what is surprising in Green's text is inevitably lost in translation, in a language, for example, with different rules of deixis. Here is a back translation into English of the published Italian translation.

> The fog was thick; a bird that had been disturbed hit a balustrade full on and slowly fell, dead, a few steps away from her.
> There it lay and Miss Fellowes looked up where seven metres from the ground there was a cloak of fog from which it had fallen, turning over once. She bent down and picked it up by a wing, then went down into a subway in front of her with the sign DEPARTURES over it, carrying her dead pigeon.

This text no longer distinguishes itself from others linguistically. What matters now is what it describes: its plot, its idealistic tendency perhaps, its moral. However, since Green does not appear to be interested in either idealistic tendencies or morals, or indeed traditional plots, it is really quite difficult to say what is left in *Party Going* when the style is gone.

If such an extreme example seems too easy, here is F. Scott Fitzgerald, introducing Gatsby's old lover Daisy and her husband Tom in *The Great Gatsby*:

> Why they came East I don't know. They had spent a year in France, for no particular reason, and then drifted here and there unrestfully wherever people played polo and were rich together. This was a permanent move, said Daisy over the telephone, but I didn't believe it - I had no sight into Daisy's heart but I felt that Tom would drift on forever seeking a

little wistfully for the dramatic turbulence of some irrecoverable football game.[9]

At first glance this may seem fairly standard prose. But the Microsoft Word spellcheck underlines 'unrestfully,' and in fact this word is not in Merriam Webster's online dictionary. It's a classic case of a word gaining meaning by not being what you expected: They drifted here and there... how? Restlessly, of course. But 'restless' suggests an impulse to be up and doing. It can be a noble attribute. 'Unrestfully' suggests not so much the impulse that drives Daisy and Tom to move – actually they only drift – but a lack of benefit from their languor. They drift without relaxing. Fitzgerald feels this mental state is sufficiently special to require a neologism to point it up.

A style, we said, requires a combination of interacting elements. What do we have? Well, a reiterated absence of knowledge or meaning: 'I don't know.' 'No particular reason.' 'I didn't believe.' 'I had no sight into Daisy's heart.' This lack of knowledge might connect up with the repetition of the verb 'drift'. One doesn't know where to go, so one drifts. Then at the heart of the paragraph is one affirmation of certainty – 'This was a permanent move' – but the claim is undermined by a blatant oxymoron, made possible by the double meaning of move: 'move house' or just movement. To read a few more pages of *The Great Gatsby* would alert us to the fact that the book is full of oxymorons – ferocious indifference, magnanimous scorn, inessential houses – suggesting a general state of precariousness.

Perhaps related to the oxymoron 'permanent move' is the other oddity in this paragraph: 'wherever people played polo and were rich together.' Standard usage has people being happy together, or sad together: emotional states. Alternatively, partners can get rich together, or get stoned together: progressive developments. But this confusion of an emotional state with a generous bank balance – 'were rich together' – is emblematic of everything that makes Gatsby's elegant world so oddly fragile, as if it existed only in the magic of words that somehow get on together despite their contradictory energies.

As with Henry Green, much of this is lost when Fitzgerald's text leaves the culture it was written in and travels around the world in other languages. I've looked at five Italian translations. None is able to convey 'unrestfully', 'permanent move', or 'get rich together'. It's surprising how much trouble they have too with an 'irrecoverable football game', a longing for an unrepeatable past that connects Tom with Gatsby and measures the distance between them: Gatsby dreams of reliving love, Tom of sporting glory. And as the separate stylistic devices disappear in translation, so does the pattern that they combined to sustain; losing the internal pattern, one inevitably loses the peculiar position the text created for itself within its culture of origin and hence its special relationship with readers. In translation, stripped of its style, Gatsby really doesn't seem a very remarkable performance.

In the past, then, and to a certain extent still today, a book by a national author sent out to reviewers who live in the same world, culture, and language would be immediately recognisable, the same way one immediately and easily places the people one meets from one's own home town and country. A critic would sense the nature of any new writer's departure from the positions available within the literary culture. For better or worse. And to an extent this kind of knowing put a limit on the hyperbole of blurbs; simply, it was self-evident what kind of animal this was. It didn't come from nowhere, but from someone among us addressing us, someone who would likely be around for a while, someone whom we would get to know. Anyone championing a new author would do so knowing that his own judgement would very much be under scrutiny, since readers could quickly assess the kind of work to which they had so enthusiastically been introduced.

Inevitably, opening up the literary world internationally and projecting novels around the globe in translation (often with simultaneous launches in a dozen and more countries) alters this situation. Whereas in the past a very personal style might have beguiled critics and declared your specialness (one thinks of the early Martin Amis), it now presents itself as a possible barrier to translation, or simply incomprehensible to those who don't share the same linguistic and cultural context. A book that is all style, like Green's, when stripped of its style hardly seems special, or particularly ambitious, like Fitzgerald's, is not going to be winning international literary prizes. There is no idealistic tendency or grandiose project to abstract from the work.

In the long run, whether through a growing awareness of this new situation on the part of writers, or simply by a process of natural selection, it seems inevitable that style will align with what can be effectively translated into multiple languages and cultural settings, or into some readily intelligible international idiom, a sort of international zone within each language. Not that there need be no style in such works, or even a flat style; on the contrary, they might go for very obviously and internationally recognisable 'literary styles', elevated registers, fancy adjectives, and elaborate syntax. But they will not be styles that require intimate knowledge of a particular linguistic context.

Two very obvious examples would be Andrés Neuman's *Traveller of the Century*, which won the 2009 Alfaguara prize, and the 2013 Booker winner, *The*

Luminaries, by the New Zealand writer Eleanor Catton.
Neuman, Argentinian, but resident in Spain, sets his work
in the early part of the nineteenth century somewhere in
Germany (neither date nor place are exactly defined),
where a mysterious traveller falls to frequenting the
cultural salon of a rich family and deploys his wit
to seduce a local and highly intellectual beauty. The
register is high, the lexical range considerable, the style
extravagantly articulated and playfully pompous, the
whole performance madly ambitious; but the knowledge
it asks of its reader is all book knowledge, general
history, and, above all, a vague awareness of what a high
prose style once was. There is no appeal to anything the
writer and reader may know and share intimately in the
here and now, though we do get some softly eroticised,
politically correct enthusiasm for internationalism. This
is what our mysterious traveller talks to his beloved about
when they are at last between the sheets.

> How can we speak about free trade, Hans pronounced
> as he lay next to Sophie, of a customs union and all
> that implies, without considering a free exchange of
> literature? We should be translating as many foreign
> books as possible, publishing them, reclaiming the
> literature of other countries and taking it to the
> classroom! That's what I told Brockhaus. And what
> did he say? Sophie asked, nibbling his nipple. Hans
> shrugged and stroked her back: He told me, yes, all
> in good time, and not to get agitated. But in such
> exchanges, said Sophie, it's important that the more
> powerful countries don't impose their literature on
> everyone else, don't you think? Absolutely, replied
> Hans, plunging his hand between Sophie's buttocks,
> and besides, powerful countries have a lot to learn
> from smaller countries which are usually more open
> and curious, that is to say more knowledgeable.
> You're the curious one! Sophie sighed, allowing

164

Hans's probing finger in and lying back. That, Hans grinned, must be because you're so open and you know what's what.[10]

Reviewing *The Luminaries*, an 800-page mystery story set in 1860s New Zealand, Catton's compatriot C.K. Stead remarks on its 'chintzy,' 'upholstered' pastiche of the nineteenth-century novel and adds:

> Every episode has its setting, decor, clothing, its period bric-a-brac, its slightly formal but often sharp dialogue. This is costume drama. It is conventional fiction but with the attention to fact and connection that the (cross-checking and online research) facilities of the modern computer permit. That apart, only the author's cultural sensitivity in dealing with Maori and Chinese characters, and an occasional anachronistic word or phrase in the dialogue ('paranoid', 'serendipitous') locate authorship in the present.[11]

In general terms Stead's comments would also be an appropriate description of Neuman's book. Removing us from the present, pastiching what the modern ear assumes the eloquence of the past to have been, the writer can appear 'stylish' without appealing to anything in his readership's immediate experience. Catton's prose has been likened to that of Dickens in *The Pickwick Papers*. But for readers who followed Pickwick in the 1830s, the book was drenched in references to the world they shared and the language itself was not so far removed from what could be heard and read every day. If one translates Dickens into another language, an enormous amount is lost; even for the Londoner reading him today, many of the references mean nothing. But Neuman's and Catton's novels have dispensed in advance with this intense engagement with a local or national readership and seem set to lose very little as they move around the world in different languages. It is in this regard alone that one has to disagree with Stead. Authorship is located in the present exactly insofar as its appeal – as in a Hollywood costume drama or indeed an extravagant computer game – is to well-established, globally shared tropes and not to any real contact with the specificity of a here and now. The comparison to the works of fantasy my students so avidly read is obvious.

Can one see now why some kind of activism, whether market-driven or undertaken with the best literary intentions, becomes necessary in such circumstances? In the absence of that supremely literary instrument – style – that particular use of a particular language in a particular moment to suggest a particular vision of a world the reading community shares, a writer has to find other ways to declare his literariness: pastiche, ideal tendencies, a wildly ambitious inclusiveness, an extravagant rhetorical gesturing. And in the absence of a public who can immediately feel the writer's position in regard to the world they live in through his or her use of language, publishers are obliged to make enormous claims for a work's literariness, usually by stressing its content and values, its plot, its range of imagery, much as in those brief explanations offered to justify the award of the Nobel: 'for the art of memory with which he has evoked the most ungraspable human destinies' (Patrick Modiano, 2014); 'for his cartography of structures of power and his trenchant images of the individual's resistance' (Mario Vargas Llosa, 2010); 'for her depiction of the landscape of the dispossessed' (Herta Müller, 2009); etc. [12]

With the constant mingling of texts from many different countries, the abundance of titles published, the presence of foreign writers writing in English, and translations from a wide range of languages, the reader is disorientated, thus in need of advice, open to persuasion. Add to that that the new global literary conversation inevitably involves fewer names than any number of separate conversations in different nations, and the stakes get higher and higher. A Dutch, or even Italian, writer trapped in their home market will not, as a rule, be able to pay his bills. A publisher who can persuade the world that Elena Ferrante is worthy of international attention can make a fortune. So a system develops in which the publishers are seeking to place a large number of products in a small number of spaces, rather than introducing a sophisticated text into a sympathetic environment that can recognise it as such. This perception that only a few books will gain access to the international conversation inevitably intensifies the atmosphere of competition in the literary world.

Activism, the aggressive promotion of literary attributes, whether genuine or merely supposed, developed in response to and is integrated with the globalisation of literature. In passing, it's evident that globalisation, which is simply an acceleration of ancient impulses, meshes very well with a certain kind of capitalism and individualism. The supreme individual, free of any cultural limitation or determination, becomes a potential reader of any book written anywhere in the world. But the more we free ourselves or suppose we free ourselves from cultural conditioning, the more we expose ourselves to a free-for-all. Since we have little to go on when we pick up a novel by a Turkish or Nigerian writer, the publishers will have to work hard to convince us that this is the book that matters, the one that should win the prizes. And of course reviewers will make their reputations by being the ones who first canonise this or that huge success: Knausgaard or Ferrante or Franzen. So no sooner does a bandwagon begin to roll than the kingmakers worldwide jump on it. Nor need they fear if they get things wrong, since their losing horse will quickly be forgotten. The turnover of literary celebrities is speeding up.

This situation, let me say, has been exacerbated by the way academic literary criticism developed through the twentieth century. Determined to present itself as scientific, to justify its presence in the academic community, literary criticism focused on the text as a detached object of study offering complex analyses of literary language and imagery while disdaining any reflection on the relationship between the writer and the reader within the larger community and the market for books, as if such things as people's tastes and publishers' instruments of persuasion were not a worthy matter for comment, or indeed part of the literary experience. Where this kind of awareness has been present, it has usually been highly politicised, as in the oceans of commentary on postcolonial literature, and more recently world literature. Eager, above all, to consolidate their own positions, academics have proved remarkably ill-equipped to record, at an anthropological level, how the business of reading and writing has been changing and in what way. It is almost comic now to see them trying to treat modern works by Neuman and Catton with the same solemnity that in the past was granted to Joyce and Faulkner, not appreciating how radically the context in which these books were produced has changed.

There are only two ways in which people relate to each other, remarked the anthropologist Louis Dumont provocatively: hierarchy and competition. By hierarchy, Dumont did not mean a simple top-down power relationship, but the kind of complex social structures which assigned to each sex, class, and caste some special role, so that each had a position that was specifically his or hers and that could not be taken away. Once a complex older hierarchy broke down, Dumont remarked, once the world became a world of equal individuals, the only possible relationship between them was competition.[13]

It's a precarious analogy perhaps, but the kind of intense interconnection of writer, language, and community created a complexity where one did not immediately think of literature in terms of winning and losing. With the loss of those connections, it sometimes seems that winning and losing is all there is.

Here is Salman Rushdie, interviewed in *The Paris Review* in 2005:

> Many people in that very gifted generation I was a part of had found their ways as writers at a much younger age. It was as if they were zooming past me. Martin Amis, Ian McEwan, Julian Barnes, William Boyd, Kazuo Ishiguro, Timothy Mo, Angela Carter, Bruce Chatwin – to name only a few. It was an extraordinary moment in English literature, and I was the one left in the starting gate, not knowing which way to run. That didn't make it any easier.[14]

It's a competition. In Rushdie's memoir *Joseph Anton* (the pseudonym that aligns Rushdie with two of the greatest writers of modern times, Joseph Conrad and Anton Chekhov), he speaks of 'his repeated failures to be, or become, a decent publishable writer of fiction', until 'slowly, from his ignominious place at the bottom of the literary barrel, he began to understand...'[15]

He was too anonymous. Rushdie sets off to India to reinforce the Indian side of his identity because he perceives this will help him to become a successful writer, and indeed he soon conceives 'a gigantic, all or nothing project' in which 'the risk of failure was far greater than the possibility of success'.[16] After the publication of *Midnight's Children*, 'many things happened about which he had not even dared to dream, awards, bestsellerdom and on the whole, popularity'.[17] Of the night when he was awarded the Booker, Rushdie speaks of his pleasure in opening the 'handsome, leather-bound presentation copy of *Midnight's Children*' with 'the bookplate inside that read WINNER'.[18]

Amit Chaudhuri has spoken of the development of forms of literary activism in contrast to market activism and this frenetic attention to self-promotion. Certainly many of us feel the need for some kind of new manner of approaching and talking about literature, a desire to retrieve it from the circus of prizes, promotions, pieties, and blurbs that it has become. For my own part I have repeatedly tried to describe the situation as it really is and by so doing to undermine that spirit of denial which likes to believe that festivals are always good, translations always enriching, prizes always positive, and so on. But one risks becoming a spoilsport, or one is accused of sour grapes. Chaudhuri has talked of a new form of championing and, of course, when any of us comes across a writer we feel has qualities that have been ignored, we want to tell the world. Here, though, the risk is that we get drawn into the promotional circus; we become excited by the idea that we too could create a star; or alternatively we despair that there just isn't the community of readers to sustain certain kinds of writers. One thinks how a writer like Bernhard never found a public in England.

Let me conclude, then, by saying that any form of literary activism has to take account of the gravitational force of this fiercely competitive world created by globalisation and its uncoupling of writer and community. There is no point in fighting this trend or yearning for some more comfortable situation in the past. Perhaps what is required is a positive vision of what literature might become as a more savvy international community of readers slowly forms. It was very much in this spirit that I have tried to do a little to champion Peter Stamm, a writer at once very much part of his Swiss community but also – thanks perhaps to the peculiar relation between Swiss German and the high German he writes in, or again to the nature of his inspiration, which prefers an extremely spare style – accessible to readers from many different cultures. No sooner, I noticed, did I speak in an excited and positive way about Stamm's work that an avalanche of mails and packages arrived more or less demanding I do the same for other writers. It was not encouraging.

1. Steven Moore, *The Novel: An Alternative History, Beginnings to 1600* (Bloomsbury: London, 2011), p. 44.

2. Robert Robertson, 'The Double World of Tomas Tranströmer', *NYR Daily*, October 14, 2011, http://www.nybooks.com/daily/2011/10/14/double-world-tomas-transtromer/, accessed September 7, 2016.

3. John Considine, *Academy Dictionaries 1600-1800* (Camberidge: Cambridge University Press, 2011).

4. Burton Feldman, *The Nobel Prize: A History of Genius, Controversy, and Prestige* (New York: Arcade, 2011), p. 67.

5. 'Shifting Notions of the Minority Language in an Era of Globalization', Panel Discussion, Conference 'Towards a Global Literature', IULM, Milano, 19 October, 2012.

6. Jorge Luis Borges, *Selected Non-Fictions*, trans. Maria Kodama (New York: Viking, 1999), p. 464.

7. Henry Green, *Party Going* (London: Vintage, 2000), p. 1.

8. Green, *Party Going*, p. 7.

9. F. Scott Fitzgerald, *The Great Gatsby* (London: Penguin, 1974), p. 12.

10. Andres Neuman, *Traveller of the Century* (London: Pushkin Press, 2012), p. 317.

11. C.K. Stead, 'The Luminaries, by Eleanor Catton', *Financial Times*, September 6, 2013.

12. All of these testimonials can be found on the Nobel Prize website.

13. Louis Dumont, *Essays on Individualism* (Chicago: University of Chicago Press, 1986).

14. Jack Livings, 'Salman Rushdie, The Art of Fiction, No. 186,' *Paris Review*, no. 174 (Summer 2005), p. 122.

15. Salman Rushdie, *Joseph Anton: A Memoir* (London: Jonathan Cape, 2012), p. 53.

16. Rushdie, *Joseph Anton*, p. 56.

17. Rushdie, *Joseph Anton*, p. 57.

18. Rushdie, *Joseph Anton*, p. 59.

The Practice of Literature: The Calcutta Context as a Guide to Literary Activism
ROSINKA CHAUDHURI

To the ongoing discussion on the convergence or divergence between literary language and the language of publishing as it functions today, I bring the Calcutta context. Not in order to bring you a tableau or 'picture of literature in Bengal' – neither, regretfully, to speak of the 'poetics of space' that inhabits the house or city of our imagination in literature – but to interrogate certain instances of writing in the past – both that which was classed as 'literary' and that which was not – in order to unsettle the narration of the making and unmaking of a modern literature here. This paper will attempt to read the creation of the practice we call 'literature' in the 'modern' Calcutta literary sphere in relation to a genre less addressed in the context of the literary nowadays: poetry. An answer to the question 'What *is* "literary" activism?' might possibly benefit from the context of past practice, throwing light on the implications of history repeating itself in new discourses. Are the values of literary activism repeated in time, and are its ends surprisingly similar in different eras? Does it always argue for a view of writing, writers, publishing, and the literary notwithstanding the market? Does the writer who militates for a chosen practice always do so in his own self-interest?

Speaking of the establishment of 'Literature' (with a capital L) in the French context, Barthes wrote, in *Writing Degree Zero*, of the manner in which 'History' 'underlies the fortunes of modes of writing'. After the demise of the classical and romantic periods came the moment of the birth of 'Literature':

> ...as soon as the writer ceased to be a witness to the universal, to become the incarnation of a tragic awareness (around 1850), his first gesture was to choose the commitment of his form, either by adopting or rejecting the writing of his past. Classical writing therefore disintegrated, and the whole of

Literature, from Flaubert to the present day, became the problematics of language.
This was precisely the time when Literature (the word having come into being shortly before) was finally established as an object.[1]

The resonance here with the situation in Bengal is intriguing, especially as modern Bengali literature too came into being around 1850, and all the more so because the process of 'adopting or rejecting the writing of [the] past' has been contaminated, in the context of the Indian writer, by the advent of colonialism. (Nevertheless, classical writing did disintegrate, and 'the whole of Literature' in Bengali, from Madhusudan to the present day, turned also to 'the problematics of language'.) To recognise that modern Literature, with the capital L on which Barthes insists, came into existence in India at about the same time as it did in France is a liberating thought, a thought that frees us substantially from the rhetoric of 'Western influence' towards an understanding of the coming of modernity along more multi-directional axes than are usually presumed to exist.

The study of literature in Bengal may be immediately traced by any historian of the field as moving on a course almost exactly parallel to and contiguous with developments in the Western hemisphere. There came into existence at almost the same time, around 1850, two activities automatically adjacent to the writing of a self-consciously new and modern literature – literary criticism and literary history. Literary criticism, written in English or the regional languages, quite often by writers themselves, but also, more and more, by new professionals in the literary sphere and newspapermen and editors of literary periodicals, took the form of book reviews, extended articles in the periodicals press, and stand-alone publications of critical essays or books. At the start, literary criticism on Bengali works was often conflated with an attempt at summing up its literary achievements, wherein Macherey's distinction in *A Theory of Literary Production* of literary criticism as an 'art' and literary history as a 'science' had not yet become operational.[2] These brief critical essays-cum-histories were quite often written, in the first instance, in the English language, arguably for the benefit of the colonial British reader, but of no mean significance to the newly English-educated classes reading them at the same time in the same language. The tradition of writing about Bengali literature in English, for instance, had been inaugurated by Kasiprasad Ghosh in the pages of the *India Gazette* in 1831 in a piece called 'On Bengali Writers'; roughly forty years later, Bankimchandra Chatterjee's two influential essays written in English ('A Popular Literature for Bengal', 1870; 'Bengali Literature', 1871) were landmarks of this particular convention (both started out as review essays). The writing of 'literary history' by writers themselves – spawned by the birth of the category of 'Literature' itself since the 1850s – was then quickly followed by professionals from the world of letters, from Akshaychandra Sarkar to Ramgati Nyayratna to Dineshchandra Sen's magisterial volume on old and medieval Bengali literature (*Banga Bhasha O Sahitya*) in 1896, which remained the landmark work in this genre for many years to come.

This was a time when the canon was being invented and put into place even as the first important modern works were making their way into the public sphere. Thus in 'Bengali Literature', Bankim starts with the medieval poets, but very quickly comes to 'the present writers in Bengali', reviewing not only the work of immediate predecessors, but also, straight-faced, the works of a 'Babu Bankim Chandra Chatarji' (*sic*), summarising his own work at great length in this article that was first published anonymously in *The Calcutta Review*. Although the story of the evolution of the language would not be complete for another fifty years, by which time both a firm conception of a 'high cultural' Bengali and a demarcated space occupied by the academic professional would take over, the fluid, excitable, and nebulous nature of the circumstances of the birth of modern Bengali literature becomes apparent from such instances, as well as the unresolved nature of many of the most important categories of analysis such as *sahitya* (literature) or *kavi* (poet). These words were reformulated and reinvented during this period to come to mean what they mean to us today, alongside other categories such as *'itihas'* [history]; we are constantly reminded that they meant something different before. Side by side, the literariness of the literary is being formulated anew, and the mapping of 'our own' literary heritage is being self-consciously undertaken in a different way to the traditional commentaries and textual analyses of the past.

LITERARY ACTIVISM, CALCUTTA STYLE

I see now that the first instance of market and literary activism I came across was embedded in my Oxford graduate research into nineteenth-century poetry in India. Henry Meredith Parker spent almost thirty years (1815-1842) in Calcutta; he was a member of the Calcutta Board of Customs, Salt, and Opium (later the Board of Revenue), and celebrated in the city for two books of poetry and his looming cultural presence in theatre, writing, and the hosting of dinner parties. Nigel Leask mentions how Byron had, in May 1813, written to Thomas Moore urging him to join the bandwagon of 'Oriental' poetry: 'Stick to the East,' he said, '...it [is] the only poetical policy.... The little I have done in that way is merely a "voice in the wilderness" for you; and, if it has had any success, that also will prove that the public are orientalizing, and pave the path for you.'[3]

178

Byron's commercial instinct was sound, proving he was an excellent entrepreneur in 'market activism'; five years later Moore's *Lalla Rookh*, which had received a gigantic advance of three thousand guineas, became a publishing sensation in London. Writing in this age of intense cultural engagement with the Orient, whose mood, as we see, was best exploited by Byron, Parker published a literary manifesto in the introduction to his second book of poems, *Bole Ponjis* [Punch Bowl], published by W. Thacker and Co. in London and St Andrew's Library, Calcutta, in 1851, militating against the vogue for 'Orientalising'. Stuck in that very East that was so much the rage in the London poetry scene, an irritated Parker waged a war of words in response to this craze for the Orient, arguing for a different sort of largely comic poetry, showing us how 'literary activism' may inhabit the most unlikely of spaces. In a classic instance of literary activism – where the writer generates a polemic against the prevalent market-created trend or taste – he warned his readers against wandering 'into realms of Orientalism, such as mine are, under an impression that she or he would there be amidst regions resembling, however faintly, those made glorious and gorgeous by Lord Byron and Thomas Moore...' On the contrary, displaying a determination to work against the dominant Western demand for certain chosen ideas and images of the East, Parker insisted his own poems were: 'of the East Easty; but of no such East as the reader has, probably, been familiar with. No "Gardens of gul in her bloom." No lands "Where all but the spirit of man is divine," – but the simple prosaic East of this every day world...'[4]

So Henry Meredith Parker's East is made up of characters such as Mr Simms, resident of Calcutta in the early nineteenth century, described in office at work and at play in various modes of recreation, or of young Bengali students debating the virtues of eating beef

(prohibited food for Hindus) on an evening circa 1827
at the Ochterlony monument in the Calcutta *maidan*.
In an age dominated by literature, Western philosophy,
religion, history, and science, all bracketed under the
aegis of 'an English education' at the Hindu College,
alias the Anglo-Indian College, the changing priorities of
the new generation are parodied relentlessly in Parker's
poem. Reacting to Sam Chund's objections to eating beef
– 'What would the goddess say? and what mamma? / Srii
might chastise me, so might my papa. / I cannot go your
lengths, indeed I can't, / Besides next week's the Shrad
for my dead aunt' – Hurry Mohun is indignation itself:

> Is this alas! the fruit of all the knowledge
> We gathered at the Anglo-Indian College?
> Was it for *this* we learned the world was round,
> That twenty shillings sterling make a pound;
> That spinning jennies, Sam, were not young ladies,
> And what a science is, and what a trade is?[5]

No Spinning Jenny ever found its way into a poem
by Southey or Byron or Moore – that much may safely be
asserted – making the argument Parker launches against
the vogue for the exotic 'Orient' to be of much broader
import, as it fights also against the all-encompassing
fashion for long narrative verse tales of adventure set in
scenes both exotic and wild (of which the Indiana Jones
series of movies seems to be the latest incarnation). The
fight of the realist literary novel against the wave of magic
realism that swept the world in the wake of Marquez in
the 1980s and 1990s could not have been more futile than
Parker's plea for a depiction of the daily world of the East
at the time.

*

To which values does this instance of literary
activism in a nineteenth-century context draw our

attention, and what were its ends? It certainly seems to be arguing for 'a view of writing, writers, publishing, and the literary notwithstanding the market', and is all the more interesting when we follow the trajectory of Parker's career, which had been launched with a bang in 1827 with an Oriental verse tale called *Draughts of Immortality*, which was aligned beautifully with the market for the Orient, written in exactly the style he attacks so ferociously in his introduction to his second volume, *Bole Ponjis*, in 1851. There is, in this turn from literary conformity towards literary activism, a strangeness that echoes the strangeness of the literary; it does seem, in Amit Chaudhuri's phrase, '*desultory*, in that its aims and value aren't immediately explicable'.[6]

Considering that in the mid-nineteenth century, poetry was almost a synonym for literature, this obsession of Parker's with the question of what should constitute poetry from the East was not surprising; it is why, in this period, market activism of Byron's sort was still possible in this genre. The relations between poetry and mass audiences were robust, and poets exploiting the market for the Orient were far better known at the time, as is always the case, than those literary activists, practitioners, and critics militating against the dominant demand. An anecdote from the same period of my research illustrates the point beautifully: when Matthew Arnold was in America, many years later, he found himself mistaken for (and 'credited to an embarrassing extent'[7] with) the poetical baggage of his namesake, Edwin Arnold, whose *The Light of Asia*, published in 1879, which tells the story of the Enlightenment of the Buddha, went through eighty editions in America and sixty in Britain by 1920, and was described by Oliver Wendell Holmes as being comparable only with the New Testament.[8] (A century later, I had never even heard of Edwin Arnold before I began researching nineteenth-century poetry in India.)

Poetry in the nineteenth century was also at the centre of the debate on what was to constitute a modern and national literature for Bengal. Bankimchandra was to address the issue in some detail in his preface to the poems of Iswar Gupta in 1885, asking, famously, 'Iswar Gupta is a *kabi* (poet). But what sort of poet?', and answering unambiguously that Iswar Gupta was not a *kabi* in the modern sense of the term, that is – and here Bankim uses the English word – Iswar Gupta was not a *'poet'*. 'Nowadays,' he continues, *'kabi* means poet, although there's a great deal of confusion about "the poetic" [*"kabitva"*]. Now, the poetic is that which in English is called *Poetry*. This is the common usage, so we are compelled to judge whether or not Iswar Gupta is a poet in this sense.'[9] Discussing the disjunction between the old and the new sense of the word *kabi*, Bankim says that in ancient times, in the *shastras*, any man of knowledge was referred to as *kabi*, whether he was a writing of theosophy or astrology. The meaning of the term has changed over time, and at the start of this century it also referred to the compositions of singer-songwriter teams, confronting each other in the contest known as *kabir lorai* or 'poets' contest'; now, however, it is used in the sense of what the English call a *poet*. Interestingly, he uses a colloquial Sanskrit expression to explain this sense of the usage: *'kabyeshu magha kabi kalidasa'* ('among poets, [the greatest are] Magha and the poet Kalidasa'). The distinction Bankim makes, therefore, is between the great poetry of India, epitomised by Magha and Kalidasa at the apex of Indian literary accomplishment, where the word is used in the English sense of the term, of 'pure poetry' so to speak, and this great poetry is opposed to both the ancient pre-modern sense of writing and the current debased sense of song. And why was Iswar Gupta not a poet in the sense that Kalidasa was a poet? Because, Bankim

182

insisted in a statement indisputably reminiscent of
the Romantic notion of poetry, 'he did not have the
ability to give form to the indistinct, soft, serious and
high aspects of the human soul; he could not articulate
the inarticulate; he was not skilled in the creation of
beauty.' [10] Bankimchandra then creates a canon of 'true
poets' for the Bengali reader, in which his contemporaries
Madhusudan, Hemchandra, Nabinchandra, and
Rabindranath are mentioned; preceding them far into
antiquity he gives us a list that ran backwards through
time from Bharatchandra, Kasiram, Krittibas, and
Mukundaram to the resonant tones of the Baishnab
poets. This moment of literary activism is remarkable in
that Bankimchandra spends a considerable amount of
time defining the new notion of the poetic, a notion with
which the poetry of the poet he is presenting to the world,
Iswar Gupta, does not synchronise. Iswar Gupta is not a
poet in the modern sense of the term, according to him.
Yet, he should not be forgotten, and Bankim makes a case
for him that establishes certain parameters in the reading
of Bengali culture more generally – the paradigm of the
authentic bard. This is literary activism not on behalf of
the literary as it is understood now, but on behalf of the
authentic selfhood of the Bengali, which is what Iswar
Gupta stands for.

FUNDAMENTAL BI- AND MULTI-LINGUALISM

If we look at modern Bengali literature as
commentators have traditionally done – that is, as arising
indisputably in part from Western literary convention, as
an offshoot or by-product – it is not surprising that this
attribution would have traditionally been denigrated by
nationalist writers. (Even so distinguished a commentator
as Sisir Kumar Das typically titled the second volume
of his *History of Indian Literature*, consisting of 815 pages
documenting the literary achievements of every Indian

language in this age, '1800-1910: Western Impact: Indian Response'.[11]) It is a historical fact, however, that all extant Indian literatures had been permeated, at different times, by 'foreign' impressions in an unavoidable and incorrigible manner, and that our literature no less than our culture has always been heterogeneous in more ways than one, as I shall try to show through the literary activism, in turn, of Iswar Gupta himself, thirty years or so before Bankimchandra did battle for him as an icon of authenticity.

The literary sphere of early nineteenth-century Calcutta was populated, apart from the commissioned academic and evangelical publications of Fort William and Serampore, by the religious and political writings of Rammohun Roy – in English, Bengali, Sanskrit, and Persian/Arabic – as well as the first English poems of Derozio and Kasiprasad Ghosh. Apart from the plethora of magazines, periodicals, and newspaper publications that dominated the printed literary productions of this era, there were also the hugely popular competing performances Bankim mentioned, the *kabir lorai*, which depended on established poets such as Iswar Gupta or Rangalal for the lyrics in their compositions. As was to be the case with the majority of India's literary practitioners who followed, therefore, almost every poet in this era oscillated between the uses of several languages to several ends, thereby serving as a salutary reminder that the practice of multilingualism in India had its antecedents in normative precolonial conditions. The milieu of modernity in which the Bengali language functioned during the early part of the nineteenth century was that of an increasingly complex and cosmopolitan Calcutta, which, as the centre of British administration, trade, and commerce, was already burgeoning with what one historian describes as a populace of 'Chinese and Frenchmen, Persians and Germans, Arabs and Spaniards,

184

Armenians and Portuguese, Jews and Dutchmen, in addition to the Indians and the British.'[12]

This was the city to which Iswar Gupta came as a child; born in 1811, he moved to Calcutta after his father died, and standard biographies take care to mention that he was never formally educated, emphasising instead his natural abilities in versification and song-writing. Iswar Gupta flourished as Calcutta's pre-eminent poet and editor until his untimely death in 1859. He regularly published poetry in the columns of his newspaper, composed songs for a *kabial* group of Bagbazaar, and collected the songs and poems of the preceding era to create an unprecedented archive of literary gleanings; he also commented, in verse and prose, on most aspects of the new life of the Bengali people in the mid-nineteenth century.

Archiving the fast-disappearing poems and songs of his forbears and attaching a critical commentary to the material he gleaned, Iswar Gupta's literary activism is to be found not only in the poetry he wrote, but also in the way he championed the work of his predecessors, the manner in which he held up particular examples for scrutiny, taking delight in and commending particular qualities in the commentary that intercut the poems presented. Iswarchandra Gupta first began to collect and publish the songs and lives of the eighteenth-century poets and song-writers Ramnidhi Gupta, Ramprasad Sen, and Bharatchandra Ray alongside that of myriad city song-writers or *kabials* in 1853, *not* making any distinction in his treatment of the 'major' and 'minor' poets, publishing them serially in the newspaper he edited till he died. Although he had plans to print these in book form, he was able to publish only one of these, on the poet Bharatchandra Ray, as a separate book in 1855.[13]

Bilingualism or multilingualism in literary composition was not a condition unique to the imposition

of British rule in India, and it is instructive to see that
Iswar Gupta commends it highly; Iswar Gupta extolled
a Hindi poem by Bharatchandra Ray that he collected in
the book, calling it 'Hindi Language Poem', and extracted
an incomplete play Bharatchandra left behind at the time
of his death, *Chandi natak*, composed in a Bengali that
consisted of a mixture of Sanskrit and Hindi. One of the
poems anthologised was simply titled 'A Poem Composed
in a Mixture of Four Languages: Sanskrit, Bengali,
Persian and Hindi' – these were obviously provisional
titles put in place by the later poet at a time when the
short poem was an almost unknown entity; Iswar Gupta
himself seems to be the first systematic proponent of it
in Bengali. Another short poem by Bharatchandra he
presents was called '*kardoraft barnan*' ['Come and Gone'
Described].[14] Iswar Gupta added a note preceding the
poem, saying, '*kardoraft* – this word is a Persian word,
which means one who has done something and who,
after having done it, has left the place' ['*kardoraft. – ei
shabdati parashya shabda, ihar artha kahar dwara e karma
hoiyachhe ebong ke e karma koriya prasthan korilo*], adding
after the poem his own comment: 'The amazing skill and
knowledge this poem displays will be appreciated only by
the knowledgeable.' The six-line poem is as follows:

Panchapadi

kamini jamini mukhe,   *nidragata shuye shukhe*
dheer shath tar mukhe,   *chumbite chumban shukhe,*
            dhire dhire kardoraft.

[The night on her beautiful face,   she sleeps in peace
The placid cheat on her face,   pleasurably plants a kiss
            Very slow, very slow, came and was gone.]

nidra hote uthe nari,   *alashe abash bhari,*

aarshite mukh heri,   *chumba chinha drishta kari,*
         bhabe bhāl kardoraft.

[When she wakes from sleep,   she is languid, inert, heavy,
On her face in the mirror,   she sees the mark of the kiss
     Very slow, very slow, come and gone.][15]

When these poems were written, Bengal was dominated by Persian and Sanskrit as the classical languages, with Bengali and Hindi as the people's *lingua franca*. Never seeming to feel the pressure of adhering to any one language, Bharatchandra mixed languages to the extent that even his admirer and anthologist, Iswar Gupta, was constrained to comment when presenting one of his poems, a century later, 'Some Persian, some Bengali and some Sanskrit – seven different imitations spoil the original' [*'sat nakale ashal khasta'*], showing how the colonial high modern with its insistence on the nationalist authenticity of one pure language was already creeping up into the literary sphere.[16] Bharatchandra himself, however, had been totally unapologetic about such usage, commenting that a great deal of pure Sanskrit inflicted as much suffering upon the Bengali language as an excessive use of Arabic/Persian words. As a result of too much Sanskrit, 'clarity would be lost, and it would cease to be entertaining', which is why he preferred to use a mixed language of different ingredients, saying, famously: 'therefore I speak a mixed language' [*ataeb kahi bhasha jabani mishal*].[17]

Arguably, then, both modern *and* early modern Bengali literature and culture is premised on a condition of multilingualism or bilingualism, and in the debate on a written language for Bengal, even Bankimchandra, almost echoing Bharatchandra, documented, in an essay called '*Bangala bhasha*' ['The Bengali Language'] published in the *Bangadarsan* in summer 1878, a mixture of linguistic registers:

The first requirement and most important quality of any writing is simplicity and clarity. The things that need to be said should be said clearly – whatever little needs to be said should be said fully – to achieve this end, words from whichever language are necessary should be used – English, Persian, Arabic, Sanskrit, rural, wild – apart from the vulgar, everything else should be permissible.[18]

Here, the only category beyond the pale for Bankimchandra is that of the immoral, rude, or low; a newly constructed banishment that would attempt to ensure the expulsion of Bharatchandra from the canon on the grounds of licentiousness. In this essay, he is positioning himself against Vidyasagar and Ramgati Nyayratna on the one hand, and allying himself to the proponents of popular language led by Tekchand Thakur, coming down firmly and unequivocally on the side of the latter. It is, in fact, a turn-of-nineteenth-century cultural imposition, arguably datable to Dineshchandra Sen, to suppose that a language should be 'pure', purged of all foreign contamination, unmixed and authentic, a desire built upon the nationalist impulse to forge a homogeneous template of cultural achievement, to create a language that was one's own, and had the strength to stand on its own.

Iswar Gupta's enterprise of collecting and highlighting what he thought was the best of the preceding poetry would inevitably have been shaped by his own practice of the craft. His poetry is well known today as a poetry of the people, of their everyday habits and peculiarities, their food, manners, dress, and carriage. This was, very specifically, a poetry of the city in a new category that had not existed before. In this Iswar Gupta had no predecessors. This poetry, or *khanda kabita* (by which was meant fragments of poems, or shorter poems, to distinguish them from the longer devotional poems of the *mangalkabya*), was a new form with new content. It was given life, literally, by the modern exigencies of the spaces of its publication, which were frequently the blank columns or half-columns in newspapers and journals that needed fillers, and it filled them up with material that related directly to the city of its birth. Into his short poems there came, alongside the Hindi or the Persian of inherited usage, the English language: English words, English sounds, dress, dance, food, and manners in nineteenth-century Calcutta, fizzing and spitting with an astonishing verve in poems on the English New Year in 1852, on Christmas Day in the city, on the Missionary Child-Eater, on the Bengali convert to Christistianity, on 'Status'.

Take, for instance, the celebrated satirical poem *ingraji nababarsha* [English New Year], written to commemorate the arrival of the English year 1852. It records, in minute detail, the sights and sounds of the celebrations in the city. Beginning with a reference to the Bengali lunar year that is losing its relevance with the coming of the English, Christian year, the poem describes the white man in his carriage on the way to church. At his side, his wife looks 'fresh' in a 'polka-dotted dress' and a feather 'flourish' ('*maanmode bibi shab hoilen phresh / pheather-er pholorish phutikata dresh*'). The detailed description has a sting in the tail, for, after describing the slippers (*shilipar*) on her white feet, the scarf around her neck, the decorative comb in her hair, and the spray of flowers that descends to her cheek, he concludes in a notorious line, '*biralakhhi bidhumukhi mukhe gandha chhute*' [cat-eyes, moon-face, bad breath]. The sound effect of fluttering ribbons (strange things to the Bengali) and flowing ease is captured:

> *Ribin urichhe kata phar phar kori*
> *dhol dhol dhol dhol banka bhaab dhori*
> *bibijaan chole jan lobejaan kore*

[So many ribbons fly fluttering away
Leaning, flowing, reclining at an angle
The beloved bibi goes her way, and one feels like
dying].[19]

*

Once we begin to look for literary activism, we
find it everywhere in the nineteenth-century literary
sphere, which contributed towards the creation of
some aspects of the Indian modern through, as well
as in opposition to, the colonial presence, mediated,
among other things, by critical notions of language
and literature. When I argue, here, that to uncover
the construction of cultural production – whereby the
dominant group constructs its reality and its history – it
is essential to interrogate the key notion of derivation
(not the old question of a derivative discourse, but
another equally old question about transition and
complex historical transaction), that too is a form of
activism. In the area of my work, the attempt to situate
the notion of 'the derived' within the old rhetoric of
the 'influence' of the English presence in India, and to
map, instead, the tradition/modernity debate (that has
structured so much of the speculative, interventionist,
or didactic practice of language, form, and style) in
such a manner that we may come up with an alternative
reading, could be said to constitute literary/critical
activism.

It is my argument that contentions between the
major literary languages of India, including the classical
and folk languages, nouveau urban and mixed languages,
colonial and 'native' languages, played an instrumental
role in the many negotiations between modernity and
literary craft in nineteenth-century Bengal. It could be
argued, therefore, that the new and changing idioms of

literary production in the nineteenth century may, rather than being located in colonial coercion and the 'impact' of Western forms, be found instead within certain newly evolving contemporary literary practices of reading and writing that became readily available to Indians from the early nineteenth century onwards. Against the grain of conventional approaches to literary criticism, it should be possible to acknowledge the enabling element in the fundamental bi- and multilingualism that allowed us to fashion the implements of our own modernity in an insistently original form. How one approaches a text is germane to any discussion on literary activism, and I want to conclude with Derek Attridge's thoughts on Derrida's strategy of reading Rousseau in *Of Grammatology*, in a head note to the extract in *Acts of Literature*:

> [it] both makes clear the necessity for scrupulous commentary of the traditional sort and urges the kind of reading he is undertaking – one that pays close attention to writing as writing, not as a mere window on some other, more 'real', reality. The domain in which writing is allowed most significance is literature, yet, as Derrida points out, literature has usually been read in accordance with the model provided by philosophy: the reduction of the text to a context, a moral, a biographical or historical origin, a formal scheme, a psychoanalytic template, a political agenda. His claim goes further than the restoration of literature's rights, however; he argues that to read as he does is to activate the movements and relations (non-logical, non-conceptual) upon which all those reductions depend. Following in the track of the wandering 'supplement' in Rousseau's texts constitutes one such activation.[20]

Activation, act, activism: re-reading Iswar Gupta's critical activism on behalf of a certain kind of literature or, indeed, reading Attridge's own act of commentating on Derrida, we see how acts of literature or activism in literary studies may relate to what Derrida calls a text's 'iterability, which both puts down roots in the unity of a context and immediately opens this non-saturable context onto a recontextualization.' [21]

In the context of the Indian modern, we then hopefully see how, setting aside the wholly understandable nationalist urge under colonial rule to discard words, concepts, and conventions that had their origin in other languages, it is possible to demonstrate that *one* of the promising signs to emerge from a cross-sectional view of Bengali literary modernity is the realisation that bilingualism or multilingualism was germane to the quest for modernity in the secular literary space of Bengal.[22] Such a cross-sectional reading creates a changed signification in the already available practices of reading, creating, instead of a binary understanding of good and bad, moral and immoral, foreign and traditional, a realisation that the production of India's many modernities involved various members of a historical situation acting together and upon each other in unexpected ways. Such a polyvalent approach can free us from the insistence that modernity is an import to be associated with British imperialism alone, showing us concretely how India's distinctive cultures and societies have always been sourced from foreign as well as regional indigenous materials. If we are to find, in the constitutive arenas of the Indian modern, some notion of creativity and specificity independently of the argument of 'Western influence', then this sort of transverse reading (itself a form of literary activism) becomes significant for the self-created identity of India's multiple modernities.

1. Roland Barthes, *Writing Degree Zero*, trans. Annette Lavers and Colin Smith (New York: Hill and Wang, 1977), pp. 2-3.

2. Pierre Macherey, *A Theory of Literary Production* (London: Routledge, 2006), p. 4.

3. Nigel Leask, *British Romantic Writers and the East: Anxieties of Empire* (Cambridge: Cambridge University Press, 1992), p. 13.

4. Henry Meredith Parker, *Bole Ponjis* (London and Calcutta, 1851), p. 139.

5. Henry Meredith Parker, 'Young India: A Bengal Eclogue' in *Bole Ponjis* (London and Calcutta, 1851), pp. 226-227.

6. From the concept note for the conference on Literary Activism by Amit Chaudhuri. See p. 6.

7. Thomas Seccombe, 'Arnold, Edwin', in the *Dictionary of National Biography*, 1912 supplement.

8. Edwin Arnold, ed., *The Arnold Poetry Reader* (London: Kegan Paul, Trench, Trubner & Co. Ltd., 1920), p. 10.

9. Bankimchandra Chatterjee, 'Introduction', *Iswar Gupter Kabita Sangraha* [Collected Poems of Iswar Gupta] (1885), reprinted in ed. Alok Ray, *Iswarchandra Gupter Sreshtha Kabita* [*Best Poems of Iswarchandra Gupta*] (Calcutta: Bharabi, 2009), p. 22.

10. Chatterjee, 'Introduction'.

11. Sisir Kumar Das, *A History of Indian Literature: 1800-1910: Western Impact, Indian Response* (New Delhi: Sahitya Akademi, 1991).

12. Ajit Kumar Ray, *The Religious Ideas of Rammohun Roy* (Calcutta: Kanak Publications, 1976), pp. 3-4.

13. Iswar Gupta, ed., *Kavivar Bharatchandra Ray Gunakarer Jibanbrittanta* (Calcutta: Prabhakar Press, 1855). Iswar Gupta published an anthology called *Kalikirtan* in 1833 that was a collection of Kali kirtans by Ramprasad Sen and others. A notice in the *Sambad Prabhakar* in 1855 had declared his intention of a 'jivan charit' on Ramprasad

Sen, with songs and notes, but this project remained unfulfilled.

14. The Persian word '*Kardraft*' may ostensibly be translated in Hindi as '*Kar do raft*' meaning to do and then to disappear, such as in '*kiya aur gaya*' [done and gone].

15. *Kabijibani, Bhāratcandra*, pp. 23-24.

16. Bhabatosh Datta ed., *Iswarchandra Gupter Kabijibani* (Calcutta: Calcutta Book House, 1958), p. vii.

17. Quoted in Haraprasad Mitra, *Bangla Kabye Prak-Rabindra* (Calcutta: The Book Emporium, n.d), p. 20. *Jabani mishal* may be translated as 'mixture of the Yavanas', where the word '*jaban*' might be interchangeably read as meaning 'foreign' or 'Muslim'.

18. Bankimchandra Chattopadhyay, '*Bangala Bhasha*' [1878] in ed., J. Bagal, *Bankim Rachanabali*, Vol.II, (Calcutta: Sahitya Sansad, 1998), p. 321.

19. Iswar Chandra Gupta, '*Ingraji Nababarsha*' ['The English New Year'] in ed. Alok Rai, *Iswarchandra*

Gupter Sreshtha Kabita [The Best Poems of Iswarchandra Gupta] (Calcutta: Bharabi, 2009), p. 84.

20. Derek Attridge, 'That Dangerous Supplement' in *Acts of Literature* by Jacques Derrida (Routledge: London, 1992), p. 76.

21. Attridge, 'That Dangerous Supplement', p. 63.

22. The realisation, for instance, that not only were the first translations of Bharatchandra and the first article on him written in English by Kasiprasad Ghosh in 1830, but that the best interpretative essays on Bharatchandra in that century too were in English rather than Bengali, adds a third dimension to the literary scene not many critics have been perceptive to. The list of Bharatchandra's admirers who wrote of him in the English language begins with Reverend Wenger who wrote on him in the *Calcutta Review* of 1850, and continues with Harchandra Datta, Rameshchandra Datta, Gourdas Bairagi,

Pramatha Chaudhuri, Nirad Chaudhuri, and J.C. Ghosh. Of all of these, it is Pramatha Chaudhuri's essay, 'The Story of Bengali Literature', written in 1917 at the request of Rabindranth Tagore, which is remarkable for its perception of the early elements of modernity in Bharatchandra.

Transnational vs. National Literature
DUBRAVKA UGREŠIĆ
Translated by *DAVID WILLIAMS*

1.

I write in the language of a small country. I left
that small country in 1993 in an effort to preserve my
right to a literary voice, to defend my writings from
the constraints of political, national, ethnic, gender,
and other ideological projections. Although true, the
explanation rings phoney, like a line from an intellectual
soap opera. Male literary history (is there any other?)
is full of such lines, but with men – being 'geniuses',
'rebels', 'visionaries', intellectual and moral bastions, etc.
– when it comes to intellectual-autobiographical kitsch,
they get free passes. People only turn up their noses
when it escapes a woman's lips. Even hip memes such as
'words without borders' and 'literature without borders'
ring pretty phoney too. The important point here is that
having crossed the border, I found myself in a literary
OUT OF NATION ZONE, the implications of which I only
figured out much later.

It could be said that I didn't actually leave my
country, but rather, by splitting into six smaller ones,
my country – Yugoslavia – left me. My mother tongue
was the only baggage I took with me, the only souvenir
my country bequeathed me. My spoken language in
everyday situations was easy to switch, but changing my
literary language... I was too old for that. However, I don't
have any romantic illusions about the irreplaceability
of one's mother tongue, nor have I ever understood the
coinage's etymology. Perhaps this is because my mother
was Bulgarian, and Bulgarian her mother tongue. She
spoke flawless Croatian though, better than many
Croats. On the off-chance I did ever have any romantic
yearnings, they were destroyed irrevocably almost a
quarter of century ago, when Croatian libraries were
euphorically purged of NON-CROATIAN books, meaning
books by Serbian writers, Croatian 'traitors', books by

'commies' and 'Yugoslavs', books printed in Cyrillic. Mouths buttoned tight, my fellow writers bore witness to a practice that may have been short-lived, but was no less terrifying for it. Indeed, if I ever harboured any linguistic romanticism, it was destroyed forever the day Bosnian Serbs set their mortars on the National Library in Sarajevo. Radovan Karadžić, a Sarajevo psychiatrist and poet – a 'colleague' – led the mission of destruction. Today, equally stubbornly and stupidly, people form Vukovar destroy plaques with the names of the streets written in both Cyrillic and Latin letters. Cyrillic letters, they say, hurt their feelings. When it comes from Muslim perpetrators, cultural vandalism is usually followed by rich media attention. When it comes from any corner of Europe, it is followed by silence. Writers at least ought not to forget these things. I haven't. Which is why I repeat them obsessively. For the majority of writers, a mother tongue and national literature are natural homes, for an 'unadjusted' minority, they're ZONES OF TRAUMA. For such writers, the translation of their work into foreign languages is a kind of refugee shelter. And so translation is for me. In the euphoria of the Croatian bibliocide, my books also ended up on the scrap heap.

After several years of academic and literary wandering, I set up camp in a small and convivial European country. Both my former and my present literary milieu consider me a 'foreigner', each for their own reasons of course. And they're not far wrong: I am a *foreigner*, and I have my reasons. The ON-zone is an unusual place voluntarily to live one's literary life. Life in the zone is pretty lonely, yet with the suspect joy of a failed suicide, I live with the consequences of a choice that was my own. I write in a language that has split into three – Croatian, Serbian, and Bosnian – but in spite of concerted efforts to will it apart, remains the same language. It's the language in which war criminals pleaded their innocence at the Hague Tribunal. At some point, the tribunals' tortured translators came up with an appropriate acronym: BCS (Bosnian-Croatian-Serbian). Understandably, the peoples reduced and retarded by their bloody divorce can't stand the fact that their language is now just an acronym. So the Croats call it Croatian, the Bosnians Bosnian, and the Serbs Serbian – even the Montenegrins have come up with an original name: they call it Montenegrin.

What sane person would want a literary marriage with an evidently traumatised literary personality like me? No one. Maybe the odd translator. Translators keep me alive in literary life. Our marriage is a match between two paupers, our symbolic capital on the stock market of world literature entirely negligible. My admiration for translators is immense, even when they translate the names Ilf and Petrov as the name of Siberian cities. Translators are mostly humble folk. Almost invisible on the literary map, they live quiet lives in the author's shadow. My empathy with translators stems, at least in part, from my own position on the literary map: I often feel like I'm invisible too. Translating, even from a small language, is still considered a profession, but writing in a small language, from a literary *out of nation zone*, now that is not a profession – *that* is a diagnosis.

The platitude about literature knowing no borders isn't one to be believed. Only literatures written in major languages enjoy passport-free travel. Writerly representatives of major literatures travel without papers, a major literature their invisible *lettre de noblesse*. Writers estranged or self-estranged, exiled or self-exiled from their maternal literatures, tend to travel on dubious passports. A literary customs officer can, at any time, escort them from the literary train under absolutely any pretext. The estranged or self-estranged female writer is such a rare species she's barely worth mentioning.

All these reasons help explain my internal neurosis: as an ON-zone-writer I always feel obliged to explain my complicated literary passport to an imagined customs officer. And as is always the case when you get into a conversation with a customs officer on unequal footing, ironic multiplications of misunderstandings soon follow. What does it matter, you might say, whether someone is a Croatian, Belgian, or American writer? 'Literature knows no borders,' you retort. But it does matter: the difference lies in the reception of the author's position; it's in the way an imagined customs officer flicks through one's passport. And although it would never cross our minds to self-designate so, we readers – *we* are those customs officers!

Every text is inseparable from its author, and vice versa; it's just that different authors get different treatment. The difference is whether a text travels together with a male or female author, whether the author belongs to a major or minor literature, writes in a major or minor language; whether a text accompanies a famous or anonymous author, whether the author is young or old, Mongolian or English, Surinamese or Italian, an Arab woman or an American man, a homosexual or a heterosexual... All these things alter the meaning of a text, help or hinder its circulation.

Let's imagine for a moment that someone sends me and a fellow writer – let's call him Dexter – to the North Pole to each write an essay about our trip. Let's also imagine a coincidence: Dexter and I return from our trip with exactly the SAME text. Dexter's position doesn't require translation, it's a universal one – Dexter is a representative of Anglo-American letters, the dominant literature of our time. My position will be translated as Balkan, post-Yugoslav, Croatian, and, of course, female. All told, a particular and specific one. My description

of the white expanse will be quickly imbued with
projected, i.e., invented, content. Customs officers will
ask Dexter whether in the white expanse he encountered
the metaphysical; astounded that I don't live at 'home',
they'll ask me why I live in Amsterdam, how it is that I,
of all people, got sent to the North Pole, and while they're
at it, they'll inquire how I feel about the development of
Croatian eco-feminism. Not bothering to read his work
first, they'll maintain that Dexter is a great writer, and
me, not bothering to read my work first either, they'll
declare a kind of literary tourist guide – to the Balkan
region, of course; where else?

   To be fair, how my text about the North Pole
will be received in my former literary community is
also a question worth asking. As my encounter with
the metaphysical? God, no. Croats will ask me how
the Croatian diaspora is getting on up there, how I –
a Croatian woman – managed to cope in the frozen
north, and whether I plunged a Croatian flag into the
ice. Actually, in all likelihood my text won't even be
published. With appropriate fanfare they'll publish
Dexter's. It'll be called 'How a great American writer
warmed us to the North Pole.'

   That literature knows no borders is just a
platitude. But it's one we need to believe in. Both
originals and their translations exist in literature. The life
of a translation is inseparable from the relatively stable
life of its original, yet the life of a translation is often
much more interesting and dramatic. Translations – poor,
good, mangled, congenial – have rich lives. A reader's
energy is interwoven into this life; in it are the mass of
books that expand, enlighten, and entertain us; that
'save our lives'; the books whose pages are imbued with
our own experiences, our lives, convictions, the times in
which we live, all kinds of things.

Many things can be deduced from a translation and, let us not forget, readers are also translators. *The Wizard of Oz*, for example, was my favourite children's book. Much later I found out that the book had travelled from the Russian to Yugoslavia and the rest of the East European world, and that it wasn't written by a certain A. Volkov (who had 'adapted' it), but by the American writer Frank L. Baum. The first time I went to Moscow (way back in 1975) I couldn't shake the feeling that I had turned up in a monochrome Oz, and that I, like Toto, just needed pull to the curtain to reveal a deceit masked by the special effects of totalitarianism. Baum's innocent arrow pierced the heart of a totalitarian regime in a way the arrows of Soviet dissident literature never could.

Every translation is a miracle of communication, a game of Chinese Whispers, where the word at the start of the chain is inseparable from that exiting the mouth of whomever is at the end. Every translation is not only a multiplication of misunderstandings, but also a multiplication of meanings. Our lungs full, we need to give wind to the journey of texts, to keep watch out for the eccentrics who send messages in bottles, and the equally eccentric who search for bottles carrying messages; we need to participate in the orgy of communication, even when it seems to those of us sending messages that communication is buried by the din, and thus senseless. Because somewhere on a distant shore a recipient awaits our message. To paraphrase Borges, he or she exists to misunderstand it and transform it into something else.

2.

Data from the International Organization for Migration changes from hour to hour, so there is no point repeating it here. Migrants make around 220 million people, maybe more. Within that figure there is a certain number (in millions) of displaced people, and a certain number of refugees. Women make up forty-nine per cent of the migrant population. It's a fair assumption that in this imagined migrant state, there would be at least a negligible percentage of writers, half of whom would be women.

Writers who have either chosen to live in the ON-zone, or been forced to seek its shelter, need more oxygen than that provided by translations into foreign languages alone. For a full-blooded literary life, such writers need, *inter alia*, an imaginary library – a context in which their work might be located. Because more often than not, such work floats free in a kind of limbo. The construction of a context – of a literary and theoretical platform, a theoretical raft that might accommodate the dislocated and de-territorialised; the transnational and a-national; cross-cultural and transcultural writers; cosmopolitans, post-national, and literary vagabonds; those who write in 'adopted' languages, in newly acquired languages, in multiple languages, in mother tongues in non-maternal habitats; all those who have voluntarily undergone the process of dispatriation – much work on the construction of such a context remains.

In *Writing Outside the Nation*, Azade Seyhan attempted to construct a theoretical framework for interpreting literary works written in exile (those of the Turkish diaspora in Germany, for example), works condemned to invisibility within both the cultural context of a writer's host country (although written in German) and that of his or her abandoned homeland.[1] This theoretical framework was transnational literature. In the intervening years, several new books have appeared, and the literary practice of transnational literature has become increasingly rich and diverse. There are ever

205

more young authors writing in the languages of their host countries: some emigrated with their parents and speak their mother tongue barely or not at all; others (for cultural and pragmatic, or literary and aesthetic reasons) have consciously exchanged their mother tongues for the language of their hosts. Some write in the language of their host countries while retaining the mental blueprint of their mother tongue, giving rise to surprising linguistic melanges; others create defamiliarising effects by mixing the vocabulary of two or sometimes multiple languages. Changes are taking place not only within individual texts, but also in their reception. The phenomenon of literary distancing is one I myself have experienced. Although I still write in the same language, I can't seem to follow contemporary Serbian, Croatian, and Bosnian literature with the ease I once did. I get hung up on things at which local readers wouldn't bat an eyelid. I sense the undertones and nuances differently to them, and it makes me wonder about the 'chemical reaction' that takes place inside the recipient of a text (in this case, me) when cultural habitat, language, and addressee have all changed. My relationship towards the canonic literary values of the 'region' has also changed. Texts I once embraced wholeheartedly now seem laughably weak. My own literary modus changed the very moment I was invited to write a column for a Dutch newspaper. That was in 1992. I was temporarily in America, war raged in my 'homeland', and the addressee of my columns was – a Dutch reader.

I don't know whether it's harder to articulate the ON-zone or to live in it. Cultural mediators rarely take into account contemporary cultural practice, in which, at least in Europe, 'direct producers' co-locate with a sizeable cultural bureaucracy – from national institutions and ministries of culture, to European cultural institutions and cultural managers, to the manifold

NGOs active in the sector. The cultural bureaucracy is primarily engaged in the protection and promotion of national cultures, in enabling cultural exchange. The bureaucracy writes and adheres to policy that suits its own ends, creating its own cultural platforms, and rarely seeking the opinion of 'direct producers'. Let's be frank with each other; in the cultural food chain, 'direct producers' have become completely irrelevant. What's important is that cultural stuff happens, and that it is managed: publishers are important, not writers; galleries and curators are important, not artists; literary festivals are important (events that prove something is happening), not the writers who participate.

Almost every European host country treats its transnational writers the same way it treats its emigrants. The civilised European milieu builds its emigrants residential neighbourhoods, here and there making an effort to adapt the urban architecture to the hypothetical tastes of future residents, discrete 'orientalisation' a favourite. Many stand in line to offer a warm welcome. Designers such as the Dutch Cindy van den Bremen, for example, design their new Muslim countrywomen modern hijabs – so they've got something to wear when they play soccer, tennis, or take a dip in the pool. The hosts do all kinds of things that they're ever so proud of, it never occurring to them that maybe they do so not to pull emigrants out of the ghetto, but rather to subtlety keep them there, in the ghetto of their identities and cultures, whatever either might mean to them; to draw an invisible line between *us* and *them*, and thus render many social spheres inaccessible. It is for this very same reason that the publishing industry loves 'exotic' authors, so long as supply and demand are balanced. Many such authors fall over themselves to ingratiate themselves with publishers – what else can they do? And anyway, why wouldn't they?

Does transnational literature have its readers? And if it does, who are they? Publishers have long since pandered to the hypothetical tastes of the majority of consumers, and the majority's tastes will inevitably reject many books as being culturally incomprehensible. If the trend of 'cultural comprehensibility' – the standardisation of literary taste – continues (and there's no reason why it won't), then every conversation about transnational literature is but idle chatter about a literary utopia. And anyway, how do we establish what is authentic, and what a product of market compromise? Our literary tastes, the tastes of literary consumers, have in time also become standardised, self-adjusting to the products offered by the culture industry. Let's not forget: the mass culture industry takes great care in rearing its consumers. In this respect, transculturality has also been transformed into a commercial trump card. In and of itself, the term bears a positive inflection, but its incorporation in a literary work needn't be any guarantee of literary quality, which is how it is increasingly deployed in the literary marketplace. Today that marketplace offers a rich vein of such books, almost all well-regarded, and their authors, protected by voguish theoretical terms – hybridity, transnationality, transculturality, cross-culturality, ethnic and gender identities – take out the moral and aesthetic sweepstakes. Here, literary kitsch is shaded by a smokescreen of ostensible political correctness, heady cocktails mixing East and West, Amsterdam Sufis and American housewives, Saharan Bedouins and Austrian feminists, the burqa and Prada, the turban and Armani.

And where are my readers? Who's going to support me and my little homespun enterprise? In the neoliberal system, of which literature is certainly part and parcel, my shop is doomed to close. And what happens then (as I noted at the beginning) with my right to defend my texts from the constraints of political, national,

208

ethnic, and other ideological projections? My freedom
has been eaten by democracy – that's not actually a bad
way to put it. There are, in any case, any number of
parks in which I can offer speeches to the birds. What
is the quality of a freedom where newspapers are slowly
disappearing because they're not able, so the claim goes,
to make a profit; when departments for 'culturally exotic'
literatures are closing, because there aren't any students
(i.e., no profit!); when publishers unceremoniously dump
their unprofitable writers, irrespective of whether those
writers have won major international awards; when
the Greeks are having to flog the family silver (one of
Apollo's temples in Athens is rumoured to be going under
the hammer); when the Dutch are fine about closing one
of the oldest departments of astrophysics in the world
(in Utrecht) because it turns out that studying the sun
is – unprofitable.

 'Things are just a whisker better for you, because
like it or not, at least you've got a kind of marketing
angle. But me, I'm completely invisible, even within
my own national literature,' a Dutch writer friend of
mine kvetches. And I mumble to myself, Christ, my
brand really is a goodie – being 'a Croatian writer who
lives in Amsterdam' is just the sexiest thing ever. But I
understand what my Amsterdam acquaintance is going
on about. And really, how does one decide between
two professional humiliations – between humiliating
invisibility in one's 'own' literary milieu, and humiliating
visibility in a 'foreign' one? The latter visibility is
inevitably based on details such as the incongruence
between one's place of birth and one's place of
residence, the colour of one's skin, or an abandoned
homeland that has just suffered a *coup d'état*. My Dutch
acquaintance isn't far from the truth. Within the
context of contemporary Dutch literature, or any other
literature, where there is no longer any context; where

there is no longer literature; where it is no longer of any importance whatsoever whether anyone reads a book so long as they're buying them; where it is no longer of any importance whatsoever what people read, as long as they're reading; where the author is forced into the role of salesperson, promoter, and interpreter of his or her own work; only in such a deeply anti-literary and anti-intellectual context I am forced to feel lucky to be noticed as a 'Croatian writer who lives in Amsterdam' and, what's more, to be envied for it.

By now it should be obvious: the little pothole I overlooked when I abandoned my 'national' literature is the sinkhole of the market. Times have certainly changed since I exited the 'national' zone and entered my ON-zone. What was then a gesture of resistance is today barely understood by anyone. (Today, at least in Europe, recidivist nationalisms and neo-fascisms are dismissed as temporary, isolated phenomena.) Of course, not all changes are immediately apparent: the cultural landscape remains the same, we're still surrounded by the things that were once and are still evidence of our *raison d'être*. We're still surrounded by bookshops, although in recent years we've noticed that the selection of books has petrified, that the same books by the same authors stand displayed in the same spots for years on end, as if bookshops are but a front, camouflage for a parallel purpose. The officer in charge has done everything he should have, just forgotten to swap the selection of books periodically, make things look convincing. Libraries are still around too, although there are fewer of them: some shut with tears and a wail, others with a slam, and then there are those that refuse to go down without a fight, and so people organise petitions. Literary theorists, critics, the professoriate, readers, they're all still here, sure, there aren't many of them, but still enough to make being a writer somewhat sensical. Publishers, editors, agents, they're all still in the room, though more and more often it occurs to us that they're not the same people anymore. It's as if no one really knows whether they're dead, or if it's us who're dead, just no one's gotten around to telling us. We've missed the boat on heaps of stuff. It's like we've turned up at a party, invitation safely in hand, but for some reason the dress code's all wrong...

Literary life in the ON-zone seems to have lost any real sense. The ethical imperatives that once drove writers, intellectuals, and artists to 'dispatriation' have in the meantime lost their value in the marketplace of ideas. The most frequent reasons for artistic and intellectual protest – fascism, nationalism, xenophobia, religious fundamentalism, political dictatorship, human rights violations, and the like – have been perverted by the voraciousness of the market, stripped of any ideological impetus and imbued with marketing clout, pathologising even the most untainted 'struggle for freedom', and transforming it into a struggle for commercial prestige.

For this reason it's completely irrelevant whether tomorrow I leave my ON-zone and return 'home', whether I set up shop somewhere else or whether I stay where I am. For the first time I can see that my zone is just a ragged tent erected between the giant tower blocks of a new corporate culture. Although my books and the recognition they have received serve to confirm my professional status, they offer me no protection from the feeling that I've lost my 'profession', not to mention my right to a 'profession'. I'm not alone; there are many like me. Many of us, without having noticed, have become homeless: for a quick buck, others, more powerful, have set the wrecking ball on our house.

After abandoning, or being expelled from, a couple of literary houses: a multicultural one, a Yugoslav one, which had been brutally destroyed, I unwillingly found myself under the roof and the rules of a Croatian, national, e.g., nationalistic one. As a writer I could not accept a house where literary values are based on the national roots, blood types of literary tenants, and fabricated literary tradition (always MALE, naturally). After having tried a literary house called 'exile', where I have been treated as a 'Croatian writer living in exile', I am looking forward to move one day into a new, global literary house that waits to be constructed by us, 'practitioners', by literary scholars, literary activists and enthusiasts; by young people who migrate, write in two or three languages, who pick their cultural references from the whole world, adopt freely different cultures and live them with passion and understanding.

This essay first appeared, in slightly different form, in the essay collection, Europe in *Sepia*, published by Open Letter in 2014.

1. Azade Seyhan, *Writing Outside the Nation* (Princeton: Princeton University Press, 2001).

The Piazza and the Car Park:
Literary Activism and the Mehrotra Campaign
AMIT CHAUDHURI

It was 1989. I was a graduate student at Oxford. I had made little progress with my doctoral dissertation and I had written a novel that had almost, but not quite, found a publisher. One of the routes that had taken me in my fiction towards Calcutta was Irish literature – its provincialism and cosmopolitanism, its eccentricity and refinement. So I was pleased when I heard that Seamus Heaney was the likeliest candidate to win the elections for the Oxford Professorship of Poetry. Paul Muldoon's anthology *The Faber Book of Contemporary Irish Poetry* had reintroduced Heaney to me: the magical early poems about the transformative odd-jobs men of a prehistoric economy – 'diviners' and 'thatchers'; the features of that economy – wells and anvils; the Dantesque political cosmology (Heaney's overt response to the 'troubles') of *Station Island*.

A diversion was caused by the nomination of the Rastafarian performance and dub poet Benjamin Zephaniah. It was a strategically absurd nomination, made in the political tradition that periodically produces a fringe contender from the Monster Raving Loony Party to clear the air. Meanwhile, Heaney himself had begun subtly to remake himself as a postcolonial poet since *Wintering Out* and particularly *North*. By 'postcolonial' I mean a particular allegorical aesthetic to do with power, Empire, violence, and empowerment: an allegory that, in Heaney's case, had seen him scrutinising, since 1971, Iron Age John Does buried for centuries in the peat and Tollund men who had once been the victims of state violence; it now also involved the glamour his words imparted to bottomless bogs and to Celtic orality. There was a hint of magic realism to *North*'s politics and poetics. In retrospect, I realise this reinvention on Heaney's part was making me uneasy.

Naturally, Heaney won by a wide margin. The poet's lectures were thronged with students and Heaney's performances often had the dazzling quality of brilliant undergraduate papers. There was another narrative unfolding in these lectures, though, which would become clearer when they were collected in *The Redress of Poetry*, some of these thoughts having already been rehearsed in *The Government of the Tongue*. It was to do with Heaney's exploration of artistic delight alongside his increasing disquiet about, and premonition of, the emptiness of the poet's life in liberal democracies. Against this he had begun to counterpoise, more and more, the exemplary aesthetic and moral pressure that East European poets experienced under punitive, totalitarian regimes. Those regimes seemed to become a kind of inverse pastoral for Heaney: enclosed, isolated, and capable, paradoxically, of producing the great artists that the West no longer did. Was Heaney at a dead end? Had he been made less creative somehow, or less powerful – not only by success, but by the inexorable collapse of those regimes that had unwittingly legitimised what for him was the only great poetry being written at that time: regimes that, one by one, began to fall almost immediately after he took up the Professorship?

A decade is a long time in the life of a culture, and much changed during the 1980s. But arguably far more changed, and changed unthinkably, between 1989 and 1993. The American writer Benjamin Kunkel, founder-editor of the journal *n+1* and the author of a book of essays on Marxism and capitalism, *Utopia or Bust: A Guide to the Present Crisis*, said in an interview published in 2014:

> ...I'm now old enough to remember when the Cold War just seemed like a permanent geological feature of the world. And then it just vanished. Then people would talk about how Japan was going to be a wealthier economy than the United States in ten years. It would have seemed totally insane that there

was going to be a black president and that gay people were going to get married...[1]

Kunkel is telling us how difficult it was, and always is, to predict the outcomes that we now take so for granted that we no longer even think about them; no longer, experientially, perceive a discontinuity. But perhaps he's also telling us how hard it is to remember – actually to feel the nearness and veracity of a time when it would have seemed 'insane' to make those predictions. The imminence of a changed world order, a new cultural order, and the ignorance of that imminence are only two features of that world to which Kunkel is referring – for that world also had an infinity of other features whose reality it is now almost impossible to recollect, let alone feel. In order to remember, we need to rely on a species of voluntary memory, that is, a willed remembering whose consequences are largely predetermined and shaped by the conceptual structures of the present; so we are led to recall large categories, but not what it would have meant to inhabit them. Kunkel is trying to imply the lived immediacy of inhabiting a moral order by one of the strategies through which we can move beyond voluntary memory – by gesturing towards, and recuperating, the unthinkable: 'It would have seemed totally insane...' In this business of recollecting the world before the free market, before globalisation, voluntary memory misleads, and the flicker of involuntary memory throws up, as ever, an array of fragments and sensations, but doesn't, in itself, instruct us in the ethics of the vanished order, an ethics we have critiqued but whose proximity we no longer sense. So it is almost impossible now to remember – as it was impossible then to predict the fall of the Berlin Wall and the advent of President Obama – that poetry was the literary genre to which the greatest prestige accrued until the mid-1980s; that one might have spent an afternoon talking with an

219

acquaintance about the rhythm of a writer's sentences (in my specific instance, the novelist I have in mind is James Kelman, the acquaintance an English graduate student in Oxford whose name I have now forgotten). In the same way, it's hard to recall that we didn't think of success in writing mainly in relation to the market, and in relation to a particular genre, the novel, and to a specific incarnation of that genre, the first novel, possibly until 1993, when *A Suitable Boy* was published, or maybe a year earlier, when Donna Tartt's *The Secret History* appeared. It is now difficult to understand these examples as watershed occurrences in an emerging order, and difficult to experience again the moral implications of living – as I lived then, and maybe Benjamin Kunkel, who is much younger than I am, did too – in an order that was superseded.

This might be because the brain or mind or whatever you call it – our entire emotional and psychological make-up – is geared to cope with death, not just our own, but especially of our loved ones, with whom we identify the founding phases in our lives. Upon a significant death, we mourn the irrevocable closure of that phase; then, pretty consistently, we find it almost impossible to comprehend what it means for that person not to be alive.

This mechanism constantly translates into our experience of the everyday. In Oxford, I recall a dimly lit car park next to the cinema on George Street that was finally turned into a fake piazza in which a market now congregates on Wednesdays. I find it difficult to recall the car park except theoretically. But I know very well that it was there. I have to rely on a moral variant of voluntary memory, on a willed excavation, to bring it back. This excavation – this ethical variation of voluntary memory – is increasingly important to those of us who have lived through a bygone epoch into this one. Without it, we accept the timelessness, the given-ness, of whatever is equivalent to the piazza in our present-day existence. In other words, voluntary memory – or that form of excavation – must take us towards what from our point of view is plausible, but essentially unthinkable: not just the past's ignorance of its own future, as in Kunkel's anecdote about a world presided upon by the Cold War and unable to conceive of its own contingency, but the past studied from the vantage point of a present in which we know the Cold War to be a historical fact, but unthinkable. To truly attest today to the existence of the car park, or our habits of reading before the free market, is, to use Kunkel's word, 'insane': or uncanny. We presume, immediately upon taking on new habits, that those habits are inborn reflexes. We are shocked to hear that poets were central to the culture; that writers once deliberately distanced themselves from material success. The past, as we reacquaint ourselves with these unthinkable facts, begins to look like that rare thing: compelling science fiction – utterly new, and unsettling. Our excavation is perhaps all the more important because we have been inhabiting, for twenty-five years, an epoch or a world in which there has been really no contesting order, no alternative economic or political model. Only through a moral variant of voluntary memory might we, who belong to a particular generation, intuit a different order and logic which isn't really recoverable, and which challenges the present one – the piazza – simply by exposing its contingency, its constructedness.

What are the features, since the 1990s, of the piazza that have almost obliterated our memory of the car park, making us doubt if it existed? Let's enumerate, quickly and crassly, some of the obvious developments in literary culture, focusing on publishing and dissemination, and the ways in which they converged with a rewriting of the literary. Let me restrict myself to

Britain, my primary location during that time, taking the developments there to be in some senses paradigmatic. For one thing, most British publishing houses, as we know, were acquired by three or four German and French conglomerates, leading to a version, in publishing, of the Blairite consensus: a sort of faithful mimicking of the absence of true oppositionality in British politics following the creation of New Labour in the image of the Thatcherite Tory party. Bookshop chains such as Dillons and Waterstones emerged, at first heterogeneous in terms of their individual outlets, then becoming merged and increasingly centralised. As many of us also know, the Net Book Agreement collapsed – that is, the agreement that had protected books from being sold under an agreed minimum price. Offers and price reductions not only became possible, they became the context for what determined shelf space and, thus, what was read. The books on price reductions and three-for-the-price-of-two offers were those that had been deemed commercial by marketing executives – the new, unacknowledged bosses of the editors and publishers – and bookshop chains, the new, unacknowledged bosses of the marketing executives.

What we were presented with, then, was a stylised hierarchy in which the author, at its bottom, was, like a monarch in a parliamentary democracy, celebrated or reviled – because, as with the monarchy, there was no real agreement on whether the author was really *necessary* – and in which even publishers and agents played stellar roles only within accommodations predetermined by marketing men and bookshop-chain bureaucrats. This is not to say that agents or publishers didn't *believe* in unlikely or unpromising books. The shift lay here: they believed in them in the cause of their untapped market potential. However, with the creation of a new marketing category, 'literary fiction', market potential would *only* be expressed in terms of aesthetic excellence. Almost no

222

publisher would say, in their press release: 'We believe this novel is going to sell tens of thousands of copies.' They would say, instead: 'We believe this novel puts the writer in the ranks of V.S. Naipaul and Salman Rushdie,' a literary formulation based upon analogies and juxtapositions that made perfect sense to the public. Belief is a sacred constituent of radical departures in literature and publishing: so it appeared, by a slight adjustment of language, as if the literary were being invested in.

Here was a commercial strategy that would not speak its name, except in the context of a kind of literary populism: 'More and more people are reading books.' At the top of the hierarchy was the figure the marketing men scrambled to obey: the reader. The word 'reader' possessed a mix of registers: it evoked the old world of humanistic individualism that had ensconced the act of reading, while, at once, it embraced the new, transformative populism. This populism worked so well in culture precisely because it didn't dispense with the language of the old humanism even though it rejected almost everything it had stood for; it simply embraced that language and used it *on its own terms.*

Who, by the way, was the 'reader'? He or she was an average person, put together by marketing via the basic techniques of realist writing (as Woolf had accused Arnold Bennett of creating characters by making them an agglomeration of characteristics).[2] The reader was, according to marketing, unburdened by intelligence; poorly read; easily challenged and offended by expressions of the intellect; easily diverted by a story, an adventure, a foreign place or fairy tale, or an issue or theme of importance. This reader was transparent, democratic, and resistant only to resistance, occlusion, obscurity, and difficulty. Writing must assume the characteristics of the 'reader': the term for this process, in which literature took on a desirable human quality, was 'accessibility'. In order to genuflect to the 'reader', who, despite being invented by marketing staff, disappointed them constantly, jacket designs had to be adjusted, and literariness programmatically marginalised. But, crucially, the notion of the 'reader' made it possible to claim that literature was, more than ever, thriving, so that it wouldn't seem that its humanistic context had been made defunct, but, instead, extended and renewed. There were more and more readers. New literatures were coming of age: 'like a continent finding its voice,' the *New York Times* had said of *Midnight's Children* more than a decade previously, though the pronouncement still seemed recent in the 1990s. Abundance was curiously repressive. Here, via the later incarnations of Waterstones and the Booker Prize, with their ambition to capture readers, were early instances of what would become a typical convergence between the vocabulary used canonically, and retrospectively, to describe a renaissance with the ethos and vocabulary of boom-time.

Speaking of renaissances, what was the academy doing at this point? By the late 1980s, critical theory and its mutations – including postcolonial theory, which would take on the responsibility of defining and discussing the increasingly important literature of Empire – had begun to make incursions into Oxbridge and other universities. The departments of English, by now, looked with some prejudice upon value and the symbols of value, such as the canon; problematised or disowned terms such as 'classic' and 'masterpiece'; often ascribed a positive political value to orality, which it conflated with non-Western culture, and a negative one to inscription or 'good writing', which it identified with the European Enlightenment. Some of this was overdue and necessary.

Meanwhile, publishers robustly adopted the language of value – to do with the 'masterpiece' and 'classic' and 'great writer' – that had fallen out of use in its old location, fashioning it in *their own terms*. And these were terms that academics essentially accepted. They critiqued literary value in their own domain, but they were unopposed to it when it was transferred to the marketplace. Part of the reason for this was the language of the market and the language of the publishing industry were (like the language of New Labour) populist during a time of anti-elitism. Part of this had to do with the fact that publishers adopted complex semantic registers. For example: from the 1990s onwards, publishers insisted there was no reason that literary novels couldn't sell. This was an irrefutable populist message disguising a significant commercial development. What publishers meant was that, in the new mainstream category of 'literary fiction', only literary novels that sold well would be deemed valid literary novels. Academics neither exposed this semantic conflict nor challenged the way literary value had been reconfigured. When, in response to political changes in the intellectual landscape, they extended the old canon and began to teach contemporary writers, or novelists from the former colonies, they largely chose as their texts novels whose position had been already decided by the market and its instruments, such as certain literary prizes.

Experts, critics, and academics took on, then, the role of service-providers in the public sphere. This dawned on me in 2005, when I was spending a couple of months with my family in Cambridge. Watching TV in the evening, possibly Channel 4, we chanced upon a programme on the ten best British film directors; the list had been created on the basis of votes from viewers. As with all such contemporary exercises, it was an odd compilation, displaying the blithe disregard for history so essential to the market's radicalism. Chaplin had either been left out or occupied a pretty low rung; Kenneth

Branagh might have been at the top. Each choice was discussed by a group of film critics and experts (such as Derek Malcolm) who, in another age, would have had the final say. Here, they neither interrogated the choices nor the legitimacy of the list; they solemnly weighed the results. Respect and a species of survival skills were their hallmark. If Channel 4 viewers had come up with a completely different list, it would have been accorded the same seriousness by the experts. They were here to perform a specific function. The programme made me realise that it's not that the market *doesn't* want the expert or the intellectual; it simply wants them *on its own terms*. The arbiter of taste and culture and the expert – whether they're a film critic, or a celebrity chef, or a Professor of English judging the Booker Prize – is a service-provider. The circumstances – such as the 'public' vote that had gone towards the list, or the six months in which the Booker judge reads 150 novels (two novels nominated by each publishing house) in order to choose the best literary novel of the year – will invariably be absurd from one point of view, and revolutionary and renovating from the point of view of the market. The expert, in a limited and predetermined way, is a requisite for this renovation. The genius of market activism lies in the fact that, unlike critical theory, it doesn't reject the terminology of literary value; it disinherits and revivifies it, and uses it as a very particular and powerful code. This accounts for its resilience.

What's interesting in this scenario is how far the consensus about the logic of the market extends, encompassing what might seem to be rents in the fabrics. Take, for example, the phenomenon of 'pirated' books in urban India, more or less coterminous with the emergence of the mainstream 'literary novel' in the nineties. 'Pirated' books are cheap copies, illegally reproduced and sold at traffic lights and on pavements. Confronting them, you have the same sense of disapproval and curiosity that you might towards contraband. In other words, the sight of 'pirated' books provokes an excitement and unease in the middle-class person that recalls, from another age, a response to the avant-garde and the out-of-the-way; the word 'pirated' adds to the aura of illegality. Only when you scrutinise the titles do you realise that pirated books are no alternative to the bookshop chain. The selection represents the most conservative bourgeois taste; popular fiction, horoscopes, best-selling non-fiction (*Mein Kampf* is perennially available), and Booker Prize winners are arrayed side by side.

Any notion of 'literary activism' positions itself not against the market, but the sense of continuity it creates. For instance, literary activism needs to proclaim its solidarity with, as well as distance itself from, the old, invaluable processes of 'championing' and reassessment. Distance itself because, in the age of the market, publishers and marketing institutions such as the Booker Prize themselves became champions. Their primary aim was to enlist the notional 'reader' in greater numbers. In one of the many semantic convergences of the period, the language of praise and championing, so fundamental to criticism and its influence, flowed, with the Booker Prize and publishing houses in the 1990s, into the market's upbeat terminology of 'bullishness'. (It would be worth knowing when betting was introduced in the run-up to the Booker results. Ladbrokes, the British betting company, seems to have been operating in the Booker arena from 2004.)

Let's have a look at how the Booker Prize morphed from a prize judged by novelists into a fundamental device for 'market activism' in the 1990s, with juries comprising politicians and comedians. The off-kilter agitation caused by the Booker was, even by the late 1980s, not so much related to the excitement of the literary, which has to do with the strangeness of poetic language (or as Housman put it, 'if a line of poetry strays into my memory, my skin bristles so that the razor ceases to act'), as it was an effect of a hyper-excited environment. The principal way in which the Booker achieved this was by confirming, and allowing itself to be informed by, the market's most value-generating characteristics: volatility and random rewards. The market never promised equitable gain and wealth for all; what it said was: 'Anyone can get rich.' The distance between equitable gain (the idea that *everyone* can be rich) and the guarantee – '*anyone* can get rich' – seems at first a matter of semantics, and non-existent; but it is very real and is reproduced exactly by the distance between the reader in the 1970s and the 'reader' in the time of market activism. In the age of full-blown capitalism, anyone *can* get rich through the market, and, also, anyone can get poor; and these occurrences are disconnected from anachronistic ideas of merit and justice. In this disconnection lies the magic of the free market, its ebullience and emancipation. So the Booker Prize implicitly proclaims: 'Anyone can win.' As long as the work in contention is a novel and is in English, both qualifications embedded in, and representing the globalised world, we can peel away the superfluous dermatological layers of literariness by agreeing that the essay, the story, and poetry are ineligible and superfluous. 'Anyone can win' suggests a revolutionary opening-up typical of the language of market activism. As the Booker's constituency – for some time now, a worldwide one – accepts the fact that anyone can win, there is, ritually, a degree of volatility about the construction, announcement, and reception of the shortlist – of late, even the longlist – which captures the agitation that propels market activism. Famous writers and critically

228

acclaimed books are often ignored; at least one unknown novelist is thrown into the limelight; one putatively mediocre novel is chosen. The book is severed from oeuvre and literary tradition, as if it existed only in the moment; the history, development, and cross-referencing that creates a literary work is correctively dispensed with.

Since the history of so-called 'new literatures' such as the Indian novel in English is tied up thoroughly (especially since *Midnight's Children*) with the Booker Prize and the manner in which it endorses novels, we subsist on a sense that the lineage of the Indian English novel is an exemplary anthology of single works, rather than a tradition of cross-referencing, borrowing, and reciprocity. The random mix on the shortlist and the incursion of first-time novelists as shortlisted authors, often even as winners, might echo the sort of championing that drew attention to new or marginal writing; while it is actually enlivened by the volatility of market activism. Each year there's the ritual outcry from critics and journalists that the judges have missed out on some meritorious works. This outcry is not a critique of the Booker; it's germane to its workings and an integral component of its activism. The culminatory outcry comes when the winner is announced; the result is occasionally shocking. Again, this phase, of disbelief and outrage, is an indispensable part of the Booker's celebration – its confirmation – of the market's metamorphic capacities; the prize would be diminished without it. This randomness should be distinguished from the perversity of the Nobel, where a little-known committee crowns a body of work marked by the old-fashioned quality of 'greatness', or rewards a writer for what's construed to be political reasons. The Nobel's arbitrariness is bureaucratic, its randomness a reliable function of bureaucracy.

Partly the Booker goes periodically to first novels or to unknown writers because its form of activism dispenses with the linear histories and body-of-work narratives that conventionally define literary histories and prizes such as the Nobel; it responds to the market's compression and shrinking of time, its jettisoning of pedigree in favour of an open-ended moment: the transformative 'now' of the market, in which anything can happen, and everything is changing. The fact that Indian writing in English since *Midnight's Children* has been handcuffed to the Booker means that it exists in this perpetual now, that its history is periodically obliterated and recreated each time an Indian gets the prize, leading Indian newspapers to proclaim every few years: 'Indian writing has come of age.' The first novel of this type, published in the 1990s, came to embody this compressed timeframe in which speculation occurs, fortunes are lost and made, radical transformation effected. Publishers who contributed significantly to market activism appropriated this sub-genre and, by often calling books that were yet to be published 'masterpieces' (the publisher Philip Gwyn Jones's pre-publication statement about *The God of Small Things*, 'a masterpiece fallen out of the sky fully formed', comes to mind), made pronouncements in terms of the market's compression of time, its subtle reframing of context and linearity, its insistence on the miraculous. The word 'masterpiece' itself became a predictive category, connected to the market's bullishness and optimism, rather than a retrospective endorsement. When a publisher proclaims today: 'The new novel we're publishing in the autumn is a masterpiece,' they mean: 'We think it will sell 50,000 copies.' No novel that's expected to sell 500 copies is deemed a 'masterpiece' by a contemporary mainstream publisher. Gwyn Jones's statement about Arundhati Roy's first novel needs, then, to be read as a prediction rather than an assessment, and a prediction made in the domain of a bullish marketplace. On the other hand, the

Booker's retrospective accolades – 'Which book would have won in 1939?' – again disrupt conventional histories and aim to bring past texts into the 'now' of the market's activism.

The most striking instance of a publishing house and author inhabiting this 'now' through a literary concept that once represented historical time is the publication of the singer Morrissey's first book, *Autobiography*, in 2013 as a Penguin Classic, the rubric evidently an authorial prerequisite. In 1992, Vikram Seth undertook a pioneering form of market activism by interviewing literary agents in order to decide who would be best equipped to auction *A Suitable Boy* to UK publishers. Notwithstanding Seth's commercial and critical success with *The Golden Gate*, he had only written his first (prose) novel. Meetings between authors and agents usually take place on fairly equal footing, with the weight of authority slightly on the side of the more powerful party. Seth's unprecedented style shifted the balance in the interests of the novel's commercial success and the sort of advance on royalties he thought it deserved. Morrissey's pre-publication mindset, two decades later, represents an evolution. No overt mention is made of figures or of the advance; it's the standard of the 'classic' that's at stake. It's as if Morrissey grasps the reification of literary concepts in the 'now' of the marketplace. Once, critics spoke ironically of the 'stocks and shares' in a writer's books being high or low with reference to their critical reputation; today, the same statement is made without irony and with a straightforward literalism. As part of this reification, however, certain words – such as 'classic' – become ironical, and come close to signifying a guarantee that needs to be fiercely bargained for. That Morrissey's hunch was right was proved by *Autobiography* climbing immediately to number one on the bestsellers' chart upon publication. It would surely be the one Penguin 'classic' to have had such an entry and such a run.

*

This, then, is what the piazza began to look like by the mid-1990s. We may have been bemused by what was unfolding in the first two years, but by the third year we believed it had always been like this. We had no memory of the car park. This no doubt had to do, as I suggested earlier, with the way the mind converts the dead into a fact: the dead are incontrovertible, but we don't know who they are. But partly it was the effect of the compressed time and space of globalisation, of inhabiting an epoch in which materiality was shrinking and our principal devices could be fitted into the palm of a hand, and periodically replaced. Personal memory, cultural institutions, and popular culture responded to this shrinkage, this ethos of recurring disposability, variously, for distinct but contiguous reasons. While literary language was acquired by publishers for the purposes of marketing, literary departments reneged, as I've said, on any discussion that connected value to the passage of time: they disavowed the 'masterpiece', 'canon', and 'classic'. Popular culture not only annexed these concepts, it produced its own terminology of eternity: for instance, the word 'all-time', as in 'all-time favourite guitarist' or 'all-time great movie director'. 'All-time', it soon became evident, covered a span of five, maybe ten, years; that is, the time of deregulated globalisation – 'all-time' was a means of managing the classic. In consonance with the eternity conjured up by 'all-time', popular culture – and even the so-called 'serious' media – abounded, and still abounds, with lists: 'ten favourite movies'; 'hundred great novels'; and so on. Lists at once mimic and annihilate the historicity of the canon; they reduce time, making it seemingly comprehensible; they exude volatility and are meaningless because the market is energised by the meaningless. Given the pervasiveness of the 'all-time', it wasn't surprising that it was difficult to give credence to the car park.

But other things were happening during the 1990s in my life that didn't quite fit in. I was rereading, and often discovering for the first time, the modernism of the Indian literatures as I prepared to compile the *Picador Book of Modern Indian Literature*. In 1992, I'd also turned my attention to Arvind Krishna Mehrotra, whose poetry I'd read on and off since the late 1970s and whose anthology, *The Oxford India Anthology of Twelve Modern Indian Poets*, published that year, seemed to be making an intervention on behalf of a discredited tradition, contemporary Indian poetry in English, without having recourse to the new interpretative apparatus. His primary intervention was the making of the anthology itself, where he brought poets and their work together in a way that redefined their relationship to each other without either explicitly rejecting or taking for granted the notion of a pre-existing canon. This was a way of looking at literary history that neither fitted in entirely with the old humanist procedures of valuation (Indian poetry in English had never anyway really been a legitimate subject of such authoritative procedures) nor subscribed to the prevalent methods connected to the postcolonial, the hybrid, or even to list-making, since Mehrotra's juxtapositions seemed to be exploring and arguing for a particular experience of the literary.

I recalled, as I was thinking of essays to include in the Picador anthology, a long, polemical critical article that Mehrotra had published in 1980 in a little magazine out of Cuttack called *Chandrabhaga* and edited by the poet Jayanta Mahapatra. The essay was 'The Emperor Has No Clothes', and I was eighteen when it came out, but I still had a sense of its central tenet: simply put, the Indian poem in English has no obvious markers of 'Indianness'. Similarly, the poem produced by the multilingual imagination has no visible hierarchy in, or signs of, the manner in which a multiplicity of languages inhabits it. With hindsight (and upon rediscovery of that issue after a strenuous search), this argument read like a prescient rebuttal of precisely one of the sacred dogmas that came into play from the 1980s onwards: that, in the case of the multicultural literary work, the admixture and its proportions were immediately noticeable, and it was therefore possible to applaud and celebrate them, rather than necessarily the work, accordingly.

Exactly when the idea came to me of getting Mehrotra nominated for the Oxford Professorship of Poetry, I can't recall, but it was obviously post-1989, with the Benjamin Zephaniah nomination pointing towards a course of action. Not that I was thinking of Mehrotra in terms of his potential comic disruptiveness; but *some* sort of unsettlement was going to be welcome. Besides, I felt Mehrotra would make for a genuinely excellent lecturer, and his self-aware position as an Indian modern made him, for me, a far better choice for the Professorship than the sort of 'great' poet who'd lost his tenancy in the emptiness of evangelical liberal democracy during globalisation.

The Picador anthology came out in 2001. The director of British Council India, in a moment of generosity, commissioned a poster exhibition as a response to it. I asked Naveen Kishore, publisher of Seagull Books, an imprint known for the beauty of its jacket designs, whether he'd take on the brief of producing the posters. Naveen created an elegant series using black-and-white photographs he'd taken himself, playing with typeface and selecting one randomly chosen quotation from pieces in the anthology per poster. One poster bore a line from Michael Madhusudan Dutt; one a remark from a letter Tagore had written; another a quote from 'The Emperor Has No Clothes'; another simply displayed the title of an A.K. Ramanujan essay, 'Is There an Indian Way of Thinking?' There were several others. Peter D. McDonald, who teaches English at Oxford and saw some of the posters I'd taken there with me, was struck especially by the Mehrotra quote that Naveen had used, a slightly edited version of this long sentence: 'Between Nabokov's English and Russian, between Borges's Spanish and English, between Ramanujan's English and Tamil-Kannada, between the pan-Indian Sanskritic tradition and folk material, and between the Bharhut Stupa and Gond carvings many cycles of give-and-take are set in motion.'

The sentence is doing something that isn't obvious at first. The back and forth, or the 'give-and-take... motion', between 'Ramanujan's English and Tamil-Kannada, between the pan-Indian Sanskritic tradition and folk material' et cetera, isn't an unexpected sort of movement – between the 'high', and the 'low' or 'popular'. It's the transverse movement *across* the sentence, connecting Nabokov, Borges, Ramanujan, the pan-Indian Sanskritic tradition, and the Bharhut Stupa to each other – characterising another kind of 'give and take' that enables these very analogies – that constitutes its departure. It signals Mehrotra's unwillingness to be constrained by conventional histories of cultural interaction or influence across the 'East' and the 'West' – so that he slyly sidesteps them or appears inadvertently to ignore them. There's a transaction between the high, the sacred with the vernacular and the profane, the sentence claims; this much is conventional wisdom. But the sentence also claims that such a transaction characterises every culture, in ways that puts cultures in conversation with each other. These conversations between cultures aren't to do with 'difference' (in which, say, the East might play the role of the irrational, the West of Enlightenment humanism); nor do they represent a conciliatory humanism, in which East and West seek versions of themselves in each other. Instead, Mehrotra behaves as if each pairing represents comparable literary trajectories that echo and illuminate each other; one of the things that the sentence declares is that the colonial encounter is hardly the only way of interpreting the contiguity between the West and the East, or even the 'high' to the 'vernacular'. The echoes that comprise the conversation ('Borges's Spanish and English... Ramanujan's English and Tamil-Kannada... the pan-Indian Sanskritic tradition and folk material') exist independently of each other, but their overlaps aren't entirely coincidental. They can only be noticed and connected in a head such as Mehrotra's, in whom, in some way not entirely explained by colonialism and the Empire, with their restrictive itineraries, these histories (catalogued in the sentence) come together. The echoes, overheard by Mehrotra, signal a liberation from those clearly demarcated histories of cultural interchange.

It was around that time that I asked Peter to read 'The Emperor Has No Clothes' in the Picador anthology, and also to consider the thought that Mehrotra be nominated for the Oxford Poetry Professorship. I hoped that Peter would be drawn to Mehrotra's larger statement, indeed to his work. This did become the case; so I'm not surprised to find an email query in my 'sent' inbox, addressed to Peter on 23 January 2009, when the opportune moment had clearly arisen:

Dear Peter,

· I notice they're looking for a new Professor of Poetry to dawdle beneath the dreaming spires. Should we conspire to get Arvind Krishna Mehrotra nominated?

Peter replied an hour later, saying he was going
to try to enlist colleagues in the department and then
proceed with the nomination, for which ten 'members
of congregation and convocation', or fully paid-up
Oxford University employees and/or degree-holders,
were required. I alerted the Irish poet-critic Tom Paulin,
who was out of sorts but still teaching at Hertford. Peter
photocopied 'The Emperor Has No Clothes' from the
Picador anthology, I poems from *Middle Earth: New and
Selected Poems* and *The Transfiguring Places* (the books, like
those of most Indian English poets, were out of print) at a
shop in Gariahat in Calcutta, and scanned and sent them
to Peter, for circulation, and also to Tom, who said he
would decide after he had investigated further.

　　Who is Arvind Krishna Mehrotra? No full account
could be given to people – and I include, here, some of
the nominators – who knew little of him and his work. All
that could be done was to put samples, the essay, and a
short biography out there and hope that this would open
up a conversation that would introduce, in the lead-up
to the elections, a new set of terms. Some might have
noticed that Mehrotra, born in 1947, was a 'midnight's
child,' but that neither his work nor life carried any news
of the nation as we'd come to understand it. The middle-
class suburb figured in the most characteristic poems.
He was born in Lahore. He grew up in a small town,
Allahabad, and was educated there and in another one,
Bhilai, and was later a graduate student in Bombay. Still
later, he'd spend two years in Iowa, homesick for India,
but there was no whiff, until the 2009 campaign, of
Oxbridge about him. Allahabad was an intellectual centre
that was moving unobtrusively, by the time Mehrotra
was seventeen and already entertaining ambitions of
being a poet, towards decline. And yet Allahabad is
where he discovered Ezra Pound and the Beat poets,
and, with a friend, brought into existence a short-lived

little magazine, *damn you/a magazine of the arts*, echoing
Ed Sanders's New York periodical from the early 1960s,
Fuck You: A Magazine of the Arts. The publication's name,
it seems to me, is intent on turning Sanders's challenge
into a Poundian imprecation, from one who clearly
shared with the narrator of 'Hugh Selwyn Mauberley'
a combative impatience about being 'born / In a half
savage country, out of date; / Bent resolutely on wringing
lilies from the acorn.' What sorts of lilies? At nineteen,
he was a youthful and exasperated satirist in *vers libre*, in
a declamatory mode borrowed from Ginsberg, opening
his long poem to the nation, *Bharatmata: A Prayer*, with:
'india / my beloved country, ah my motherland / you
are, in the world's slum / the lavatory.' It was 1966, two
years after Nehru's death, a time in which the late prime
minister's projects of industrialisation and austerity
continued doggedly to be pursued. Then, around 1969-70,
something magical happens, and, in rhythms and imagery
that glance knowingly both at French surrealism and
American poetry, Mehrotra begins to produce his first
mature poems, which are often parables about suburban
Allahabad:

> This is about the green miraculous trees,
> And old clocks on stone towers,
> And playgrounds full of light
> And dark blue uniforms.
> At eight I'm a Boy Scout and make a tent
> By stretching a bed-sheet over parallel bars...
> ('Continuities')

At least two things strike us as we acquaint
ourselves with Mehrotra's life and oeuvre. The first
has to do with movement. How does a person who has
moved relatively little encounter and even anticipate
the contemporary world of ideas and letters – in an age
without the fax and internet, in which the speediest
epistolary communication is the telegram? It's a mystery

that has no adequate explanation. Yet scratch the surface of the life and the history that produced it, and you find that Mehrotra exemplifies not an aberration but a pattern. It's a pattern that defines both India and much of literary modernity, and Mehrotra embodies it in the singular way in which he traverses the provincial and the cosmopolitan. This would have always made it difficult to present him in the campaign as a postcolonial who – like Derek Walcott, according to his supporters – had somehow transcended his identity into the realm of universality. ('With Walcott, you need only to remember the name,' an English professor had said dreamily to students.) Mehrotra, like Allahabad, was an anomaly, and modernity was local and anomalous. The second thing that becomes clear quickly is Mehrotra's indifference to creating an authentic 'Indian' idiom in English. Instead, like the speaker of a later poem, 'Borges,' he seems content to let 'the borrowed voice / [set] the true one free'. In an email to me he once admitted that, as a young man, he'd turned to French surrealism because he wanted to escape 'the language of nightingales and skylarks'. The same could presumably be said of his lifelong preoccupation, as both a poet and translator, with Pound, William Carlos Williams, and the emphatic dialogue of American cartoons. What's notable is the historical and creative intelligence latent in this statement: the notion that neither the English language nor Western culture is a continuous and unbroken entity, that each is heterogeneous and will contain *within* itself breaks and departures (such as French surrealism and the diction of Pound). No break need be made from it, because that's probably impossible; instead, a break might be effected *through* it by deliberately choosing one register or history over another. Modernism and Pound's poetry, then, aren't absolutes for Mehrotra; they constitute, instead, a breakdown in 'the language of skylarks and nightingales'.

This breakdown will resonate very differently for an Indian – for whom 'Western culture' is an ambivalent but real inheritance – from the way it will for a European to whom that inheritance is a given. It also means that the Indian poet in English will be less of a creator busy originating an authentic tongue, and more like a jazz musician, listening acutely to the conflicting tonality – nightingales, skylarks, the Beat poets, Pound – of what surrounds and precedes him. Out of this curious tradition (which in no way precludes Indian writing: Mehrotra's translations include versions of Prakrit love poetry, of Kabir, and of the contemporary Hindi poet Vinod Kumar Shukla, and it's often at the moment of translation that the registers I've mentioned are counterintuitively adopted), he must make something of his 'own'.

The enervating, bewildering, and thrilling elements of the Mehrotra campaign are too many in number to enumerate here. Let me recount a few points, some of which are already familiar to those who kept track of the event. We ended up recruiting a mix of well-wishers and personal contacts, all of them distinguished in their fields, as supporters, some of them already admirers of Mehrotra. Among the latter were the novelists Geoff Dyer and Toby Litt and the Romanticist Jon Mee. Tariq Ali was made to reacquaint himself with the work and became one of the most vocal supporters of the candidacy; Tom Paulin joined the campaign once his investigations confirmed the value of the candidate; Wendy Doniger and the philosopher Charles Taylor discovered Mehrotra for the first time and came on board; Homi Bhabha pledged support and mysteriously vanished; old friends and recent acquaintances including the scientists Sunetra Gupta and Rohit Manchanda, the historians Shahid Amin and Ananya Vajpeyi, the political thinker Pratap Bhanu Mehta, and the literary scholars Rajeswari Sunder Rajan, Swapan Chakravorty, Uttara

Natarajan, Rosinka Chaudhuri, and Subha Mukherjee
– all 'members of convocation' – put in their signatures.
A lot of leg-work was put in by Dr Sally Bayley, then a
part-time lecturer at Balliol College, and she didn't seem
to mind offending the faculty's inner circle, comprising,
among others, Hermione Lee and my excellent former
supervisor Jon Stallworthy. I was thinking of approaching
another literary friend, the poet Ruth Padel, for a
signature, when, curiously, she announced her candidacy
and approached me for mine. Ruth is charming, and
a good poet and speaker, but her hands-on approach
to her own nomination *was* unprecedented; nominees
are historically aloof from electioneering. Whether her
style was an appropriation of the methods of market
activism, to which the author's cooperation in, and
production of, PR is oxygen, I can't decide; some form of
activism it certainly was. Later, after the whole abortive
2009 elections were over, Tariq Ali, in a fit of anger,
would, in an email to me, call Padel's a 'New Labour-
style campaign', a style manufactured in the 1990s and
discomfiting to the old Left.

    Still in the early days of the lead-up to the
elections, I wrote a sonorous paragraph that was only
slightly tweaked by Peter: 'Arvind Krishna Mehrotra is
one of the leading Indian poets in the English language,
and one of the finest poets working in any language.
Influential anthologist, translator, and commentator,
he is a poet-critic of an exceptionally high order.
Mehrotra has much to say of value – of urgency – on
the matter of multilingualism, creative practice, and
translation (in both its literal and figurative sense),
issues that are pressingly important in today's world.
He is not an easy "postcolonial" choice, for he emerges
from a rich and occasionally fraught world history of
cosmopolitanism; but he is proof – as critic and artist
– that cosmopolitanism is not only about European

ecleticism, but about a wider, more complex network of languages and histories. For these reasons he would make an excellent, and timely, Professor of Poetry at Oxford.' This was circulated widely and put in the flyer; Peter sent it out along with the poems and the essay into the English faculty. By now, the official candidate, Derek Walcott, was in place. Poems by the three contenders appeared in the *Oxford Magazine*, chosen by Bernard O'Donoghue of the 'official' camp, but enough of a devotee of poetry (and a gentleman) to convey his admiration for Mehrotra's verse to Peter.

One thing Mehrotra had on his side as a writer was age – he was sixty-two. In the time of Romanticism and in the Modernist twentieth century, early death or suicide was the writer's sole means of unfettering themselves of conventional valuation and breaking through instantaneously. In the shrunken time of globalisation, in the eternity of the piazza, when the constant cycles of boom and bust that governed the market ensured that many economic and cultural lifetimes could occur in a decade, the writer needed to simply survive, to grow old, so that he might outlive those cycles, the piazza's eternity, into a mini-epoch (maybe a period of bust) when the literary is again visible. This crucial task, of growing old, Mehrotra had performed perfectly. Just as the market had triumphantly annexed and put to use the language of literary valuation disposed of by literature departments, the literary activist after the 1990s must ideally study the patterns of the free market, its repetition of boom and bust, its unravelling, to employ those rhythms on behalf of the literary. In the (often self-destructive) unpredictability of globalisation, the literary writer's function is to wait; and not die.

The story of the 2009 elections threatened to become sordid in the contemporary manner reserved for celebrity when *The Independent*, and consequently *The*

Sunday Times and other papers, carried a report about
how a dossier had begun to be circulated about Walcott's
past misdemeanours: in particular, his alleged sexual
harassment of two students, one at Harvard University
and the other at Boston, in 1982 and 1996 respectively.
These instances, however, were no secret. Before very
long, Walcott withdrew from the race, with Padel earning
great resentment from the 'official' camp as she was
accused of first alerting the press to Walcott's undeniable
history – a charge she strenuously denied. Many in the
'inner circle' pointed out that the only honourable course
of action for the two remaining candidates now was to
withdraw. Among those who advocated this course of
action was *a different* Peter McDonald: the Irish poet and
Christ Church lecturer. (I've always believed that Oxford
is a place of inconvenient doppelgangers.) All this time,
another upheaval was taking place, unreported: various
faculty members were discovering, via the emailed scans,
a compelling poet and essayist in Mehrotra. So much
so that Mehrotra became the first contender who, as a
losing outsider, gained as many as 129 votes. Padel won
handsomely with 297 votes on 16 May and in so doing
became the first woman to be elected to the post in 301
years. She resigned nine days later, admitting, after her
involvement in the matter became undeniable: 'I did not
engage in a smear campaign against [Walcott], but, as a
result of student concern, I naively – and with hindsight
unwisely – passed on to two journalists, whom I believed
to be covering the whole election responsibly, information
that was already in the public domain.' Tariq Ali and
others wondered why Mehrotra wasn't made Professor
by default, as did a *New York Times* editorial on 26 May,
which pointed out: 'The only person who comes out well
in all of this is ... Mehrotra... Oxford would do well to
confirm him and allow everyone to move along until the
next election, five years hence.' But Oxford declared the

elections invalid, so paving the way for Geoffrey Hill's
uncontested appointment to the post the next year:
another 'great' poet hobbled in some ways by the political
order under liberal democracy, envious, occasionally,
of the authoritative suffering caused by a now-historic
totalitarianism.

What the 2009 elections are largely remembered
for is Padel's radical, discredited, *sui generis* style, leading
at first to success and then disgrace, but which widened
the arcane sphere of the professorship into the logic
of the epoch: the activism of the marketplace, where
volatility now takes on the incarnation of literary value,
now of justice, but remains otherwise irreducible. It is
remembered for those regal, glacial categories or objects,
such as Walcott's reputation, and, on closer examination,
the undemocratic 'inner circle', that transcended
the workings of the market, but were vulnerable for
precisely this reason and in a way appropriated. As for
the Mehrotra campaign, which approached the press
only on behalf of a poetic and critical practice and not
ethnicity or identity, and which fell on neither side of
the dichotomy, its fate, despite its impact, was to be not
properly noticed and remembered. Perhaps it's integral
to literary activism that it not be properly remembered
or noticed, but experienced, uncovered, excavated, and
read?

I should mention, before I conclude by reflecting
on our adventure, that there was an attempt to push
Mehrotra's candidacy into a postcolonial rubric, and
then also to claim that he threatened to split the valuable
'postcolonial' vote. That his candidacy was deliberately
distanced from such a positioning – echoing Mehrotra's
own description of the Indian multilingual poem as
something that possesses no reliable signs of identity –
should be something we consider when we account for
what the aims of literary activism are. The official Oxford

244

dispensation didn't know what to make of Mehrotra, as he didn't come with mainstream markers of literary pedigree; nor was he a hero of the new peripheries; nor did he embody market style. His behaviour as a candidate was impeccable, but the nature of his candidacy was on more than one level resistant. If resistance, or difficulty, enlarges our notion of literature, then the inner circle was, in turn, resistant to such an enlargement. After Walcott's withdrawal, it instructed its members and students – despite the fact that many of them were increasingly aware and appreciative of Mehrotra's merits – to abstain from voting: otherwise, there was every chance that Mehrotra would have won.

Our intention – the pronoun includes Peter D. McDonald, myself, and Mehrotra, who had graciously accepted our proposal in the first place – was, I venture, never to win. This doesn't mean that the campaign pursued a romantic courtship of failure; not at all. Rather, our marshalling of people and resources was worldly and political but being liberated from the thought of victory meant our activities could take on dimensions that would otherwise have been proscribed to it; it allowed Mehrotra to plot and devise his lectures in the way we had plotted the campaign, as a deliberate long shot that *should* succeed. To the literary pages of the *Hindu* Mehrotra proclaimed that he would 'broaden the scope' of what had been a 'Eurocentric' (an unusual word-choice for Mehrotra) job, and that he wasn't losing sleep over the imminent results. As it happens, Mehrotra and I had a long-distance phone conversation not long before the voting, and he said to me that he'd had a sleepless night at the not-wholly-improbable prospect of winning. It would have been a disaster – for him. In his way, Mehrotra was miming the elusiveness and difficulty of the literary as Padel had the methods of the market. This threw a kind of light, for me, on the event.

1.   David Wallace-Well, 'How Benjamin Kunkel Went from Novelist to Marxist Public Intellectual,' Vulture.com, http://www. vulture.com/2014/03/ benjamin-kunkel-marxist-novel-utopia-or-bust.html

2.   Virginia Woolf, 'Mr Bennett and Mrs Brown,' in Virginia Woolf, *Selected Essays* (Oxford: Oxford University Press, 2008), p. 32.

Forms of Fidelity:
Poetry Translation as Literary Activism
JAMIE MCKENDRICK

It may seem odd to consider the activity of poetry translation within the context of literary activism. That phrase suggests polemical criticism, manifestos, public protests, and other interventions such as anthology-making that seek to effect change in the literary realm, whereas poetry in translation, by contrast, conjures images of ill-paid labour, commercial losses, the reticence of publishers, and a dearth of reviews.

And yet, not only is translation a central place where a form of passionate advocacy can be found, where the linguistic contours as well as the perspectives of a culture may be challenged and even expanded, but it can also be a kind of cultural catalyst. Ezra Pound is the embodiment of more than one kind of literary activism: *a caposcuola* for the Imagistes, a central figure for the Vorticists and for Modernism itself, an untiring polemicist writing on poetry, sculpture, and music (leaving aside his baleful economic and political propagandising), but it's arguable that his collection *Cathay* (1915), a translation of classical Chinese poems, changed the literary map just as profoundly.[1] They represented a challenge of a radical nature to prevailing ideas about poetry. By importing perspectives from far afield but also by rethinking the ways in which such perspectives might become apprehensible and audible within his own environment, Pound challenged the literary culture of his day.

Though I have plenty of reservations about Robert Lowell's *Imitations* (of which more later), that book too has been profoundly influential not only on subsequent translating practice but also, and relatedly, in sweeping aside linguistic and cultural barriers.[2] Of course there's an argument for respecting those barriers rather than sweeping them aside, but for the moment I'm considering the impact of the work within the Anglo-speaking culture.

Within almost every generation of poets a claim could be made for the transformative and challenging effects of translation. After all, in terms of the genesis of 'modern' English poetry, two of Thomas Wyatt's versions of Petrarch's 'Whoso List to Hount' and 'My Galley, Chargèd with Forgetfulness' stand as superb and paradoxically originary creations, formative for the whole development of the sonnet as well as for a native lyric tradition.

Although for the most part reviews ignore the translator as a creature best neither seen nor heard, and translators themselves are content – or resigned – to remain as invisible as glass through which another world may appear, it's not surprising that every now and then quarrels rage within the vocation's confines that make it far from a peaceable kingdom populated by ghosts or ghost-writers.

A 2011 article in the *New York Review of Books* blog by Tim Parks, the English novelist and now retired translator of Italian, picks a quarrel with a culture of poetry translation thriving in the absence of any knowledge of original languages, which he accuses of being irresponsible, and goes on to highlight some of the more casuistical claims that support these endeavours.[3] I'm flattered – well, both flattered and irked – that he also takes issue by proxy with one of my own declarations from long ago, which had been quoted by the Scottish poet Robin Robertson in the introduction to his translations of Tomas Tranströmer – these being the main target for Parks's attack.[4] As the argument interests me, in both senses, I'd like to quote at length:

> Robertson also calls on the British poet Jamie McKendrick who, he feels, is 'surely right' when he says 'The translator's knowledge of language is more important than their knowledge of languages.' How vague this remark is! Does it mean that the translator

has one kind of knowledge of how language in general achieves its effects, and another of the nuts and bolts of the different languages he knows, the first kind being 'more important' than the second? If that is the case, then to what degree more important? Wouldn't the two, rather, be interdependent and mutually sustaining? These perplexities apart, the thrust of McKendrick's argument is clear enough: we are sweeping aside the objection that a profound knowledge of a foreign language might be required to translate its poetry, or prose for that matter, thus clearing the path for a translation by someone who is an expert in the area that counts: our own language.

In my defence I should say that had Parks bothered to look up my remark's original context, he would have seen that it was very much in a dialectic with contrary statements, and part of an argument not that different from his own. Immediately preceding the sentence he quotes, I had written: 'If you can't hear the sound of the original (however impossible that is to reproduce in the target language) how on earth, short of some unearthly promptings, are you going to know by how far you've missed it or what you need to do to move your own version closer?'[5]

I still feel somewhat torn in this dispute: I think Parks is right about the cavalier manner in which numerous poets brush aside the question of their competence in another language by claiming that the poet somehow trumps the humble translator – 'It does seem,' he observes, 'that a serious issue is being dispatched with indecent haste here.' It is assumed that the poet-translator is able mysteriously to intuit the dynamics of a poem without knowing the language, and that such knowledge might even be an encumbrance to the swiftness and depth of a presumably telepathic rapport. And yet I'm impressed by the translations of some of the poets his arguments would seek to expose, and feel that their practice should be defended. Their practice, that is – not their theory.

To give a quick résumé of these theories, if they could be called that, I'd say their founding father was Robert Lowell's *Imitations*, which is an assemblage of free translations from several European languages, from poets that include Rimbaud, Pasternak, and Montale. Probably no book of poetry translations in the English-speaking world has been as influential since Ezra Pound's *Cathay*. Both poets share an ignorance of the original languages, though Pound based his work on Ernest Fenollosa's notes. In Lowell's introduction he speaks about 'tone' as though this were the exclusive preserve of the poet-translator: 'Boris Pasternak has said that the usual reliable translator gets the literal meaning but misses the tone, and that in poetry tone is of course everything.'[6]

> Parks also cites this argument and comments wryly:
> Here the 'of course' skates over the fact that tone
> is always in relation to content: if the content were
> altered while diction and register remained the same,
> the tone would inevitably shift. One notes in passing
> the disparagement of the 'usual reliable translator'
> – the fellow knows his foreign language, but doesn't
> understand poetry.

What seems to me even more questionable about Lowell's use of Pasternak's statement is that only adept speakers of a language are likely to infer tone, by which we understand the emotional colouration of words, and yet Lowell is boldly asserting that only poets, regardless of their linguistic competence, have access to this elusive quality of another language. One example where this regal confidence has led Lowell astray is his translation of Montale's 'L'anguilla' – 'The Eel'. Not only does Lowell mistakenly splice another thirty-line Montale poem with a completely different topic on to what is perhaps the

252

most celebrated example of twentieth-century Italian poetry, but he completely misunderstands the final lines of the original poem and ends up saying almost the opposite to Montale.[7] Despite these serious flaws, Lowell achieves effects of sinewy brilliance 'threading / delicate capillaries of slime', and you could set some of his lines very much to his advantage against most other English translations of the poem, including those of translators with a good knowledge of Italian. But it's a high price to pay, and the theoretical justification that precedes it makes one even less willing to pay.

Many of Lowell's followers reproduce both the hubristic and the aggressive-defensive quality of his introduction. Perhaps the most influential in Britain at the time of writing is Don Paterson, who has published *The Eyes*, a translation of Antonio Machado and then *Orpheus* – a translation of Rilke's *Die Sonette an Orpheus*. I should say at the outset that these are two outstanding works, inventive, supple, and, in both cases, lifted by Paterson's deft handling of the sonnet and his skill with rhyme, a formal intelligence that arguably makes him one of the best translators of the Spanish as well as of the German poet. My dissent is confined to the accompanying essays to both collections – the theory not the practice. And I really believe the two can be divorced, especially as the latter may well have been devised defensively (against all those pedants Eliot warned Lowell about) and perhaps a shade naively. To adapt Lawrence's remark, we should trust the translations, not the accompanying paraphernalia, and yet these arguments become influential when a practitioner of Paterson's gifts makes them.

On the front cover of *The Eyes*, there's no mention at all of Machado (just as Rilke is absent from the cover of *Orpheus*).[8] Whether this signals his publisher's preference to steer the book's reception away from the

dowdy straits of translation or Paterson's own feeling
that these are really his and not Machado's poems, it's
alarming that the cover should erase the name of arguably
twentieth-century Spain's foremost poet and sport only
that of his translator. I can think of no other country
where this kind of usurpation could happen.

In his 'Afterword', Paterson declares:

These poems are versions, and not translations. A
reader looking for an accurate translation of Antonio
Machado's *words*, then, should stop here and go out
and buy another book – again, probably Trueblood's,
which although it isn't poetry, at least gives a more
reliable reflection of the surface life of Machado's
verse.[9]

In this and the following passage, Paterson makes
far too neat a distinction between 'surface' and depth,
'lexis' and 'vision', 'literal meaning' and 'spirit', and I
would disagree that Alan Trueblood's translations are not
poetry, or that he was essentially trying to do something
significantly different from Paterson. Translators of
poems, whether or not they are accomplished poets,
don't just plonk down the literal word and think their job
is over. No more than Paterson would Trueblood consider
the 'surface life of the verse', or mere verbal accuracy,
to be an adequate response to the original. It is true that
Paterson has allowed himself more liberties, though
he confesses further on that Trueblood's 'solid literal
translations have more poetry in them than most poems,
because of the integrity and self-delighted purity of his
enterprise' and apologises for having on two or three
occasions 'stolen lines of his because they seemed pretty
much unimprovable'. With this mixture of swaggering
critique and honest generosity, it's clear that Paterson
is tying himself in knots in order to maintain what is in
essence a specious distinction between a translation and
a version. Having compared the two, poem by poem, in

254

most cases I prefer Paterson's translations to Trueblood's, from which they have evidently profited, so I'm far from having any objection to Paterson's practice.[10]

The same argument, only in a slightly more exaggerated form, resurfaces when Paterson in his *Orpheus* introduction employs the ugly gerund 'versioning' to distinguish his practice from that of jobbing translators (and it's a term that is now brandished about by a younger and older generation of his admirers). The argument in both the Machado and Rilke books is often acute and observant about language, but it's his assumption that only poets are really qualified to translate, which is suspect and, perhaps unwittingly, fosters a kind of linguistic insularity that Britain can ill afford, given the dwindling of language teaching in schools, the imperilled position of language departments in universities, and the general disregard for other languages that has long been a feature of British cultural life. I rather think the same could be said of America. The excuse of having a language that enjoys global sway and the resulting prestige is no excuse. And besides, such incuriosity about other languages is, I'd argue, a severe handicap for poets and writers in general. There are many examples of *non*-poets' translations of poetry that are of the highest standard and from which most poets could learn a great deal – you only have to think of Constantine Cavafy in Edmund Keeley and Philip Sherrard's translation or Zbigniew Herbert translated by John and Bogdana Carpenter.

Political questions lie very close to the surface of translation. The perpetual tussle between domesticating and estranging strategies in translation, which has been highlighted by various contemporary theorists, often starts from the assumption that it is a battle between the prestige of two cultures and languages, that what is going on is somewhat similar to colonial appropriation if English is the target language in question. Whereas for the translator of poetry (of poetry especially but not exclusively) it's very often the deviation from normal usage that can characterise a particular style, and that sets a whole other kind of procedural difficulty in motion. The theory in this operates at some distance from the real interests of the job, and so offers a facile politicisation of the métier. The hegemonic status of English, the argument would go, flattens out the local elements and particularities of other languages and cultures for a kind of insular readership – insular here referring just as much to the continental US.

And yet, especially between Romance and Germanic languages, the cultural differences are not that insurmountable, and only in rare instances require footnotes. Translations from remoter languages and cultures may well stand in greater need of explanatory apparatus. More often the problems facing a translator of poetry have to do with slight shifts in conventional usage – say, an unexpected preposition or an eccentric word-choice that signals a calculated departure from the norm, but which might risk sounding like inept translation if literally rendered. Such subtle alterations can be the lifeblood of a poem and yet are the kind of things about which a poet-translator with no knowledge of the language would be blithely unaware. With these kinds of micro-problems the whole political discourse that argues on the macro-scale about the unwieldy blocks of different languages becomes inappropriate. Such is the complexity of the task, most of the time, that having some kind of aprioristic ideological or theoretical position about translation is likely to be irrelevant or distracting. Decisions have to be taken on the hoof, on a one-by-one basis, with a kind of pragmatism which I'd like to hope could also include aesthetic discrimination. There is, however, a politics of sorts in this refusal of ideology: not simply a fidelity to the original text, because we understand that fidelity to one aspect or element can be a betrayal of another, to sound, let's say, at the cost of lexical accuracy, or vice versa, but a fidelity to an aesthetic whole. No sooner have I risked a phrase like this than I realise how open it is to attack, how close I'm getting to the arguments of those poet-translators who work without knowledge of the other language. But still I can think of no other way of putting it. This aspiration to a deeper kind of fidelity is an attempt to respect not just the alterity of another language and culture but also that of another individual sensibility. The translator's task is to listen out for what is happening on as many levels as possible and tentatively to move the target language in the right direction. If it puts strains on the receiving language well and good, but those strains have to be such that the reader can still intuit something of what made the original poem of value.

To return to Parks's argument, he begins with Robertson describing 'a process wherein his Swedish girlfriend gives him a literal line-by-line translation into English, then reads the Swedish to him to give him "the cadences," after which he created "relatively free" versions in English'. And yet Parks ends with what he obviously believes to be a telling contrast with the husband-and-wife team of Robert and Jean Hollander, who have adapted, he claims with I'm not sure how much accuracy, Sinclair's earlier version of Dante's *Commedia*. He invites us to try an experiment: to look into a book which he says is 'misnamed' – Dante's *Inferno*, a gathering of poets who have attempted a canto each:

> Sometimes it is Heaney's *Inferno*, sometimes it is Carolyn Forché's, sometimes it is W. S. Merwin's, but it is never Dante's.
> Then dip into the 1939 prose translation by the scholar John Sinclair. There is immediately a homogeneity and fluency here, a lack of showiness

and a semantic cohesion over scores of pages that give quite a different experience. To wind up, look at Robert and Jean Hollander's 2002 reworking of Sinclair. Robert Hollander is a Dante scholar and has cleared up Sinclair's few errors. His wife Jean is a poet who, while respecting to a very large degree Sinclair's phrasing, has made some adjustments, under her husband's meticulous eye, allowing the translation to fit into unrhymed verse. It is still a long way from reading Dante in the original, but now we do feel that we have a very serious approximation and a fine read.[11]

It's strange that Parks seems unaware that he has come full circle and proposed a model of scrupulous collaboration that almost exactly replicates the one he began by gently mocking. The fact that this second team are married doesn't make the translation, *per se*, more respectable, and nor does the presence of two 'scholars' on this second squad guarantee anything about the translation. In the case of Dante, there's an argument, and one that Benedetto Croce makes forcefully, to free up the *Commedia* from the encrustations of centuries of scholarship. When he says of the Hollanders' translation 'now we do feel that we have a very serious approximation and a fine read', we realise that, in his hands too, 'a serious issue is being dispatched with indecent haste', and his clinching finale is an anti-climax that leaves the whole question of quality unresolved. Having more people at work by no means ensures the superiority of that venture over the individual poets' cantos, or for that matter over Robertson's Tranströmer. As it happens, I think highly of the Hollanders' translation but I would suggest a counter-experiment: to read the Hollanders' translation of the Inferno cantos xxxii and xxxiii and compare it with Seamus Heaney's *Ugolino* in *Field Work*.[12] If we allow Heaney a few vivid departures from the original, such as

'carnal melon' – like a gory anagram of 'Menalippo' –
his image of Ugolino sinking his teeth into Archbishop
Ruggiero's skull:

> Gnawing at him where the neck and head
> Are grafted to the sweet fruit of the brain,
> Like a famine victim at a loaf of bread.
> So the berserk Tydeus gnashed and fed
> Upon the severed head of Menalippus
> As if it were some spattered carnal melon

This is both far more Dantesque and far more
compelling than the Hollanders':

> We had left him behind when I took note
> of two souls so frozen in a single hole
> the head of one served as the other's hat.
>
> As a famished man will bite into his bread,
> the one above had set his teeth into the other
> just where the brain's stem leaves the spinal cord.
>
> Tydeus gnawed the temples of Melanippus
> with bitter hatred just as he was doing
> to the skull and to the other parts.[13]

Not only does Heaney have a finer sense of the
line, but his rhymes (head/fed/bread) give the reader
a secure sense of Dante's *terza rima*, which is the
miraculous engine of the original. Parks's idea that the
Hollanders have adapted Sinclair's prose 'to fit into
unrhymed verse' betrays scant respect for anything we
should want from, or associate with, a poem. While
Heaney's botanical 'grafted' as well as his 'sweet fruit of
the brain' are his own inventions, which foreshadow the
'spattered carnal melon', the whole texture of the verse

259

is far closer to Dante's. The Hollanders' line, 'where the brain's stem leaves the spinal cord', rather too coolly anatomical, is no less of an invention for the Italian 'là 've 'l cervel s'aggiunge con la nuca' – literally 'there where the brain joins itself to the nape'. The first quoted line by the Hollanders is dull pentametric filler and the last two are especially flat. Though you could claim that the phrases 'he was doing' and 'the other parts' are more literal than Heaney's, they fail to give the sinister feel of the grey and bloody matter in Dante's 'e l'altre cose' – 'cose' meaning 'things' rather than body parts, *things* he would prefer not to specify.

The Russian poet Osip Mandelstam describes this canto as 'enveloped in the dense and heavy timbre of a cello like rancid, poisoned honey' and Heaney's version, however he deviates from the literal, gives us access to these acoustics.[14] He knows about the visceral hatred of internecine warfare and his lines carry that sinister freight unerringly. If Parks can hear nothing of this, he should step a great deal more warily into the zone of poetry translation.

Dwelling at such length on a blog entry may seem excessive but it has been republished in a book of essays, and even if Parks pays scant attention to elements that are among the most crucial in poetry translation – such as form, sound and linguistic texture – his arguments regarding the unexamined premises of poet-translators deserve serious attention.[15]

I began with the claim that translation could be a form of literary activism but I should also stress that I don't consider the translation of well-established figures such as Montale, Machado, Rilke, or Tranströmer, however valuable, to qualify, though I wouldn't altogether exclude that possibility. Perhaps among those works that have inherited the mantle of Lowell, Tom Paulin's *The Road to Inver* is the most original, the most like literary activism – a gathering of translations from Pessoa to Mayakovsky, all shamelessly and entertainingly wrestled into his own quirky vernacular.[16] Among translations published in the Britain over the past two decades, however, none seem to me to earn this title as surely as do those of the poet Michael Hofmann, whose exemplary volumes of Durs Grünbein, Günter Eich, and Gottfried Benn have carried these three very distinct and divergent voices into English and made them audible for the first time, combining passionate advocacy with an equal depth of knowledge both of German and English.[17]

To return to the instance of Pound's translations with which I began, one conspicuous aspect that I have left without comment is the temporal distance that his Chinese translations have had to cover. Inevitably, this entails dealing not only with linguistic and cultural difference but also with the even more formidable distance between eras. (Elsewhere, Pound's translations from Cavalcanti, which make that distance evident even when addressing moments that are relatively straightforward in the original, seem to me often wilfully obscure and archaic.) How does one simultaneously preserve that distance and discover proximity and connection? Among the most engaging work of this kind, a literary activism that approaches alchemy, are A.K. Ramanujan's translations from Classical Tamil (c. 100 BC-250 CE) and Arun Kolatkar's translations from various Marathi poets.[18] Kolkatar's version of the thirteenth- and fourteenth-century poet Namdev manages to sound at once chthonic and contemporary:

> in the beginning
> is the ant
> mouth of the triple river
> is the mouth of the ant[19]

Arvind Krishna Mehrotra's translation of the first- and second-century CE Mahārāshtrī Prākrit anthology

Gāthāsaptaśatī is another exemplary work. Since we've been considering the costs of fidelity in translation, I'll end with one of his sinuous and vivid versions:

> Let faithful wives
>   Say what they like,
> I don't sleep with my husband
>   Even when I do.[20]

1. No longer in print as an individual volume, but included in Ezra Pound, *The Shorter Poems of Ezra Pound* (London: Faber and Faber, 2001), pp. 13-146.
2. Robert Lowell, *Imitations* (London: Faber and Faber, 1962).
3. Tim Parks, 'Translating in the Dark', from *NYR Daily*, November 30, 2011, http://www.nybooks.com/daily/2011/11/30/translating-dark/
4. Tomas Tranströmer, *The Deleted World*, trans. Robin Robertson (London: Enitharmon, 2006).
5. Jamie McKendrick, 'Sinister Experiments?' in *Poetry News* (Winter 2002/3), www.poetrysoc.com/content/publications/poetrynews/pn2003/translation/
6. Lowell, *Imitations*, p. xi.
7. Lowell, *Imitations*, pp. 125-127.
8. Don Paterson, *The Eyes* (London: Faber and Faber, 1999).
9. Paterson, *The Eyes*, pp. ix-x.
10. For a fuller exploration of Paterson's translations,

see Xon de Ros, *The Poetry of Antonio Machado: Changing the Landscape* (Oxford: Oxford University Press, 2015), pp. 178-238.
11. Parks, 'Translating in the Dark'.
12. Seamus Heaney, *Field Work* (London: Faber and Faber, 1979), pp. 61-64.
13. Dante, *The Inferno*, trans. by Robert and Jean Hollander (New York: Doubleday, 2001), p. 547.
14. Osip Mandelstam, *The Collected Critical Prose and Letters*, ed. Jane Gary Harris (London: Collins Harvill, 1991), p. 427.
15. Tim Parks, *Where I'm Reading From: The Changing World of Books* (London: Harvill Secker, 2014).
16. Tom Paulin, *The Road to Inver* (London: Faber and Faber, 2008).
17. Durs Grünbein, *Ashes for Breakfast*, trans. Michael Hofmann (London: Faber and Faber, 2006); Gunter Eich, *Angina Days: Selected Poems*, trans. Michael Hofmann (New Jersey: Princeton University Press, 2010); Gottfried Benn, *Impromptus: Selected Poems*

and Some Prose, trans. Michael Hofmann (New York: Farrar Straus Giroux, 2013).

18.   A.K. Ramanujan, *Poems of Love and War* (New Delhi: Oxford University Press, 1996).

19.   Arun Kolatkar, *Collected Poems in English* (Tarset: Bloodaxe, 2010), p. 298.

20.   Arvind Krishna Mehrotra, *Collected Poems 1969-2014* (New Delhi: Penguin Books, 2014), p. 206.

Literary Surrogacy and Literary Activism:
Instances from Bengal
SWAPAN CHAKRAVORTY

Perhaps I ought to begin with a definition of, or at least an explanation of, what I mean by the phrase 'literary surrogacy'. Surrogacy is a word much in use in ART, which in this case is not about matters aesthetic, but an acronym for Assisted Reproductive Technology. A woman unable to bear children pays or persuades a surrogate mother to carry a child for her. The latter may carry an embryo created using in vitro fertilisation, and as a result be biologically unrelated to the baby. Alternatively, the surrogate may be inseminated naturally or artificially, although in the latter case she would be biologically related to the offspring. The difference between gestational and traditional surrogacy may be of little importance to my purpose. However, the core sense of surrogacy, that is, a substitution of the designated functionary with one who is better able to serve the function on the former's behalf, underlies my use of the phrase.

That brings one to the question of 'literary activism'. Literary activism may be thought of in different ways: the critics' affirmation of aesthetic value against the judgements of the marketplace (for instance, the Leavisite activism of *Scrutiny* and the early reviews in *The Cambridge Quarterly*); the 'market activism' of literary agents, publishers, and booksellers, including those who sail against the current and challenge corporate media houses and lucrative awards (for instance, André Schiffrin's New Press and Zero Press); the writings that form part of the activism fuelled by partisan positions in politics or aesthetics (for instance, the many forms of post-Marxist and radical feminist approaches to what in innocent times was called 'literature'); the *avant-garde* activism within the literary field of experimental writers and little magazines (for instance, the Pre-Raphaelite movement and its short-lived journal *The Germ* or Wyndham Lewis's almost forgotten periodical *Blast*);

the academic re-evaluation of the canon (evident, for instance, in postcolonial criticism).

I have deliberately put together an unsorted mix of instances from the West since these may be expected to be less unfamiliar to a large section of readers. One could cite parallel instances of 'literary activism', such as the focus on *dalit* literatures in the many Indian languages.[1] A good point of departure, if I were to take the Indian case, would be if we would identify a broad notion of 'literary activism' with what Rabindranath Tagore called the *karma mārga* in *sāhitya*. Tagore was delivering the Presidential Address at the Bengal Literary Conference in Vārānasi in 1923, the first held outside (then undivided) Bengal, a decade after he had won the Nobel Prize and after chairs of Bengali had been instituted in European universities such as Philipps-Universität Marburg. It was a heady time for modern Bengali writing, and Tagore, while being modest about his merits as President, was also pleased that the Bengal Literary Conference, started in 1907, was being taken to other parts of India. The organisers, Tagore implied, were literary activists. More explicitly, Tagore spoke of three paths or *mārgas* in literature: *karma* or work, which consisted of organising conferences, editing and publishing periodicals (I guess he would have included reviews and translations); *jnāna*, or knowledge, which consisted of studying history, philosophy, and antiquity and their relationship to literature (again, my informed guess is that he would have included all forms of literary scholarship); and *srishti*, or creation, that is, writing poetry, fiction, drama, and non-fiction of 'aesthetic' merit.[2]

Tagore went on to say that he was merely a traveller on the creative path (the collection of essays in which the address, part-copied by Pradyot Sengupta, was first included was titled *Sāhityer pathe*, i.e., 'On the Road to Literature'), but we should not be misled by Tagore's disingenuous protestations. Tagore was one of the leaders of the agitation against the proposed partition of Bengal in the first decade of the twentieth century, coinciding with the boycott of British goods. He was active in the movement known as *swadesi*, the editor of several serious periodicals including the political magazine *Bhāndār* during the *swadesi* phase. He was a leader of the reformist Hindu monotheist sect known as Brāhmo Samāj. He was one of the first producers of experimental stage plays. He was also an indefatigable writer on religious, political, and educational issues and the translator of the medieval Hindustani poet Kabir, the medieval Anglo-Saxon poet Caedmon, the eighth-century Chinese poet Li Po (or Li Bai), and the twentieth-century modernists Ezra Pound and T.S. Eliot. He founded a modern university and was an early enthusiast in the field of national education. He was a printer and publisher and became a pioneer of house-style in Bengali publishing. He was also a book designer and illustrator and wrote graded language primers (for learners of English and Bengali), a book on the Bengali language, another on prosody, and an educational text on science. He also founded an art school and gallery; was a composer and musicologist; and a sharp, and occasionally intransigent, critic of literatures in ancient Sanskrit, Pali, English, medieval Hindustani and Maithili, and medieval and modern Bengali.

This list might appear to be a tedious iteration of the school drop-out's daunting versatility, an annoying habit of which Bengali-language speakers seem not to tire. There is, however, a crucial purpose the list might serve. Tagore is protesting too much, but he seems impelled to do so because of the pressure he feels to sunder *karma* and *jnāna* from *srishti*, to deny the sustaining role that literary activism and scholarship necessarily played in his literary 'creation'.

Tagore was not the only one during his time and in the immediately preceding years to enlist literary activism in the service of literary production. If you are looking for an assembly floor for literary activism, Bengal is the place for you. Every major writer in Bengal, from Rāmmohun Roy (1774-1883) and Bankimchandra Chattopādhyāy (1838–1894) to Iswarchandra Vidyāsāgar (1820-1891), like Tagore, ran their own presses and journals. These printing houses were not always established in Kolkata, the colonial capital, or in the major city that is now the capital of Bangladesh, Dhaka. It is useful to recall that the period during late eighteenth- and early nineteenth-century Bengal when printing hit the undivided province was more than colonial: its nature was more multicolonial. Bengali movable types were first used in 1778 in a press in Hugli (a Dutch settlement), the Baptist missionaries from Britain in Srirāmpur (a Danish outpost about 102 km from Kolkata) started printing in 40 languages on paper produced at their own mill in 1800. To get back to nineteenth-century Bengali literary activism, Chattopādhyāy's press was set up in the old town of Kanthālpārā, Naihāti (about 40 km from Kolkata), while Tagore's press, gifted by citizens of Omaha, Lincoln, started operations in Sāntiniketan, Bolpur (about 155 km from Kolkata). Translators of the *Mahābhārata* and compilers of Bengali encyclopedias such as Haridas Siddhāntabāgis (1878-1961) and Nagendranāth Basu (1866-1938) installed presses and ran publishing houses from Kolkata. To cite one last name, the internationally recognised scientist, entrepreneur, and President of the science segment of the 1913 Bengal Literary Conference, Praphullachandra Rāy (1861-1944), who taught from 1889 to 1916 at Presidency College and later at Calcutta University, ran his own steam-powered press at Bengal Chemical and Pharmaceutical Works, a company he had himself pioneered.

Why then did Tagore feel the need to disjoin literary *karma* from *srishti*, knowing full well that he was as committed to the former as he was immersed in the latter? The question involves that of particular historical moments, such as the moment when early nineteenth-century Bengali writers were exposed to print and colonial education at the same time, that have induced such investments in literary activism. In the wake of the moment cited as an example, pressure mounted to introduce broader forms of activism, political or otherwise, that would employ literature not simply as an instrument of propaganda but as a *surrogate*, something capable of bearing the weight of, or mediating the purport of, that which would otherwise be ineffectual. Literary activism at such moments functions as what I am calling 'literary surrogacy', important in its own right, but also as part of a transferred projective epithet.

'Creativity' for the colonial modern such as Tagore was a category that needed to be imagined as one that could speak over the shoulders of colonial pedagogy and hegemony, and also one that could not be entirely subsumed by the early nationalist project. Indians and Bengalis lost out to the Europeans when it came to material power driven by *karma*, but *srishti* could draw them to a secret compact with their Western models and peers in an imagined popular front of resistance against the might of the champions of *karma*. The paradox was that without *karma* there was no new clearing in which they could locate *srishti*. Even the want of a standardised prose, of orthography and punctuation, of diglossic conventions, impeded the consonance of the 'creative' and the resistive potencies of 'literature'. Hence, the Tagorean disclaimer, however weak and unconvincing, that he was really a creative sojourner without a foot in either literary activism or scholarship.

In a more general sense (and, I hope, a positive sense), I consider literary surrogacy as instances of what I would like to call 'defection'. Defection is deviation; a perceived lack, a defect that needs to be fixed, a void that needs to be filled. Speaking of the distinction between literature and philosophy, the philosopher Alain Badiou identifies literature, not in itself but within philosophy, as that which fills such a void in philosophical language. It is both a defect in philosophy and a defection from it that allows literature to function as its surrogate. Here is the relevant passage translated from Badiou's 1992 essay 'Le Recours philosophique au poème':

> The poem occurs in philosophy *at one of its points*, and this localization is never ruled by a poetic or literary principle. It depends on the moment at which the argument places the unpresentable, and where, by a torsion prescribed by the argument, the nudity of the operations of the true is only transmissible by a return, always immoderate, to the pleasure of sense, which is always also a pleasure of the senses. The literary in philosophy is the directed transmission, the vectoring, through an effect of sense, of the following: the relation of a truth to sense is a defective or void relation. It is this defection that exposes philosophy to the imperative of a localized fiction.[3]

Badiou's immediate concern is the eruption of the poetic in philosophy, when knowledge and prediction coincide, when one is drawn outside-of-self in order to name the incalculable, in order to name the chance that is undecidable. The problem is internal to the ontology of philosophical language and involves the limitations of critical discourse, of what Leavisites were fond of calling the 'synoptic' use of language. The philosopher, in this situation, may not resort to poetry *qua* poetry. Rather, she would turn into a philosophical activist, a rebel bent on breaching the fences of one's discipline and risking the rejection of the market and the academy. It is possible, as Derek Attridge says, that the philosopher may in this case function like Jacques Derrida, a 'lover' of the texts that he deconstructs.[4]

I would like to think that the 'hermeneutics of suspicion' to which Professor Attridge refers, the impulse to detect ideological seams in the silences of the text, may provide room for identification with the literary representation, while simultaneously allowing the distance one needs for reflection. The latter demands critical withdrawal from that which threatens to immerse the reader, and the withdrawal may risk self-division. Georges Poulet wrote in his essay 'Phenomenology of Reading' that every thought needed a subject to think it. The reader knew that the ideas of the texts she read were external to her being as subject, yet internal to her consciousness. 'Whenever I read, I mentally pronounce an *I*, and yet the *I* which I pronounce is not myself.'[5] A similar paradox of proximity and distance in one's response to literature was addressed in a different way by Ernst Cassirer in *The Philosophy of Symbolic Forms*. The work allowed the reader, thought Cassirer, to look at the world at a remove by turning it into a concept. The concept moved its object 'into a kind of ideal distance': it needed to annul 'presence' in order to arrive at 'representation'.[6]

The observations of the two Western philosophers remind me of the great commentary on Ānandavardhana's *Dhvanyālokah* by the *saiva* philosopher Abhinavagupta (*c*. 10th–11th century CE). Abhinavagupta, in his commentary on Ānandavardhana's *Dhvanyālokah* (*c*. 9th century CE), had used the word *sahṛdaya* to denote the ideal reader or audience of poetry. The *sahṛdaya* feels at one with the subject matter (or, if the poet is the subject, with the poet). Sensitive listeners achieve this sense of oneness by clearing the speculum of the mind through a disciplined study of the way poetry works – a statement in English that may serve as paraphrase of Abhinavagupta's Sanskrit: *kāvyānuśilanābhyāsa-vaśād viśadibhute mano mukure varnaniya tanmayibhavana-yogyatā te hṛdaya-samvādabhājah sahṛdayāh*. Abhinavagupta was fashioning a definition of *adhikārin*, that is, those who possessed what in Anglophone criticism is often called 'literary competence' or 'cultural competence'. Such competence enables recognition of the codes through which poetry, or any literary work, affects the consumers of the text.[7]

Abhinavagupta also composed a great commentary on the *Nāṭyaśāstra*, a Sanskrit text on dramaturgy attributed to Bharata (*c*. 8th century CE for the text extant, although composition may be plural, the earliest segments dating back to earlier centuries). Abhinavagupta interprets Bharata to mean that the theatre is not materially unmoored, although it is unconcerned with the narrowly particular. When Kālidāsa describes fear, it is not the poet's or the deer's, but an abstract *bhāva* or mental state arrived at through the appropriate devices, verbal or otherwise. Hence, the cultured viewer or *sahṛdaya* arrives at a state of mind that recognises anxiety yet enjoys it as dissimulation. This is an attitude Subodh Chandra Sen Gupta, the Shakespearean critic, has described as a 'combination of absorption and aloofness'. Drama, therefore, creates identity at a distance. As Sen Gupta points out in connection with the views of Abhinavagupta, *all* art is dramatic and lyrical at the same time. Art is expression of personal affect, yet it is dramatic, 'because it is only by viewing his impressions from a *distance* that the artist can give them universal form'.[8]

What has all this got to do with literary activism, or worse, with literary surrogacy? I shall try to list the points I consider worth examining, then briefly remark on three instances from twentieth-century Bengal. First, literary representation, by virtue of its ontological function as staging an absent presence, appeals to a relation of void with the programmatic moves of any overt literary or political activism in the academy, the market or in the polity. Second, the literary surrogate, whether remaining an intractable reprobate or co-opted by the market or the academia, while releasing itself in an idealised conceptual space, paradoxically appeals to textual pleasure. The surrogacy hence takes on the nature of a supplement, a surplus that might undermine its own activist intent or outlive it. Finally, the surplus in its turn energises the literary industry through evaluations, translations, and adaptations, outgrowing the activism of the moment of genesis yet stimulating, and aligning itself with, new forms of literary activism at the moment of impact. The literary surrogate, without any attempt at a cheap quibble, is the genuine mother of activisms, including lapsed ones.

In what follows, I shall look briefly at three moments of genesis: the *swadesi* movement in undivided Bengal in the first decade of the twentieth century, the literary movement of the so-called Hungry Generation in West Bengal in the early 1960s, and the Bengali literature of the Maoist movement in the decade that followed the peasant uprising in Naxalbari in 1967. We could easily have chosen other moments, such as the many movements launched by *avant-garde* little magazines in Bengal since at least the inception in 1914 of *Sabuj Patra*, edited by Pramatha Chaudhuri. However, I would like to think that the moments of impact of the three forms of activist literature I have chosen are to this date coterminous with their moments of genesis. The first concerns the configuration of a Bengali language and history that would piece together an absent cultural nation; the second was a visceral reaction against the

275

decorous silences of that effort; and the third was allied to a violent political programme to voice the muffled rage of the people excluded from the cultural idea of a nation, a population with whom even mainstream Marxists seemed unable to engage.

*

The agitation against Lord Curzon's proposed partition of Bengal, tabled in December 1903, gathered steam in 1905 and culminated in the movement known as *swadesi*, which signified reliance on indigenously produced goods and resources and the boycott of British imports. The movement succeeded in that the plan had to be rescinded in the face of popular protests. For a short while, Rabindranath Tagore led street marches (one ended at the Nakhodā Masjid, the landmark mosque in north Kolkata), wrote songs to unite Hindus and Muslims and fanned the flames of the popular upsurge. In a parallel development, Lord Curzon had passed the University Bill in 1901-2. The Bill sought to bring Calcutta University under direct government control. It inspired the movement demanding education on national lines and under national control and led to the founding of the National Council of Education, Bengal, the institution that in 1956 became Jadavpur University. Two eminent writers came together in the movement: Aurobindo Ghosh, a poet who wrote in English and plotted an armed insurrection, and Rabindranath Tagore, who was soon disenchanted with the thoughtless headiness of the movement. His version of *swadesi* was attacking the root of the problem in the heart of *des*, that is, the country, in the Bengal villages. This is clear from his influential lecture *Swadesi samāj*, read at the Minerva Theatre in June 1904. The poet was then forty-three years old. Notwithstanding the fact that there are Indians who stubbornly maintain in the face of facts that Tagore was virtually unknown before he won the Nobel Prize in 1913, the crowd was so large that mounted policemen had to be deployed and the same essay read again nine days later at Curzon Theatre, the auditorium near College Street Market, renamed Alfred Theatre (later Grace Cinema). Tagore had more faith in the neighbourly community or *samāj* rather than the political state, and withdrew from the movement and from the National Council. He was to divert his activist energies to rural reconstruction and his school in Sāntiniketan. Tagore made many enemies with his withdrawal from, and his critique of, the movement he had once led. The most stinging riposte came from his admirer Rāmendrasundar Tribedi, a writer, scientist, and Secretary of the Bangiya-Sāhitya-Parishat, the Bengali literary academy set up in the wake of the movement. Bangiya-Sāhitya-Parishat was a monument to the most ardent moment of literary activism in Bengal. The academy was designed to house a library and a museum, which would be far from simply 'literary'. It would be a place that would offer an impressive conspectus of the reconfigured history of the Bengali nation. It would, to put it fancifully, moor the Bengali to an imagined lineage, just as the paintings, portraits, and maxims on the walls and ceiling of his library allowed Montaigne, enthroned in the chair he called 'mon siege', to recall the canonical legacy of European thought.[9] To return to Tribedi's essay, he used for his rejoinder the same title that Tagore had given to a polemical essay against the movement: *Byādhi o pratikār* (the disease and its remedy).[10]

Bengal had seen literary activism earlier, especially when Bankimchandra Chattopādhyāy's journal *Bangadarsan* (1872-1883) attempted to fashion a discerning reading public for literature in Bengali. But Bengal had seen nothing on this scale before. Presses and reviews were started; nationalist sentiments inspired

songs, poetry, and fiction; antiquarian activities such
as the recovery of old Buddhist manuscripts in Bengali
by Haraprasad Sāstri in 1916 and the study of ruins
in northern Bengal by Barendra Anusandhān Samiti
founded in Rajsāhi by Akshay Maitreya in 1910 flourished.
The Bangiya-Sāhitya-Parishat – established in 1893
along the lines of the Asiatic Society of Bengal with an
indigenous thrust and instituted through public initiative
– received new impetus; the Banga-Sāhitya-Sammelan
or Bengal Literary Conference followed suit. Bengali
theatres found new patrons and the National Council of
Education, Bengal established its college with the poet
and revolutionary Aurobindo Ghosh as its founding
principal.

One of the new journals dedicated to the cause
was *Bhāndār*, a political magazine edited by Tagore –
the only political journal he would ever agree to edit.
The magazine carried a segment in which a topical
question was placed before leaders of the movement and
contributors for debate. In the April-May 1905 number,
the inspirational leader of the agitation Surendranāth
Bandyopādhyāy (or Banerjee) raised the question: how
does one link the people at large – the words used were
'public' and *prākritajan* – with the public initiatives
of the name. There were many strategies proposed.
Rāmendrasundar Tribedi thought that literature would
serve as the missing link. Despite the bewildering variety
of languages in India, it would be possible to convince the
people of the Punjāb, Rajputānā, Madras, and Bombay
that the same stories of Rāma, Krishna, and the Purānas
are the shared legacy of Bhārata, or the Sanskrit word
used in the *Vishnu Purana* (2.1.31; the alternative toponym
is Bhāratvarsha) to denote what we now call the Indian
peninsula. The new literature excludes the aspirants
to this nascent public sphere. Instead, writers should
propagate these stories, along with those of the Sikhs,

Mārathās, Rājputs, and, oddly enough, China, Japan, France, and Germany.[11]

This is a candid attempt at literary surrogacy, the declaration of a 'programmatic intention' and a 'final intention' – I borrow the terms from the textual scholars Michael Hancher and George Thomas Tanselle – that seeks to enlist the 'active intention' of a work of art, and even prescribe its aims, in the interest of a nationalist project that is unable to engender the bond that would unite the identity of its constituency.[12] One of the respondents in the number was the editor himself. Although a *swadesi* enthusiast at this stage, Tagore was distinctly uncomfortable with the political enlistment of literature without addressing the ills that plagued the community or *samāj* as opposed to the political state or *rāshtra*. No wonder disillusion with the movement would follow sooner than he had foreseen. Tagore had always been a bad joiner.

One result of this disenchantment was his novel *Gorā*, the undisputed masterpiece on which he spent four years (1907-1910). *Gorā* is an immense book. Its themes and debates unfold in endless conversations and narrative turns involving Gorā, his friend Binay, the young Brāhmo woman Sucharitā and her dignified father Pares, and Gorā's parents – Krishnadayāl and Ānandamayee. For Gorā, Bhāratavarsha is the figment of a place, race, nation, and community. He constructs a purist notion of a Hindu past and a pristine brahmanical creed that together drive his passion for service and renunciation. After a stint in jail in service of the imagined nation, he prepares for a dramatic expiation in order to rid himself of desire, including his sexual attraction towards Sucharitā. It is at this moment that the truth is revealed to him by Krishnadayāl, who thinks that he is about to die. Gorā cannot perform his last rites, since Gorā's biological father was an Irishman who had died during the great rebellion of 1857. Born to a refugee mother sheltered by Ānandamayee and Krishnadayāl and who died after giving birth to a son, Gorā had been brought up to believe that he was born a Hindu.

The truth has an oddly liberating effect of Gorā. 'He has no mother,' says the text, 'no father, no country, no race, no name, no lineage, no deity.'[13] In the strange directionless emptiness Gorā sat, silent. There was no country left for him in his imagined India, the doors of all temples were now closed to him. A renewed life follows almost immediately after. He is born in a new Bhāratavarsha, a country that is also identical with the mother-surrogate Ānandamayee, who had sheltered a dying stranger and raised the latter's son as her own. Gorā simultaneously reclaims his country and mother. The reclamation also redeems his desire. Gorā takes Sucharitā's hands in his own in the final lines of the novel.

Gorā starts with a burden of literary activism, but is released into the indeterminate freedom of literary surrogacy. This 'indeterminate freedom' is what the mission statement of the symposium proposed as *its* way of characterising 'literary activism' – this is suggested in the statement by the phrase 'the strangeness of the literary', and by its claim that 'literary activism may be desultory, in that its aims and value aren't immediately explicable'. The statement is close to my understanding of 'literary surrogacy' in that the 'programmatic' and 'final intentions' of the work or the author, what the work or writer sets out to do or affect, may deviate from the 'active' intentions, that is, the way in which the author may be understood to be wishing her work to be read by the reader at the time of composition or later. Surrogacy, that is, may supply a defect, yet defect from, activism in unpredictable ways.

The text wins, not because Tagore had no programme of his own; of course he had. But the

280

novel still speaks to the inchoate idea of freedom from
a constricted and exclusivist idea of Bhāratavarsha.
The lost way to a liberating Bhāratavarsha still haunts
the contemporary Bengali poet, who had since seen
Bengal divided and the stupendous mass migrations and
sectarian riots that followed. I end this section with a
quotation from the contemporary poet Sankha Ghosh:

> Which is my country, where the stable corners
>   of the earth
> Which eyes cloud the heart's sky as I gaze into them
> From country to country, across times, where is
>   my home
> And you want to find my bloodline?
> ('Jābāl Satyakām')[14]

*

My remarks on the other two moments in the
literary activism will be briefer, and are intended simply
to illustrate the notion of literary surrogacy I have
proposed. The name 'Hungry Generation' was claimed to
have been derived from a phrase in Chaucer's translation
of Boethius' *De Consolatione Philosphiae* or *Boece* ('Whan
it was in the sowre hungry tyme...'), which was made to
serve ideas of cultural atrophy popularised by Oswald
Spengler's *Der Untergang des Abendlandes* (*The Decline of
the West; 1918-1923*), although an allusion to Keats's line in
'Ode to a Nightingale' ('No hungry generations tread thee
down') is not unlikely.[15] The first group of self-proclaimed
Hungry writers became active in Patna in 1961 (with
colleagues known as *bhukhi pidi* writing in Hindi), while
a circle of writers started writing in a similar rebellious
vein in Howrah and Kolkata since at least 1962. The Patna
circle included Samir Ray Choudhury, his brother Malay,
Sakti Chattopādhyāy, and Debi Rāy (also belonging to

Howrah), while Kolkata Hungryalists such as Saileswar Ghosh, Subo Āchārya, and Bāsudeb Dāsgupta were publishing kindred pieces in other magazines in the early 1960s. There are contesting claims of the origin of the movement ever since the diffuse movement fell apart after a decade or so of energetic writing, but the disputed accounts of genesis are of minor relevance to my purpose.[16] The Hungryalists, as they came to be called, gained notoriety when five 'scruffy' young men were arrested by the police in 1964 on charges of obscenity and made it to the pages of *Time* magazine (it was *Time* that described them as 'scruffy').[17] There is a popular notion that they were close to the beatnik poet Allen Ginsberg,[18] although in later life they strongly denied having anything to do with Ginsberg's amorphous fascination with the 'spirituality' of the East.[19] In any case, Ginsberg reached Patna for the first time only in 1963. Ginsberg befriended many Bengali poets at the time and introduced a few to the joys of an LSD trip. Some of his friends subscribed to the iconoclastic poetry magazine *Krittibās*. There were fellow-travellers in both camps such as Sakti Chattopādhyāy, Sandipan Chattopādhyāy, and Utpalkumār Basu, not counting the occasional renegade, but the two groups are better studied as distinct.[20]

Although the young rebels were released (because of the rumoured intervention of a once-liberal Indira Gandhi), Hungry writers were more than a blip on Bengal's literary radar. Thanks to Ginsberg, Larwence Ferlinghetti, and such friends, their scandalous activities were discussed in international literary circuits. Hungryalist attacks on bourgeois hypocrisy, and their outraged expressions of social disgust and sexual angst were translated and included in anthologies. The eminent Indian poet Arvind Krishna Mehrotra considered the movement important enough to establish a Hungry Generation Archive at Northwestern University, which

282

contains typescripts of poems by Malay Ray Choudhury and the correspondence on the subject between Mehrotra and the American poet Howard McCord.[21] A few leaders of the movement have continued to write, although they are not as 'hungry' as they once were. Their rebellion against strait-laced Bengali decorousness was also a familiar form of political protest against poverty and repression that had gripped the state, and the regimented political formations that pretended to fight them.

From 1971 to 1984, seven collections of Hungry writing were published by the Kolkata Hungryalists. These carried the writings of the major Hungry writers, and also contributions from interviews of writers they cared about, ranging from William Burroughs to the novelist Amiyabhushan Majumdār, translations of Antoine Artaud and Henry Miller (among others), and essays by emphatically non-Hungry writers such as the poet Sankha Ghosh. An edition of the seven collections was published in 2011, with the Hungryalist Saileswar Ghosh raging in his editorial introduction against renegades such as Malay Rāy Choudhury, Utpalkumār Basu, and Sandipan Chattopādhyāy (the latter had apparently driven away Saileswar Ghosh and Subhāsh Ghosh when they went to meet him at his house after securing bail), and the easy capitulation of powerful *Krittibās* writers such as Sakti Chattopādhyāy and Sunil Gangopādhyāy to the blandishments of big media houses.[22] The collections, however, were a late crop, and ignored major contributions by a few pioneers. The recent compilation, ironically, was brought out by the unapologetically commercial publishing firm Dey's, located right across the street on which Sanskrit College (now University) stands.

The Hungry Generation was not a minor episode in Bengali modernism, nor was it a mere catalyst for an evolving literary taste. Even during its initial anarchic phase, it produced literature of genuine quality. The early work of Sakti Chattopādhyāy, Debi Rāy, and Utpalkumār Basu have long been admitted into the canon, and several poems by Malay Rāy Choudhury, Phālguni Rāy, and Subo Āchārya, I suspect, deserve no less. My interest at this point is less with the arguable 'literariness' of their works than with the activism that drove them to risk poverty, opprobrium, and imprisonment (in 1965 Malay Rāy Choudhury was handed a jail sentence in the lower court but acquitted by the High Court two years later[23]).

A good instance, especially for those unfamiliar with Hungry writing, is the high-pitched sample from the 1967 curtain-raiser to the magazine *Khudhārta* (hungry), titled *The Hungry Resistance First Collection* and edited by Saileswar Ghosh:

> Have you considered that the world no longer needs art, that there is a dreadful plot afoot to kill all poets! Capitalism x (industry) x communism are breeding castrated fathers all the time. Ours is not just the howl of one generation – it is the scream of the whole of hungry India. People are losing the courage to speak out, everyone knows what would happen if you dared tell the truth. The insurance companies advertise – cancer, death, insure yourself today – but every human being is being driven crazy under the heavy foot of a daily death, but this enormous crime is going unnoticed. Cautious reader, you can see that the so-called poets and writers of Bengal are insuring themselves, buying insurances, you may see them at the lakes, parks and restaurants in the evening, after nine they are slinking home.
>
> 'Hunger is a fraud' – well, all of life is. There is no wonder in that. Who had tried to purify this rotten nation and how – we have forgotten those lessons learnt in school. Those who would die immediately would not be hungry, that's simple enough. The

ones who would live and would want to live would
cry 'hunger', complain, curse, demand, throw their
arms and legs about – the bourgeoisie have made life
obscene and anaemic – none but criminals are free.
...Freud the atom bomb Jean Paul Sartre can all go to
hell. Remember, this is the fight to defend freedom.
The only sorrow that is personal is freedom: come,
the angry sad insulted proud ego-free martyrs of a
loveless world, let us build a strong resistance.[24]

I think this sample should suffice. This was
certainly a variety of literary activism, but was it also
surrogacy for a broader programme? More important,
did the surrogate leave behind a supplement or surplus
once the cause was no longer immediate? Certainly, as
Saileswar Ghosh points in his introduction to the 2011
collected edition, the movement cleared the decks for the
co-option of sexually explicit fiction that was published
by mainstream popular magazines and commercial
publishing houses. When the novelist Samares Basu,
once a foot soldier in the Marxist cultural front, was
being accused of selling out to big media houses and
making money by peddling obscene novels, established
mainstream writers such as Santoshkumār Ghosh were
quick to point out that Basu's novels were far more
layered than the Hungryalist productions, and that the
mature novelist succeeded where the young Turks had
palpably failed.[25]

Hence, the Hungry writers were surrogates, or at
least midwives, for one form of literary activism that was
soon co-opted by the market, a market that was keen to
build an informed readership for the new urban fiction,
although neither the original Hungryalists nor Samares
Basu were urban writers to start with and were able to
ignore the demands of bourgeois Bengali rhetoric. A
nuanced and reasoned argument was put forward by
Sankha Ghosh in the 1972-1973 Hungry collection. In

an essay titled 'Sabda ār satya' (word and truth), Ghosh observed that the Hungry movement certainly demanded to be assessed in its historical context, as a reaction against the atrophy of the literature that had lost touch with the immediate as much as it had with the past. At the same time, literary activism had to rid itself of its self-imposed role of *false surrogacy*. It needed to break away from the clichés that defined the established habits that were being challenged, and to look inward in order to outgrow its own deafening slogans. Literature must redeem itself from repressions, but, like the Maoist urban guerillas in Kolkata at the time who struck at the city before energising itself in the villages, the Hungry generation ran the risk of infructuous surrogacy. The supplement in the surrogate function of the text that characterised the 'literary' rather than the 'activism' was hence surrendered.[26] Pradip Chaudhuri, a Hungryalist writer well versed in French, wrote a spirited rejoinder in the collection accusing Ghosh of self-contradiction and bias against radicals.[27] It seems that Chaudhuri misses the point when he tries to calibrate the degrees of extremism in literary activism rather than address the question of supplementarity. Supplementarity, as Derrida reminds us, characterises the literary as a form of writing that inscribes textuality within the text.[28] Such laying bare of text, of the texture of the text, results in openings and openness that override the programmatic aims of mere activism. Literature is most active when it outstrips the activist intent.

*

It is hardly surprising that Sankha Ghosh should have been thinking of the imminent defeat of the Naxalite uprising when writing of the Hungry movement. The Naxalite cause was an implacably political one unlike the Hungry movement: poets such as Saroj Datta and

Dronāchārya Ghosh lost their lives, as did Timirbaran Singha, a young pupil of Sankha Ghosh. We are thinking here of the literature produced to further the war against the state, such as the writings of Saroj Datta, Nabārun Bhattacharya, Abhijit Sen, Saibāl Mitra, and Dronāchārya Ghosh, that is, the writings of activist-authors involved in the movement rather than of powerful writers who chose the movement for their theme but were not themselves Naxalites. The latter group would include some of the most important names in Bengali literature of our times: Samares Basu, Mahāswetā Devi, Sankha Ghosh, and Debes Rāy, among others. In time, the Naxalite setting informed much docu-drama, prison narratives, and a clutch of films by *avant-garde* directors such as Mrināl Sen, Utpalendu Chakrabarty, and Gautam Ghosh.

The Naxalites suffered no disquiet about the role of literature in the movement. It was not surrogate activism, but a way of undermining the 'over-indulgent story of middle-class modernity'; it sought to be writing that 'narrate the lives of those who are excluded' from that story.[29] Surrogacy and activism are sought to be joined in the consciousness of what the Naxalites liked calling 'the New Man'. Dronāchārya Ghosh announces, Hamlet-like, that all forms, pressures, saws of all books are erased from the revolutionary's memory as he assumes this new life:

All the old words are discarded today.
Armed revolution glows firm in belief.
This is the only path of liberation.
There is no other word in our hearts.[30]

Even in this inadequate translation (by Sumanta Banerjee), one sees that the materiality of language is sought to be enlisted as a weapon of the revolution: surrogate and agent are one. What the failure of such activist poetry to affect the 'final' purpose alerts us to is the distance Abhinavagupta's cultivated *sahṛdaya* requires for recognising the poetic codes even while identifying with the text, since cognition of the literary text is self-cognition; as Gadamer taught us, what the text says, must be what it says *to us*.[31] This is especially clear if one compares the literature set against the uprising written after its defeat – the works, for instance, of Mahāswetā Devi (*Bashāi Tudu*), Samares Basu (*Mahākāler Rather Ghodā* / The horse of the chariot of time), Saibāl Mitra (*Agrabāhini* / Advance guard), Debes Rāy (*Samay Asamayer Brittānta* / Chronicles of time and disjointed times), and Abhijit Sen (*Holud Ranger Surjo* / Yellow-coloured sun). The revolutionary rediscovers in these texts the plenitude of literary surrogacy that overruns the projective impulse of ideology and, at moments of repeated impact, resists adoption by a market that must, to recall a phrase I once heard a teacher at Jadavpur University use, follow its followers in order to lead.[32]

1. For collections of *dalit* literature in English or English translation, see K. Satyanarayana and Susie Tharu, eds, *The Exercise of Freedom: An Introduction to Dalit Writing* (Delhi: Navayana, 2013); K. Satyanarayana and Susie Tharu, eds, *Steel Nibs Are Sprouting: New Dalit Writing from South India Dossier 2: Kannada and Telugu* (Noida: HarperCollins, 2013); Tapan Basu et al., eds, *Listen to the Flames: Texts and Readings from the Margins* (New Delhi: Oxford University Press, 2016).

2. Rabindranāth Thākur, 'Sabhāpatir Abhibhāshan', *Sāhityer Pathe*, 'Parisisishta', *Rabindra-Rachanābali*, vol. 23 (Kolkata: Visva-Bhārati, 1354 BS), pp. 467-477; p. 467. For an English translation, see Rabindranath Tagore, 'Presidential Address', trans. Swapan Chakravorty, in Sisir Kumar Das and Sukanta Chaudhuri, eds, *Essays on Literature and Language*, The Oxford Tagore Translations (New Delhi: Oxford University Press, 2001), pp. 310-319.

3. Alain Badiou, 'Philosophy and Art', *Infinite Thought: Truth and the Return to Philosophy*, trans. and ed. Oliver Feltham and Justin Clemens (London: Continuum, 2005), p. 79.

4. See Derek Attridge, 'The Critic as Lover: Literary Activism and the Academy', pp. 45-70 of this volume. See also Derek Attridge, 'Introduction: Derrida and the Questioning of Literature', in Jacques Derrida, *Acts of Literature*, ed. Derek Attridge (London: Routledge, 1992), pp. 1-29.

5. Georges Poulet, 'Phenomenology of Reading', *New Literary History*, 1 (1969), p. 56.

6. Ernst Cassirer, *The Philosophy of Symbolic Forms*, 3 vols, trans. Ralph Manheim (New Haven: Yale University Press, 1953), vol. 3, p. 307.

7. See J.L. Masson and M.V. Patwardhan, *Aesthetic Rapture: The Rasādhyāya of the Nātyasāstra* (Poona: Deccan College, 1970), p. 6. See also Sushil Kumar De, *History of Sanskrit Poetics*, 2 vols (1925; 2nd edition, Calcutta:

Firma KLM, 1960), vol. 2, p. 135.The requirements of the culturally competent are listed in Bharata, *Nāṭyaśāstra*, 27.49. See my 'Being Staged: Unconcealment through Reading and Performance in Marlowe's *Doctor Faustus* and Bharata's *Nāṭyaśāstra*', *Philosophy East and West*, 66.1 (2016), pp. 40-59. The idea of cultural or literary competence is important for such Western critics as Jonathan Culler. See his *Structuralist Poetics: Structuralism, Linguistics and the Study of Literature* (Ithaca: Cornell University Press, 1975), pp. 113-130.

8. See S.C. Sen Gupta, '*Hamlet* in the Light of Indian Poetics', *Aspects of Shakespearian Tragedy* (Calcutta: Oxford University Press, 1972), p. 144; and S.C. Sen Gupta, 'Shakespeare's Sonnets', *Shakespeare Manual* (Calcutta: Oxford University Press, 1982), p. 156.

9. See Michel de Montaigne, *Essais*, Book 3, Chapter 3; *Essais de Montaigne*, vol. 2, ed. Maurice Rat (Paris: Editions

Garnier Frères, 1962), p. 249.

10. Tribedi was challenging Tagore's arguments in the latter's essay 'Byādhi o pratikār' published in the magazine *Prabāsi* in Srāvana 1314 BS (July-August 1907), and later included in *Samuha-Parisista*; see *Rabindra-Rachanābali*, vol. 10 (Kolkata: Visva-Bhārati, 1348 BS), pp. 623-35. Tribedi's rejoinder was carried in *Prabāsi*, Āswin 1314 BS (September-October 1907). See *Rāmendra-rachanā-sangraha*, eds Sunitikumār Chattopadhyāy and Anilkumār Kānjilāl (Kolkata: Bangiya-Sāhitya-Parishat, 1964), pp. 617-634. On the museum proposed for Bangiya-Sāhitya-Parishat, see Rāmendrasundar Tribedi, 'Mātrimandir' (read at the Bengali Literary Conference in Kāsimbājār in 1314 BS and first published in *Upāsanā*, 6, 1315 BS), pp. 522-535.

11. See *Bangabhange jijñāsā o janamat: Bhāndār-sankalan*, ed. Hirendranāth Chakrabarti (Kolkata: Netaji

290

Institute of Asian Studies, 2011), pp. 16-18.

12. See Michael Hancher, 'Three Kinds of Intention', *Modern Language Notes*, 87 (1972), pp. 827-851; and G. Thomas Tanselle, 'The Editorial Problem of Final Authorial Intention', *Selected Studies in Bibliography* (Charlottesville: University of Virginia Press, 1979), pp. 309-354. Hancher speaks of three kinds of authorial intention: *programmatic*, in which the author intends to make something or the other; *active*, in which the author intends to be understood as acting in some way or other; and *final*, in which the author intends to cause something or other to happen.

13. Rabindranāth Thākur, *Gorā, Rabindra-Rachanābali*, vol. 6 (1347 BS; repr.; Kolkata: Visva-Bhārati, 1363 BS), p. 566. My translation.

14. Sankha Ghosh, 'Jābāl Satyakām', *Sreshtha Kabitā*, (1970; enlarged edition, Kolkata: Dey's, 1978), p. 79. My translation.

15. For the source of the term, see Malay Rāy Choudhury, 'Anil Karanjāi o Postmodern Painting', *Hungry Sāhitya Āndolan: Tattva, Tathya, Itihās*, ed. Pranabkumār Chattopādhyāy (Kolkata: Pratibhās, 2015), p. 255. See also Malay Rāy Choudhury, 'Hungry Pratisandarbha', *Hungry Sāhitya Āndolan*, p. 262; Sakti Chattopādhyāy's 1965 deposition before the Presidency Magistrate of Bankshal Court, Kolkata, against Malay Rāy Choudhury in 1965, *Hungry Sāhitya Āndolan*, p. 126; *Hungry Generationer Srashtāder Khudhārta Sankalan: Sātti Pratisthānbirodhi Sankhyā*, ed. Saileswar Ghosh (Kolkata: Dey's, 2011), p. 18. For the phrase 'Whan it was in the sowre hungry tyme', see Geoffrey Chaucer, *Boece*, Book 1, Prosa 4, lines 80-81, *The Works of Geoffrey Chaucer*, ed. F.N. Robinson (1933; 2nd edition, London: Oxford University Press, 1957), p. 324.

16. The alternative accounts are represented by the recent collections, *Hungry Sāhitya Āndolan*;

and *Hungry Generationer Srashtāder Khudhārta Sankalan: Sātti Pratisthānbirodhi Sankhyā*.

17. *Time*, November 1964; see *Hungry Generationer Srashtāder Khudhārta Sankalan: Sātti Pratisthānbirodhi Sankhyā*, p. 32. For the early history of the Hungry Generation, see pp. 17-30.

18. See Bill Morgan, *The Beats Abroad: A Global Guide to the Beat Generation* (San Francisco: City Lights, 2015), pp. 188ff.

19. See *Hungry Sāhitya Āndolan*, pp. 310, 428. See especially Malay Rāy Choudhury, 'Allen Ginsberg-ke Hungry Āndolan Kibhābe Prabhābita Korechhe' (How Allen Ginsberg was influenced by the Hungry movement), *Hungry Sāhitya Āndolan*, pp. 324-338.

20. Malay Rāy Choudhury, 'Krittibās Theke hungry āndolan: bānglā Kabitār Pālābadal', *Hungry Sāhitya Āndolan*, pp. 276-288.

21. See Malay Rāy Choudhury, 'Allen Ginsbreg-ke Hungry Āndolan Kibhābe Prabhābita

Korechhe', p. 337; and Saileswar Ghosh, 'Hungry Generationer Srashtāder "Khudhārta"', *Hungry Generationer Srashtāder Khudhārta Sankalan: Sātti Pratisthānbirodhi Sankhyā*, p. 18. On the archive at Northwestern University, <http://www.library.northwestern.edu/documents/libraries-collections/special-collections/Hungry-Generation-guide.pdf>, accessed on 1 July 2016.

22. Saileswar Ghosh, 'Hungry Generationer Srashtāder "Khudhārta"', pp. 27, 152. Ghosh made this remark in the Bengali magazine *Des* in 1965.

23. For the depositions and records of trials, see *Hungry Sāhitya Āndolan*, pp. 119-141; and <https://hungryalist.wordpress.com/2011/12/09/hungry-generation-case-papers>, accessed on 1 July 2016.

24. 'Parisista 2', *Hungry Generationer Srashtāder Khudhārta Sankalan*, p. 614. This is from the *The Hungry Resistance First Collection* (1967). My translation.

25. Saileswar Ghosh, 'Hungry Generationer Srashtāder "Khudhārta"', p. 23.

26. Sankha Ghosh, 'Sabda ār Satya', *Hungry Generationer Srashtāder Khudhārta Sankalan*, pp. 258-264.

27. Pradip Chaudhuri, 'Sabda o Gopan Satya: (athabā calling bell jāder ātankita kare)', *Hungry Generationer Srashtāder Khudhārta Sankalan*, pp. 265-268.

28. Derrida says this of Rousseau's writing while discussing the question of supplementarity. See Jacques Derrida, *Of Grammatology*, trans. Gayatri Chakravorty Spivak (Baltimore: The Johns Hopkins University Press, 1976), p. 163.

29. Sharmilā Purkāyastha, 'Creative Engagements: Literature and Politics in Bengal (1967-1975)', PhD thesis, University of Delhi, 2015, p. 300.

30. Dronāchārya Ghosh, 'Our Paths', trans. Sumanta Banerjee, *Thema Book of Naxalite Poetry* (Kolkata: Thema, 1987), p. 72.

31. Hans-Georg Gadamer, *Philosophical Hermeneutics*, trans. and ed. David E. Linge (Berkeley: University of California Press, 1976), pp. 100-101.

32. The professor was Sipra Sarkar, who taught history at Jadavpur University, Kolkata.

I wish to thank Sharmilā Purkāyastha for permission to quote from her unpublished thesis. I am grateful to Moloy Rakshit for leading me to sources, and to Amit Chaudhuri for suggesting improvements and pointing out errors.

293

Epilogue

Literary Activism:
Where Now, What Next?

JON COOK

1.

As the other contributions to this volume show, 'literary activism' quite deliberately eludes any summary definition and, thus, may prove frustrating to those in search of quick answers. It is not, in the first instance, a contribution to literary theory or criticism (although it raises questions pertinent to both, about the role and purpose of criticism, for example); nor is it an attempt to contribute to the growing body of work about the teaching of creative writing (although it might ask whether the demand to produce work acceptable to commercial publishers should be the guiding maxim of judgement in a creative writing class, or even its tacit concern). It certainly harbours an element of resistance, and not just to the way the literary marketplace currently operates, but also to how literature is taught, researched, and valued within the academy. But this element of resistance does not express itself in the formulation of a new position in whose name a new set of dogmas and methods can be promulgated. The work of literary activism, whose beginnings this volume announces, is more varied and more unsettled than the formulation of any definition or doctrine might suggest. No single line of enquiry or emphasis runs through the essays collected here. There is certainly an attempt to find new freedoms of thought and questioning, even if there is, at the same time, a reservation about their possibility. While some of the essays offer the beginnings of an analysis of the literary world at a certain moment of 'globalisation', there is equally a series of questions about whether such a thing as a literary world exists and, if it does, where its current boundaries lie. These may seem large and theoretical issues. In fact they are all practically concerned with who reads what and why, with the practice of writing at a particular contemporary moment, and with the activities and institutions that shape an understanding of what literature is and what it can do.

In his introduction to this volume, Amit Chaudhuri provides a striking and provocative formulation of why a form of literary activism – an activism on behalf of an idea of literature – is needed now. It arises as a response to another phenomenon, the 'market activism' that has become an increasing force over the last two decades and more in shaping what literature is and how it gets valued. Different reactions to market activism are evident in many of the essays in this collection. All seek a distance from its claims and energies, sometimes through a quiet scepticism, at others through satirical or sardonic invocation. The range in view is probably familiar to many readers: the mesmeric power of money as news starts to circulate about the latest six- or seven-figure advance; the writers who become celebrities and the celebrities who become writers; the impatient talk about 'outmoded' forms ('biography is dead'; 'Black British fiction had its day in the 1990s'); to be hailed as 'new'; to write a 'masterpiece'; to get a large advance; to become a literary personality; to be the headline act at a literary festival: all these have become the hallmarks of literary success and significance.

In his essay, David Graham outlines some of the economic changes that have produced this climate. They include, crucially, the integration of many independent publishing houses into large media conglomerates, all working at a global level in terms of their market reach. A once-independent publishing house in Britain, Jonathan Cape is now part of a larger publishing company, Random House, which is itself part of a newly merged company, Penguin Random House, a merger that brings together Penguin – owned by Pearson plc and 'the largest book publisher in the world' according to its website – and Random House, in turn owned by the German

298

media conglomerate Bertelsmann. The same is true for HarperCollins, now part of Rupert Murdoch's News Corp empire. Between them, these groups account for a great many of the books sold in the world today. Their effects on the work of a literary publishing are immense, if little discussed or known. They include a transformation in the rate of profit expected of a publishing house. In her book *The World Republic of Letters*, Pascale Casanova, citing research on the publishing industry, indicates the scale of this change: the average profit of publishing houses in the 1920s in Europe and the United States stood at around four per cent.[1] Now it is set at somewhere between twelve and fifteen per cent. And with this change go others: the increasing importance of marketing directors in deciding which books are published; a heightened attention to sales figures as an indication of a writer's value; and, over the past decade, a precipitate decline in the advances offered to 'mid-list' literary novelists. Integrated into large corporations in this way, the publication of literary fiction is a very small part of a much larger activity that includes the production of films, computer games, or television programmes, often now brigaded under the single heading of a 'content' that seeks its relay and distribution across as many media platforms as possible. It is clear by now increased profit margins have not resulted in the freeing up of resources for literary publication. If anything, the opposite has happened.

Reflecting on these changes and others, including the emergence of Amazon and the abolition of the Net Book Agreement, David Graham argues that a chain has been broken, a chain that linked authors to agents, agents to editors, editors to booksellers. It rested on an assumption about the activity of publishing literature, whereby the proceeds of a bestseller would be used to offset the commercial risks of literary authorship. To take just one example from Britain, this publishing model sustained the work of William Golding, a novelist whose career began with a major publishing success, *Lord of the Flies*, and was followed by some years of relative obscurity before a late flowering of his authorship. In all this, as John Carey's biography of Golding makes clear, his relationship with his editor, Charles Monteith, was crucial to the making – let alone the publication – of his work.[2] It is doubtful whether a literary career such as Golding's would survive in today's marketplace. That obliviousness to the past, other than as a form of heritage, which Amit Chaudhuri notes as a feature of market activism, is unlikely to register this as a loss.

But market activism is not just a phenomenon of economic changes in the publishing industry. These may be one of its necessary conditions, but another is the buzzy interdependence of media and markets. As a result, market activism has become a distinctive idiom in literary culture, a way of talking about what is happening, what is notable, what we should be excited about and why. In an essay first published in 1992, 'The Novelist Today: Still at the Crossroads', David Lodge provided an early commentary on the nature of this change. His essay revisits another, 'The Novelist at the Crossroads', first published in 1969, where Lodge argued that the choice confronting the modern novelist was predominantly between two kinds of imagination and form, one he called 'fabulation', the other 'realism'.[3] By 1992, the situation had changed yet again. The novelist no longer had to choose or mediate between two aesthetic possibilities, but between many. Lodge describes this as an 'aesthetic pluralism', a 'situation in which everything is in and nothing is out'. While this led to what he regarded as an openness to different styles, it had a downside too, the absence of any 'consensus about aesthetic value' and the kinds of debate that would inform its making. In its absence, something else took over, 'a somewhat materialistic notion of success, as measured by sales, advances, prizes, media celebrity, etc'.[4]

Lodge writes as if he is trying to keep an increasingly pressing set of worries at bay, or, at least, under control. The balancing act between the 'artist' who writes a novel and the 'man or woman of business' who publishes it is felt to be increasingly difficult to sustain.[5] In a postscript to the essay, written in 1995, literary and financial values have become ever more confused, a situation exemplified for Lodge by the publication and reception of Martin Amis's novel *The Information*, an event that combined large advances with stories of betrayal and friendships undone as Amis moved from one literary agent to another. The book itself seems to dissolve in the scandals and celebrations that surround its publication. Lodge finds little to offer by way of resistance to these circumstances other than a note of caution. Something unstoppable, energetic, and threatening seemed to have invaded the precarious autonomy of the literary sphere.

More than two decades after the publication of Lodge's essay, the culture of 'sales, advances, prizes, media celebrity, etc' has become normative. What is hidden in that 'etc' are claims about the powers of markets in general that Lodge does not directly discuss in his essay and perhaps underestimates. In the late twentieth century it was part of the rhetoric of markets that they were hailed as 'drivers of innovation' and not simply as a means of circulating commodities. If markets possessed this capacity in general, then why shouldn't it apply to literature as well as to computers and cars? The modernist assumption that markets did exactly the reverse of this was itself reversed.[6]

In his introduction to this volume, Amit Chaudhuri notes how the power of market activism has resulted in a kind of linguistic takeover of the terms of critical judgement, just as the validity of those same terms was being questioned in university departments of literature. The announcement of a new work as a 'masterpiece' became commonplace. But the claims of the market to be remaking culture didn't end there. Just as it appropriated established terms of value, it at the same time became the champion of the 'new' in another and more politically loaded sense. The egalitarianism and openness of the new literary market was underlined by the discovery of 'new voices' from different parts of the world, each 'new voice' a contributor to the emergence of a global literature that would overcome the old condescensions and omissions of the European and American cultural elites.

What is true of writers could also be true of readers. The market would come to speak in the name of a readership whose rights to finding an accessible literature would be made paramount. Traditional distinctions between elite and popular values would be dissolved as the best work was made available to the widest possible readership. In his essay, Tim Parks quotes the words of a festival director, filled with confidence about a test of value: 'If a work is good it will reach out to everyone the world over.' He records his own scepticism about this claim, detecting a marketing ploy in what looks like a celebration of a new kind of democracy in the world republic of letters. Do all good literary works 'reach out' in this way? Might not some deliberately refuse to do so? And, if we believe in the festival director's vision, do we lose some of those particularities of knowledge and idiom that make literature worth reading?

The 2013 publication of Morrissey's memoirs, *Autobiography*, by Penguin is one instance of how weird and yet seamlessly acceptable the co-option of words such as 'classic' and 'masterpiece' has become; it also exemplifies the interactions of celebrity and authorship under the dispensation of market activism. The former lead singer of the The Smiths insisted that his book should be published immediately as a Penguin Modern Classic. From his point of view it's not hard to understand why: if his songs and albums had been hailed as classics, why shouldn't his memoirs? The word was a way of saying about something not just that it was good, but very good – perhaps, even, a shade better than a 'masterpiece'. But this market-driven use of the word 'classic' takes on an odd resonance when applied to a work of literature. The hint of paradox already at work in the notion of a 'modern classic' is heightened to a point where it becomes a contradiction in terms: an 'instant classic'. The idea, for some essential to the meaning of the word, that the judgement of something as a 'classic' could only arise over a period of time, in the movement of reception and reading across generations, becomes null and void. It is another instance of that flattening of time into a present which makes different pasts almost unthinkable, which Amit Chaudhuri notes as a feature of the world of market activism in his essay on literary activism and the Mehrotra campaign. The piazza replaces the car park. A past where, for example, 'writers deliberately distanced themselves from material success' can only be approached as if it were a kind of fiction. By the same token it becomes hard to imagine a time when words such as 'masterpiece', 'classic', or 'original' were anything other than promotional terms in a marketing strategy to boost the sales of a book and the reputation of its author. It's worth noting, too, who has the power – in the world of market activism – to decide how a word will be used. Like Humpty Dumpty in Lewis Carroll's *Through the Looking Glass*, when Morrissey uses the word 'classic' it will mean 'just what I want it to mean – neither more nor less'.[7]

One response to these concerns about market activism might be to say that they are just the expressions of a misplaced anxiety. We have been here before. Frequent defences of literature have been mounted by identifying the commercial marketplace as its enemy. The current situation is no exception. In the eighteenth century, Alexander Pope wrote a satire on the literary marketplace: *The Dunciad*. The poem delivers a grotesque series of visions, many of them animated by the fear of an overproduction of books and the debasement of literature by commerce, a condition where there is 'A Lumberhouse of books in ev'ry head / For ever reading never to be read'.[8] Writing some two hundred years later, Q.D. Leavis, in her book *Fiction and the Reading Public*, offered a less gleeful, but equally acerbic, analysis of the effects of what she called 'The Book Market' on the experience of reading. Noting the way that bestsellers offer 'ideal companionship to a reader by its uniquely compelling illusion of life in which sympathetic characters... touch off the warmer emotional responses' and the literary agent's maxim that 'the principal character' of any commercially successful novel must be 'likeable', Leavis goes on to argue that a culture of reading shaped in this way makes an engagement with the work of D.H. Lawrence or Virginia Woolf almost impossible.[9] Examples of this kind of response, often now dismissed as elitist, could be multiplied. The true value of literature is repeatedly defined against its malign but necessary counterpart, the literary marketplace.

More recently, and from the perspective of a literary and cultural history that starts with the emergence of national literatures in sixteenth-century Europe, Pascale Casanova thinks we have come to the end of the line, a terminal point where commercial imperatives now threaten to bring the history of this antagonism to an end. According to Casanaova, the kinds of anxiety and the anger that provoked Pope – or, later, Leavis – belong to an earlier phase of the history of literature and commerce. What she detects in the late twentieth century is a new kind of market power, one where the 'form of books themselves' is modified by market forces that give the appearance of literariness at the same time as the 'very idea of a literature independent of commercial forces' has been put into question.[10] Casanova would probably agree with the argument put forward in this collection by Dubravka Ugresic. Literature has been eviscerated by markets and an eerie simulacrum has come to take its place.

What might we make of these historical precedents? Is there a danger of crying wolf, or has the wolf actually arrived? And how would we know if it had? The history of literature's relationship with commerce is long and complicated. To think that this history's exclusive theme is about the threat of market forces to ideas of literary value would be radically to misconstrue the role that markets have played in supporting modes of authorship and in developing genres, most notably the modern novel.[11] Like other histories, this one abounds in the striking of poses and the manufacture of hypocrisy. But, nonetheless, elements of resistance and antagonism have always been present, sometimes in the sense that the operation of literary markets inevitably degrades literary taste, sometimes in the wish to make the scale of literary production less industrial and more closely aligned to specific communities of authors and readers. But that latter response, born out of the need to remake literature on a smaller but freer scale and evident in the essays in this collection by Tim Parks and David Graham, invites comparison with another account of authorship that has to do with the emergence of a particular idea of literature during the period of European Romanticism. Here what is at issue is not so much an idea about how an author is connected or not to a community of readers, but to a particular idea of authorship itself.

The Italian writer Roberto Calasso is one among many critics who have given a name to this idea. In his book *Literature and the Gods*, he sees it at work in a number of mainly European writers, Holderlin, Baudelaire, de Lautreamont, Mallarme, and Nabokov, among them. What all these writers share, in the midst of their many differences, is a certain intransigence. Calasso calls this 'absolute literature', which he glosses as 'literature at its most piercing, its most intolerant of any social trappings'. Often attracted to parodic or sardonic idioms, blurring distinctions between the serious and the comic, disturbing amicable relations between author and reader, this literature was also repeatedly attracted to a strange possibility, hence the title of Calasso's book. Far from being dead, the gods were alive and well, but in a new guise, no longer a family on Olympus, but a multitude, 'a teeming crowd in an endless metropolis', living in stories and 'scattered idols', inhabiting pages and screens, including the computer screen, which Calasso sees as a 'new kind of Centaur', where the mind 'grows used to seeing itself as an unlimited theatre'.[12] Their presence disturbed the ongoing routines of time. The French surrealist Louis Aragon's *Paysan de Paris*, first published in 1926, seeks them out in the cafés, hotels, parks, and arcades of the city, places where he can discover a 'sense of strangeness', of 'rare thresholds... that unite the data of my sense... with the unconscious'.[13]

Calasso's idea of an 'absolute literature' hints at another hesitation or even recoil in response to the pressures of market activism. There is a kind of sociability about market activism that invites us to join, to subscribe, to turn up, to attend. Reading groups and festivals are two obvious manifestations of this affable, rivalrous behaviour that makes literature into the occasion for a gathering. But there is another possibility, that this sometimes pleasurable, sometimes enforced sociability threatens to overwhelm a special solitude or separation that is a condition for the writing and reading of literature. A letter from Doris Lessing gives a clear expression to the difficulty:

> Things have fallen so that it seems positively precious to remind people not writers that writers' capital, their storehouse, their essential fuel, is a kind of brooding and solitary silence, which sometimes has to bemaintained over many months, an inner concentration that is easily overthrown and dispersed.[14]

In the concluding pages of *Literature and the Gods*, Calasso contemplates an ancient image, one that illuminates the nature of the 'inner concentration' that Lessing wants to guard: a young man writes on a tablet, below him a severed head watches him as he writes, and to one side the Greek god Apollo is also present, a laurel rod in one hand, the other reaching out towards the writer. For Calasso, this scene becomes an epitome for the writing of literature:

> Literature is never the product of a single subject. There are always at least three actors: the hand that writes, the voice that speaks, the god who watches over and compels.... A continuous process of triangulation is at work between them. Every sentence, every form is a variation within that force field. Hence the ambiguity of literature because its point of view is incessantly shifting between these three extremes, without warning us, and sometimes without warning the author.[15]

That much-loved figure, the reader, is singularly absent from this scene. Nor is there any insistence on the craft of writing. Instead authorship arises in the midst of processes that are beyond the writer's control. 'The god who watches over and compels' is a metaphor for that presence which compels the writer's attention, a turning away from concerns about what will please readers towards a strangeness that a number of contributors to this volume have argued is at the centre of any serious literary art.

Perhaps the questions provoked by the distinction between market activism and literary activism can be briefly and provisionally summarised through this epitome. What happens if the insistence and volubility of the market takes the place of the 'god who watches over and compels'? What if, in the writing of modern literature, there is always an uncertain boundary between the one and the other, and one that could be breached without our even being aware of it? It is not simply that something might be lost if such an event were to occur. A future could be foreclosed as well, one that finds an inspiration in the kind of authorship that Calasso records and celebrates in his book. What is at issue then in the critique of market activism is not simply an acknowledgement that, to use a clumsy phrase, 'market forces have taken over', but an analysis of what at least some of the consequences of that take over have been. If David Lodge, writing in 1995, was apprehensive about market success becoming the default criterion of literary value, what he did not anticipate was the appropriation by the market and its surrogates of a language of value and the creation of a new, foreshortened and limiting experience of time and history.

2.

The questioning of market activism marks one point of orientation in understanding the concerns of literary activism. But there is another, directed towards the role of universities and the place of literary studies within them. Once the university might have been

308

imagined as the place that protected and encouraged
an idea of literature that stood apart from, and even
opposed, the notions of literary value promoted by
markets. That assumption can no longer be taken for
granted, as many of the essays in this collection make
clear. The pieces by Derek Attridge and Peter McDonald
focus on the role of criticism inside and outside the
academy. Saikat Majumdar's essay raises a question
about the place of a particular, non-specialist kind of
authorship in universities that are increasingly concerned
with specialism and the development of a professional
cadre of academics. And Amit Chaudhuri identifies
a form of literary activism that disturbs assumptions
about literary value and prestige that are enacted in the
appointment of prominent literary chairs such as the
Oxford Professorship of Poetry.

Derek Attridge identifies one powerful
interpretative trend in the recent history of literary study
in universities, 'the hermeneutics of suspicion'. This
critical stance enjoins a certain wariness in reading. The
pleasure we take in a text may all too readily be a form of
ideological complicity with forms of power that oppress,
distort, and mutilate. Critical work is both an exposure of
this complicity and a wake-up call to readers to be alert
to the mystifications and concealments that make literary
works what they are and also shape the interpretative
traditions that grow up around them. We are constantly in
danger of being fooled or of fooling ourselves. Criticism
needs to guard against this deception. This cautionary
stance can be accompanied by a more exuberant version
of a disillusioning criticism, one that seeks to liberate
subversive energies in works that critical traditions have
deliberately ignored.

As Attridge himself acknowledges, some powerful
and influential critical work has been written under this
rubric. The discipline of these kinds of reading can be

exacting and their results illuminating. But suspicion
can have its shortcomings too, above all by imposing
theories of literature that have the effect of limiting or
even proscribing certain kinds of response. A version
of the dilemmas posed by the circular nature of literary
interpretation becomes evident, one in which our initial
presuppositions about what literature can or should do
shapes what we discover in a particular work.

What Attridge proposes as an alternative to the
hermeneutics of suspicion is the idea of the critic as lover.
It is striking that, in his autobiographical account, this
idea comes to him by way of what a friend and colleague
called him rather than as a critical position deliberately
adopted. His essay is, in a sense, an account of how
he came to acknowledge that calling and recognise its
validity. The very thought of the critic as lover may
provoke unease. It immediately seems to unsettle the
assumption that the academic study of literature should
be based in professional expertise and not on an affective
relation to what is studied. How could a rigorous study
of literature accommodate the feelings of the critic?
Isn't there a risk that criticism will turn into a display of
sensibility, rather than a knowledge of the text?

An implicit response to these questions comes
through Attridge's account of what the goal of a loving
criticism might be, what he identifies as 'an *affirmative*
criticism, one that operates – with as much sophistication
and care as any other approach – to understand, explore,
respond to and judge what is of value in works of
literature'.[16] And, it is worth adding, that this is not the
work of a single individual, but a group, one engaged
in a dialogue about what of value a literary work might
produce or disclose.

This insight might be developed in different
directions. The critic as lover can become the critic as
advocate (and hence a kind of activist), arguing the case

310

for contemporary authors in a way that Attridge himself has done. While there are instances of this advocacy in the pages of many journals and magazines such as *The New Yorker* or *The London Review of Books*, they rarely lead to the kind of sustained thinking about the work of one author that Attridge has in mind when he writes about his advocacy of the South African writer Zoë Wicomb. Reviews sustain our sense of the plurality of literature. By their nature they are usually drawn to one publication rather than a body of work. They are punctual in the sense that they can capture the excitement or the disappointment that comes at the moment of publication. More often than not, they seek to patrol the boundaries of existing reputations rather than challenging prevailing literary tastes. Only rarely do they offer any insight into what a particular authorship might tell us about the potentials and values of literature more generally and its cultural resonance. What, above all, is missing is that quality of debate – and the notion of debate is not simply equivalent to controversy – that Attridge, at the conclusion of his essay, sees hopefully as a task that university departments of literature are best placed to undertake, a debate that begins in the experience of literature as 'deeply felt and highly valued' and is sustained through the exploration of that experience with others.

If Attridge's essay identifies another possible form of literary activism in the work of the critic, it also raises a question about the institutional contexts that shape the reading of literature. In his essay, Peter McDonald reminds us that this meaning is never arrived at through an unconstrained dialogue between well-intentioned readers. Any attempt to discover a new language of criticism needs to consider 'the media and the institutions through which that language might find its way into the public domain'.[17] Using Maurice Blanchot's essay 'The Task of Criticism Today', he traces both the changing institutional contexts of the essay's publication and reception, one that moves from debates in the French Left in the 1950s to the academic world of literary theory in the 1970s, and its continuing challenge and relevance to thinking about what it means to read critically.

Writing in the 1950s, Blanchot anticipated some of the problems that continue to vex the activity of criticism and the purpose of the critic. Neither equal to the 'day-to-day knowledge' of journalism nor the 'scholarly knowledge of the university', criticism is a kind of intellectual orphan. Blanchot rejects the idea that criticism should shuttle back and forth between Grub Street and the academy, whether by disseminating specialist knowledge to non-specialists or as a voice of 'higher values'. Bereft of both institutional location and scientific credentials, criticism risks losing all identity. But its very weakness can become source of its strength. Neither delivering judgements on the basis of criteria external to the text, as is the case with the 'hermeneutics of suspicion', nor concerned with an appraisal on the basis of canonical literary values, criticism will instead, in Blanchot's words, belong 'to the movement by which the work comes to itself, searches for itself, and experiences its own possibility'.[18]

Blanchot's understanding of a literary text endows it with a special kind of life. It is not, as one kind of traditional aesthetics might have it, a harmony awaiting our delighted contemplation. Nor is it an enigmatic object that requires interpretative decoding. Nor, again, is it mainly the product of dominant ideologies or a reaction to them. It is in a state of potential or movement, but one that arises in the midst of multiple, even paradoxical conditions: finding what it is, searching for what it is, realising its possible configurations. But it's not just anything, not just what we want to make of it. There

312

will be realisations of its potential that are true to it, and others that are not.

This conception of the literary work in Blanchot's essay, and Peter McDonald's commentary on it, opens up a fascinating historical constellation. Blanchot's proposal for a criticism that endlessly discovers the work and its own purpose in response to undogmatic acts of reading has historical affiliations. One of them is in Oscar Wilde's essay 'The Critic as Artist', where criticism is identified as a 'creation within a creation', but one that calls for a 'surrender' that is absolute 'to the work in question'.[19] Another is with the work of Walter Benjamin, and his reactivation in the 1920s of the idea of 'immanent critique'. Contrasting this approach with the idea of a criticism that would judge a work by an external and prescribed set of criteria, Benjamin argued that the method of criticism engages in a dialogue with the work, discovering, in the process, its 'inner form' or 'presupposition'.[20] Neither of these were given by the rules of genre, or indeed less explicit conventions about what a literary work should be. The 'inner form' of Shakespeare's sonnets, for example, does not derive from his variation on the inherited rules of a fourteen-line poem, but the complex work of mourning and resistance that they undertake. 'Inner form' consists in that distinctive relationship to the world to which the work bears witness. The dangers of this unfolding dialogue between work and critic were as evident to Benjamin as its potentials. The procedure is fraught with risk because the destination or outcome of this dialogue cannot be known in advance. It may break down, or swerve away from the work in question, or be reduced to silence.

If these comparisons suggest that the idea of criticism in Blanchot's essay is not eccentric or unprecedented, and if they also give some suggestion of the resources that might be available in the invention of a new critical language, one adequate to what Amit Chaudhuri describes as the 'strangeness' of the literary, they also return us to a problem that is both literally and symbolically one of location. Wilde's 'The Critic as Artist' is again a helpful precursor because of the way it deliberately connects a style of criticism to its setting. The piece is cast in the form of a dialogue that takes place at night in 'the library of a house in Piccadilly, overlooking Hyde Park'. Its two participants are both aesthetes, critics as lovers in more than one sense. Its style includes extravagant displays of critical sensibility as well as the familiar antinomian form of Wilde's paradoxes: 'The mere creative instinct does not innovate, but reproduces'; 'It is very much more difficult to talk about a thing than do it'; 'to do nothing at all is the most difficult thing in the world', and so on.[21]

Alongside these defiances of late-nineteenth-century English pieties, there is another, more ambivalent conversation at work. Wilde acknowledges but also resists Matthew Arnold's understanding of what the critic should be and do. This is as evident in the style and tone of 'The Critic as Artist' as in its direct skirmishes with Arnold's ideas. Both measure a distance from the sometimes weary and sometimes ironic seriousness of Arnold's formulation of the ethical work of the critic, and, in doing that, they distance themselves too from the idea of translating criticism into a pedagogy or curriculum that can be taught in schools and universities. Wilde draws on Arnold's ideas only to transform them. Arnold was a cosmopolitan, but he nonetheless insisted on the public and educational responsibilities of criticism in the development of a national culture. Wilde created an idea of criticism that is more wayward and more intransigent than Arnold's. While he agreed with Arnold that criticism should follow 'the law of its own nature,

314

which is to be the free play of the mind on all subjects that it touches', he thought that Arnold had given too restrictive account of what that 'free play' might be like. He also rejected Arnold's claim that: 'The critical power is of lower rank than the creative.'[22]

These differences are reflected in the form of Wilde's essay. 'The Critic as Artist' is an adaptation of a Socratic method, a dialogue whose purpose is to expose the fragility of orthodox beliefs about the role of criticism and the identity of the critic. But the setting of the dialogue also deliberately opens it to what is contingent and of the moment: the pleasures of a cigarette and a moonlit walk in the park, or that longing to be elsewhere that is, for Wilde, a part of the attraction of art. The dialogue celebrates the kind of thinking that occurs at night and unfolds at leisure. It has moments of illumination and of distraction. The two participants in the dialogue flirt with each other as they argue. They are late-nineteenth-century pagans, devotees of the 'critical spirit of Alexandria' and its invention of modernity. The subtitle of the dialogue when it was first published – 'with Some Remarks on the Importance of Doing Nothing' – gives another indication of how at odds it is with the requirements of a Protestant work ethic and single-minded devotion to the public duties of the critic.

The way of living and thinking celebrated in 'The Critic as Artist' is unlikely to find much welcome in a modern university preoccupied with outcomes, impacts, and measurable returns on investment. Whether the 'critic as lover' can find a place there is no clearer. Derek Attridge is hopeful. Peter McDonald, in his Sancho Panza voice, is less so, citing a number of changes both within and outside the university that threaten the possibility of the kind of critical attention described by Blanchot. The circulation of opinion in the blogosphere, universities run as businesses, 'taste arbiters' who are 'media celebrities';

all these are signs that we may be living at the end of the era that made universities into at least the provisional home for an idea of literature that was not catered for by the marketplace.

In his essay on the postcolonial university, Saikat Majumdar brings together a parallel set of concerns, although seen from a different historical and cultural perspective. The critic as lover becomes the critic as 'amateur'. Majumdar traces the vicissitudes of the relative status of the amateur and the professional in the history of taste and in the academic study of literature within universities in the twentieth century. The figure of the amateur became an uneasy presence in the academy, at once relegated as an example of the type of approach that the university must exclude if literary criticism was to become a professional academic discipline, and yet refusing to go quietly, a reminder of a 'powerful anti-professional strain... that has militated against the institutionalization of critical activity as an academic discipline'.[23] The question posed by Majumdar, and one whose history he traces through the different careers of two writers, Nirad C. Chaudhuri and Arvind Krishna Mehrotra, is whether the kinds of ambivalence that allowed literary intellectuals to be both inside and outside the academy, either fleeing the classroom or finding subtle ways around it, can persist in the twenty-first century when universities across all their disciplines are engaged in a relentless process of professionalisation, and one that makes specialism – rather than an idiosyncratic eclecticism – the hallmark of success.

Haunted by the possibility that the interplay between the professional and the amateur may come to an end in the passing of the kind of attentive reading that has been its essential basis, Majumdar, like MacDonald and Attridge, holds to at least the possibility that literary study in universities will prosper, more especially in those

316

Indian universities where English literature was first studied as an academic discipline.

In these essays, as elsewhere in the collection, we can catch glimpses of what this study might look like in the future. Rosinka Chaudhuri provides a history of a literary modernity that came into being in Bengal at the same time as a similar invention was taking shape in France. There was the same encounter with problems of language and classical form as in France, but, in the situation of Bengal, it was 'contaminated... by the context of colonialism'.[24] As she acknowledges, this is a liberating thought precisely because it frees us from the idea of modernism as an exclusive property of the West. It also opens up the possibility of a more discrete and discriminating understanding of the nature of modern literature, one that will find its sources in Calcutta and Beijing as much as in Paris, London, or New York. Modernity is at once dislocated from its traditional settings and relocated in new ones. This, rather than the weary formula of questioning the canon, opens up possibilities for a new understanding of the relations between a cultural milieu and literary originality.

Swapan Chakravorty's essay shows how these possibilities might be realised in his commentary upon three instances of literary activism in twentieth-century Bengal. Each of these instances – the *swadesi* movement, the Hungry Generation poets, and the Naxalite movement – illuminate the intricate relationships between literary and other kinds of activism. Chakravorty's analysis shows how a literary activism can, in certain circumstances, act as a surrogate for a political task that politics itself cannot perform. He cites the example of the appeal amongst some adherents of the *swadesi* movement to the idea of traditional and time-honoured narratives: the 'stories of Rama, Krishna, and the Purānas' would provide a common bond amongst the linguistically and culturally heterogeneous people 'of the Punjab, Rajputana, Madras, and Mumbai'.[25] But, while alerting us to the important question of what literary activism might be a surrogate for, Chakravorty also reflects on the way that the 'activism' of a literary text is never simply punctual, defined by a historical moment, task, or programmatic intention. Texts outlive the contexts of their initial making and consumption. His essay reminds us that literature can be 'most active when it outstrips its activist intent'.

Laetitia Zecchini's essay on translating the work of Arun Kolatkar provides another example of how we need news maps for the location of literary originality. Kolatkar, a visual artist as well as an experimental poet, wrote in a local argot of Marathi and Hindi as well as in English. His work refused the imperatives of nation-building in postcolonial India. Instead he created a distinctively modern literature that needed to be in Bombay in order for its character to emerge. It provided the context for his fusion of an intensely local speech with a form and idiom drawn from elsewhere; in his case, the work of his contemporaries and immediate forbears in the United States. All this was done in a spirit of resolute indifference to the literary marketplace and to the trappings of reputation.

If this awakening to a history of the different locations of modernism is one possibility for the future study of literature, another comes in a quotation, cited by Amit Chaudhuri, from Arvind Krishna Mehrotra: 'Between Nabokov's English and Russian, between Borges's Spanish and English, between Ramanujan's English and Tamil-Kannada, between the pan-Indian Sanskritic tradition and folk material, and between the Bharhut Stupa and the Gond carvings "many cycles of give and take are set in motion"'.

In his commentary on this passage, Chaudhuri notes how it invites us to think of the 'cycles of give and take' in at least two ways: as between, say, Nabokov's English and Russian, but also between that and Ramunajan's English and Tamil-Kannada, or the 'Bharut Stupa and the Gond carvings'. These openings on to a way of thinking about literature and culture are as helpful for what they bypass as for what they recommend. Distinctions between high and low culture and between imperial and subordinate cultures are put in abeyance in the name of another kind of reading: one that will move reciprocally rather than progressively between the texts it engages, so not leaving Nabokov's Russian texts and moving on to his work in English, but discovering the one in the other, moving back and forth between them. In avoiding logics of subordination and of historical sublation, the 'cycles of give and take' propose a new rhythm of attention, one that accepts that writing occurs between languages rather than simply within them, one that discovers the resonance of one text within another by way of a certain kind of comparative daring and engagement. One value of these may lie in their apparent unpredictability. Textual energy need not and does not simply follow the lines that are laid down for it by nation or empire.

These different ideas about the current state and the future possibilities of criticism, when aligned with one another, present a sketch – and that is all it is at the moment – of what the study of literature might look like in the coming decades. This sketch will obviously need to be elaborated, but some of its main lines are clear: a criticism that thinks with and about literature rather than holding it at a suspicious distance; and an openness, therefore, to the idea of the critic as lover or artist rather than sceptical judge; an engagement with the different places in which a modern literature has emerged that moves beyond the familiar sites of London, Paris, and New York; and an historical and comparative understanding that is open to the 'cycles of give and take' described by Arvind Krishna Mehrotra. This assumes – as Wilde did in 'The Critic as Artist' – that criticism is an inherently cosmopolitan activity and that it assumes a bilingual, if not polyglot, writer and reader. While this latter assumption is taken for granted in the Indian context, it becomes much more problematic when we move to the United Kingdom, where a resolute attachment to a single language runs deep.[26]

3.

The idea of a literature written between languages, crossing different cultural boundaries and genres while it resists the imperatives of the market, illuminates another aspect of literary activism: the role of the translator. In this volume Laetitia Zecchini and Jamie McKendrick provide case studies of the translator as literary activist, while Derek Attridge shows how closely aligned the idea of the critic as lover is to the work of the translator. All of them unsettle assumptions about what is marginal and what is central. They remind us that the mental maps of literature that we carry around in our heads are often highly selective. Without the work of the translator we might not know of, let alone be able to read, the work of contemporary novelists writing in Afrikaans. As with Laetitia Zecchini's translations of Kolatkar's poetry into French or Jamie McKendrick's translations of Italian poetry into English, literary translation can open up a new horizon for our understanding both of where contemporary literature is being written and what it means to be 'contemporary'. A geographical and a conceptual disturbance go hand in hand. The 'contemporary' is no longer defined as simply what is being published now in the world of major international publishers, one in which the novelist Michel Houellebecq is marketed in translation as 'France's leading literary export'. Translation can and certainly does follow in the wake of this kind of promotion, but it can also bring to our attention work that is less easily branded.

The further connections of literary translation to ideas about literary activism can only be briefly noted here. The work of attentive reading that is a precursor to any serious translation provides one instance of the kind of criticism envisaged by Blanchot, The text in translation can be an example of that 'movement whereby a work... experiences its own possibility'. But whether it is or not will depend upon the translator's understanding of the activity of translation itself. On the one hand there is the import/export model, a process of finding word-for-word equivalents between the first language of a text and its second, and then revising the result in ways that accommodate the translated work to the linguistic traditions and generic conventions of the second language.

But, as John Berger has recently argued, translation is not, or, rather, should not be a two-way process. It involves, if the translation is to have value, a third element as well: a return to what Berger calls the 'pre- verbal'. Language is not, according to this view, simply one articulate surface that can be recoded in another to which it can be made equivalent. Translation can occur within a very different configuration. Call it, for the sake of brevity, the relation between the articulate to the inarticulate, or, following Wittgenstein, the indissoluble relation between a language and a 'form of life'. To translate this dimension of language is to go from the words of the original text to what Berger describes as 'the vision or experience that prompted them' and then move that over into another language.

The engaged translation described by Berger bears an uncanny resemblance to Arvind Krishna Mehrotra's movement of 'give and take' between one work and another, one author and another, one culture and another. Translation is a form of migration, a movement back and forth between languages. One language has to be persuaded to give space to an experience witnessed in another. What this calls for is a testing and adjustment, an acknowledgement of the living body of language, which is usually ignored when translation is imagined as a process of recoding.

The example of translation becomes for Berger an epitome of the relation of the writer to language in general. The writer at work proposes words to a language that has its own distinctive power and being:

> After I've written a few lines I let the words slip back into the creature of their language. And there, they are instantly recognized and greeted by a host of other words with whom they have an affinity of meaning, or of opposition, or metaphor or alliteration or rhythm. I listen to their confabulation. Together they are contesting the use to which I put the words I chose. They are questioning the roles I allotted them. So I modify the lines, change a word or two, and submit them again. Another confabulation begins. And it goes on like this until there is a low murmur of provisional consent. Then I proceed to the next paragraph, another confabulation begins...[27]

'Confabulation', a mixing up that is also a separating out, a questioning followed by a 'provisional consent': Berger's account of how writing proceeds includes as its necessary ground an attention to language that is prior to any notion of craft or technique. In this respect, at least, it shares something of the spirit of the essays collected in this volume which all invite us, in their different ways, to take a step back or to one side and consider what our relation is to the languages of markets and media, of literary criticism and translation, and of literature itself.

While the essays in this volume offer different accounts of the literary activist as writer, critic, translator, publisher, or cultural gadfly, it also raises some questions for further exploration and enquiry. One is whether the form of criticism proposed in various essays in this volume will find a place in universities, bearing in mind that this question will be decided as much by what happens to the study of literature in Indian universities as in those in Europe and the United States. If that were to be the case – if, that is, literature remains a significant subject of study in higher education – then two other questions emerge. One is what kind of criticism it might be and the other is what its relation be to 'creative writing', now an established presence in many literature departments in Britain and the United States?

It is too early to give definitive answers to either of these questions. But the context in which they might be asked has become clearer. Within many of the essays in this volume, there is a call for or a defence of an affirmative criticism, one that concerns itself with the value of literary experience. But this cannot happen under the guise of a nostalgic return. Literary works need to be freed from the spell cast upon them by entrenched habits of reading within the academy. What this might look like is at least anticipated in the work of writers like Wilde, Blanchot, and Benjamin. The question of creative writing has a slightly different bearing. It is the subject in universities where the pressures of the contemporary literary marketplace are strongly felt, whether in the links that grow between creative writing programmes and publishing houses, editors and agents, or in a pedagogy that takes what will be acceptable to publishers as a guiding maxim. But then there is another possibility, one that creates a constitutive tension within the subject that needs to be more fully understood. Drawn to the marketplace on the one hand, creative writing also harbours the impulse to encourage kinds of writing that would find little or no place with mainstream publishers. It maintains the promise of an alternative or experimental literature that has been a recurrent motif within the idea of literary modernity itself.

One purpose of literary activism might be to insist that these questions are raised in ways that counteract the dull excitements of the literary marketplace and the heavily managed intellectual life of the neo-liberal university. But it does this within the context of another question. In his essay Swapan Chakravorty cites Rabrindranath Tagore's Presidential Address to the 1923 meeting of the Bengal Literary Conference. Tagore describes three 'paths' for literature: *karma*, or work, the organisation of meetings, publishing, and editing; *mana*, or the historical and critical study of literature; and *shrishti*, the work of creation. Tagore did all these three things, while, as Chakravorty makes clear, sometimes pretending to himself and others, that he only did the third. In doing so, he raised an important question about the extent to which the three paths correspond to a division of labour in the literary sphere between publishers and organisers, scholars and critics, and novelists, poets, and dramatists. We might accept this division of labour as the way things are and valuably so. Or we might, as many of the essays in this collection do, put this division in question in the quest for a kind of writing and reading that cannot be contained within its boundaries.

324

1.   Pascale Casanova, *The World Republic of Letters*, translated by M.B. Debevoise (Cambridge, Mass: Harvard University Press), p. 170.

2.   See John Carey, *William Golding: The Man Who Wrote Lord of the Flies* (London: Faber and Faber Limited, 2009).

3.   David Lodge, *The Novelist at the Crossroads: And Other Essays on Fiction and Criticism* (London: Routledge and Kegan Paul, 1971), pp. 18-19.

4.   David Lodge, 'The Novelist Today: Still at the Crossroads?' in *The Practice of Writing* (London: Vintage Books, 2011), p. 11.

5.   Lodge, 'The Novelist Today', p. 16.

6.   Ezra Pound's poems 'Mr Nixon' and 'EP Ode Pour L'Election de Son Sepulcre' are two examples of this modernist assumption. For another work concerned with this question, see Henry James, 'The Lesson of the Master' in *The Figure in the Carpet and Other Stories*, ed. Frank Kermode (London: Penguin Books), pp. 113-189.

7.   Lewis Carroll, *Through the Looking Glass* (London: HarperCollins, 2010, first published 1871), p. 80.

8.   Alexander Pope, The Dunciad, Book III, ll. 189-90, in *The Poems of Alexander Pope*, ed. John Butt (London:Methuen 1965), p. 414.

9.   Q.D. Leavis, *Fiction and the Reading Public* (London: Chatto and Windus, 1932), pp. 222-223.

10.   Casanova, *The World Republic of Letters*, pp. 171-172.

11.   For one account of the connection between formal innovation and a new kind of literary commerce in the eighteenth century, see Ian Watt, *The Rise of the Novel* (London: Pimlico 2000, first published 1957), pp. 35-60.

12.   Roberto Calasso, *Literature and the Gods*, trans. Tim Parks (London: Vintage Books, 2001), pp. 21-23.

13.   Louis Aragon, *Le Paysan de Paris* (Paris: Gallimard, 1926), p. 153.

14.   Doris Lessing, 'For the Attention of John Boothe',

typewritten letter available at The British Archive for Contemporary Writing, UEA.

15. Calasso, *Literature and the Gods*, p. 192.

16. See Derek Attridge, 'The Critic as Lover: Literary Activism and the Academy', pp. 45-70 of this volume.

17. See Peter D. McDonald, 'What about Criticism? Blanchot's Giant-Windmill', pp. 91-107 of this volume.

18. For a translation of Blanchot's essay, see 'The Task of Criticism Today', *Oxford Literary Review*, Vol. 22, issue 1, pp. 19-24.

19. Oscar Wilde, 'The Critic as Artist', *The Soul of Man Under Socialism and Selected Critical Prose*, ed. L. Dowling (London: Penguin Books, 2001), p. 237.

20. Howard Caygill, *Walter Benjamin: The Colour of Experience* (Abingdon: Routledge, 1998), p. 36; Walter Benjamin, 'Two Poems by Friederich Holderlin', *Selected Writings, Volume 1, 1913-26*, eds M. Bullock and M.W. Jennings (Cambridge and London: Harvard University Press, 1996), p. 18.

21. Wilde, 'The Critic as Artist', pp. 213, 230, 231, 253.

22. Matthew Arnold, 'The Function of Criticism', *Essays in Criticism* (London: Everyman Library 1964), p. 20, p. 11.

23. See Saikat Majumdar, 'The Amatory Activist', pp. 109-146 of this volume.

24. See Rosinka Chaudhuri, 'The Practice of Literature: The Calcutta Context as a Guide to Literary Activism', pp. 173-196 of this volume.

25. See Swapan Chakravorty, 'Literary Surrogacy and Literary Activism: Instances from Bengal', pp. 265-294 of this volume.

26. For a more detailed discussion of questions of translation, see Clive Scott, *Translating the Perception of the Text* (London: Legenda, 2012).

27. John Berger, 'Writing is an off-shoot of something else', *The Guardian*, 12 December 2014.

Appendix I
An Exchange of Emails

Following the event on 'literary activism' on 15 October 2015 at St. Hugh's College, Oxford, some of the writers who'd spoken that day – Tim Parks, Kirsty Gunn, Peter D. McDonald, and Amit Chaudhuri – found themselves exchanging emails on questions that had arisen during the talks and panel discussions. A selection from the exchange, largely unedited and almost entirely in its original form, is included below. The point of including this conversation is not to showcase its intrinsic merits, or the merits of the symposium from which it arose. It's to allow this volume to include the unrehearsed moment; to not only be a platform for the finished performance, but to make space for the spontaneous – less polished – conversations that occur in the green room. Another reason of interest might be that it's an exchange between writers and an academic – the two don't generally mix.

A couple of references might need a further note. *The Novel: A Survival Skill* is a critical work by Tim Parks, published by Oxford University Press in 2015, a few months before the event at St. Hugh's. 'The Origins of Dislike' is the name of a lecture by Amit Chaudhuri, as yet unpublished.

From: Tim Parks
Sent: 18 October 2015
To: Amit Chaudhuri

Thanks Amit. It was a big surprise to me. I'd kind of given up hoping that a conference could be not only interesting but important for me. It was important to be reminded of the need to be able to fail. Three or four times I tried to write a blog about this, but gave up because it seemed out of left field. But I'll go back there now.

...

From: Tim Parks
Sent: 19 October 2015
To: Amit Chaudhuri

In a world where we wish to pretend that everything is the
same when everything has changed, surely the historical
novel has a special place, as an anchor of conservatism.

...

From: Amit Chaudhuri
Sent: 19 October 2015
To: Tim Parks

Dear Tim,

That's a great insight in the context of our recent
discussions. 'An anchor of conservatism' is a succinct
and acute way of describing what's going on now with
fictional representations of history.
        As you might know, the historical has a particular
prestige in the realm of Anglophone Indian fiction. It's
something one has had to deal with.

...

From: Tim Parks
Sent: 21 October 2015
To: Amit Chaudhuri

Well, Amit,

I just read through your Dislike piece. Obviously, it's interesting to me in all kinds of ways, the culture clash, the choice of pet hates and obscure teachers, etc.

I wonder about 'temperament', which I think is a little more accessible to analysis than you allow here. I would like to look at each writer's temperament along the lines I use in *The Novel: A Survival Skill*, the semantic polarities galvanizing their choices.

But this only brings us to the really curious things. I have always been deeply suspicious of Renaissance art, something I tried to persuade people of when I curated the show Money, Beauty, and Boticelli in Florence, suggesting how perverse the pact between art, religion and money was in that period that kicked off the bourgeois temperament – I understand bourgeois as the person who believes that one is never obliged to choose between being good and being rich.

And I have always LOATHED historical novels for their inherent falseness and illusion of control... And all this leads me to wonder if we two aren't somehow both tied into the whole semantic of good and evil in a way that obliges us constantly to expose people who are showing off their goodness or integrity, while in fact we feel that they are up to no good and complacent with it.

...

From: Tim Parks
Sent: 21 October 2015
To: Amit Chaudhuri

And perhaps this is why we both like Lawrence so much, so much, in fact, at least in my case, that like isn't the right word.

...

From: Amit Chaudhuri
Sent: 23 October 2015
To: Tim Parks

...I found a book of essays by you in my office in UEA, unopened. It had been sent to me, but, of course, I'm in Calcutta most of the time. I opened and read a piece in about the 'story'. My God! I have been attacking 'storytelling' kitsch for ages. In 2009, I said 'Fuck storytelling' at an international convention in Delhi, and offended a British Asian literary journalist – not because I'd used an expletive, but because I'd desecrated a sacred principle of human empowerment and community.

...

From: Tim Parks
Sent: 24 October 2015
To: Amit Chaudhuri

Yep, people hate it. I'm not against stories, but against the piety that they are somehow necessary. They are another part of experience. Out there. This silliness that the world needs stories is clearly self-serving and makes no sense at all.

I've been thinking about your formulation that the language of literary appreciation has been appropriated for marketing purposes. I would go further, the idea of literature is a essentially promotional.

The nearest I got to this in that book was, 'The idea of greatness is a marketing tool. See Franzen.'

We have to forget the word literature. I think this was my problem with your 'literary activism'. When I see the word literary, I am immediately suspicious.

...

From: Tim Parks
Sent: 28 October 2015
To: Amit Chaudhuri

I've been thinking of your dislikes in art and your hostility
to stories. Could it be that what unites them is that
Western habit of manufacturing pathos, that complacent
appreciation of our own compassion in the face of
suffering, and the faint suggestion that pain is redeemed
in beauty.
          Just a thought

...

From: Kirsty Gunn
Sent: 7 November 2015
To: Tim Parks; Peter McDonald

Dear Tim.
          Thank you so much for sending me your *The Novel:
A Survival Skill*. I am thoroughly enjoying the premise of
the entire project and am interested deeply in the ideas
you are following...
          For a long time now, I have been talking about
what I call 'psychic imperative' in the work of major
novelists (for you are right, this idea of the individual
having something at stake pertains to the relationship of
writer to novel in a way it doesn't to other art forms, so it
seems to me... or rather, other art forms require different
kinds of negotiations that are abstracted through those
other forms in ways literary work can't be...) – psychic
imperative being a kind of engine to the novel – and
identifying it as present in those works of literature I
admire. So – yes! I am with you in the conversation of

your book and when I am finished – soon – will write again.

   Thank you again for sending it. I am cc-ing in Peter by way of continuing literary-activism thoughts – and wish I had Amit on this system too, but alas he is on my other email address system that I'll forward this note from... For it appears that these ideas may well build on the St. Hugh's discussions pertaining to the ideal of a readership that may yield to individual rather than economic forces, along with the sort of start-from-scratch critical thinking Peter was proposing in his talk, and with his ideas of a literature and criticism that may speak back to itself as though containing a dialectic debate.

   All interesting. How good it is that we've all met!
   Kirsty

...

From: Tim Parks
Sent: 9 November 2015
To: Kirsty Gunn; Peter McDonald

Dear Kirsty,
   Thanks so much for this. The book is yet to be reviewed, so it's a relief to hear it makes sense to another writer.
   Psychic imperative makes sense, yes. I suppose what one wrestles with is the different nature of that imperative for different writers. I'm presently reading Attwell's new book on Coetzee and it's most intriguing how elusively he (Coetzee) positions himself in all relationships.
   I'm sure there is an element of this in other art forms. But with novels the narrative itself reflects the story of the behaviour behind the writing.

I wonder if we can't extend 'literary activism' to a reflection on the ways we use literature, partly to position ourselves in relation to other writers and readers. To feel who we are. While the big publishers just want the crowd in agreement...

Again thanks for writing. Would be great to get together in London sometime. I'm talking about a book of essays on Italian literature at the Italian Cultural institute this Thursday evening, but alas all was organized way back and I'm there and gone in day...

All best, Tim

...

From: Peter McDonald
Sent: 11 November 2015
To: Tim Parks; Kirsty Gunn

Dear Tim and Kirsty,

I've been meaning to thank you for the book as well, Tim, which I have now started reading. So much to say, I have no idea where to start. A proper response would really mean another book, but, for what it is worth, here are three brief points, which amount to nothing more than immediate and personal reaction to the introduction and the sections on Joyce and Coetzee.

1. I am in complete agreement with you about the grim state of academic criticism. In fact, I have spent my career trying to keep out of that world. Not easy when you collect a salary from a literature department. I don't really know what it is that I do, but it is not literary criticism pure and simple.

2. In broad methodological terms, I am 'instinctively' (?) wary of positing some or other clearly identifiable inner drive or 'psychic imperative' to any writer, particularly as part of a move to explain or

335

interpret her or his work. I have no doubt that these
forces exist, but I suspect there are many of them, that
they are seldom coherent or stable, and that they are
largely opaque to the writers themselves. This doesn't
come from any lofty theoretical position. A few sentences
form a letter Joyce wrote to his brother in 1907 have
always haunted me, though there are, of course, many
other such statements you could cite: 'I have certain ideas
I would like to give form to: not as a doctrine but as the
continuation of the expression of myself which I now
see I began in *Chamber Music*. These ideas or instincts
or intuitions or impulses may be purely personal. I have
no wish to codify myself as anarchist or socialist or
reactionary.' I have always been struck by his refusal to
define his guiding energies as either personal or political,
private or public, or even to settle on a single term for
them.

      3.   Having said this, I find your argument and
way of proceeding very engaging, even though I don't
feel I could, in good faith, make it myself. It is the kind
of argument you can and should make as a writer. As
an academic, admittedly now of the old, almost wholly
marginal civil-service school, I have always believed it
is my job to make a case for the public value literature.
In saying this, I don't mean to deny that it has a private
value to many people, in fact, many private values. I
am simply identifying the focal point of my own work,
which is now looking increasingly anachronistic at a
time when the idea of the public university is in ruins.
(We of course also need to bear in mind that for the past
forty years or so academic literary criticism has been
deeply suspicious of literature's public value, and, in
some cases, hell bent on destroying it, but that is another
story.) This sounds like a fully worked out professional
position—it is partially worked out!—but it really goes
back to my first responses to reading Coetzee when I was

19, a biographical experience, if you like, that has kept me going thus far.

As I said, there is too much to say, but I hope this at least makes some sort of start. I now need to finish the book!

All best,
Peter

...

From: Tim Parks
Sent: 11 November 2015
To: Kirsty Gunn; Peter McDonald

Thanks for this Peter. I reply at once because at a loose end this morning, trying and failing to work. And because I'm over the moon that the book has found readers like yourselves.

I understand all your reservations. I even share them. Just two remarks. In the chapters on Hardy and Dickens, I try to show how this approach can fit in with 'academic standards'. The Hardy chapter is the most effective I think. An earlier version was published as an academic paper with the Hardy Journal. I mean, a conflict is identified, which is undeniable, by considering the plots, and the lexical fields, a conflict that clearly evolves and is clearly in a curious relation to the life. I mean, I think in those chapters I take it beyond any sense of what my personal reaction might be, though at the end I admit how conflicted I am in response to Hardy and suggest that other people are bound to respond to such a fierce confusion/dilemma in different ways.

As for public value. I am with you. The problem is that this value is so often interpreted as some sort of automatically uplifting, always politically and morally positive force. While I suspect that the public value has more to do with the engagement we are drawn towards with worlds quite different from our own. At some point in the book I did get to this. Can't remember where. For example, our different responses to the Hardy conundrum would be the value.

About Coetzee, I'm sure you're right that he means the papers as some kind of object lesson of the writerly life. And I wanted to ask you whether you didn't find that – it sounds weird to use the word for Coetzee – naive, even endearing. As if the old idea of the man of letters and the world it presupposes hadn't been blown away this last fifty years. I have a strong aversion towards the idea of preparing my papers for someone else's examination, living in function of posterity's take on me. But I suppose that's not something I need worry about anyway.

Still, I'm thoroughly enjoying it, and Attwell himself.

...

From: Kirsty Gunn
Sent: 11 November 2015
To: Tim Parks; Peter McDonald

So much to respond to here, Peter, but for now just let me make it clear: the very reason I use that term of mine 'psychic imperative' is because it is not something that can [be] codified or understood in exactly those ways you talk about in your Joyce quote. It s an engine, a driving force that we need not associate with some biographical detail or other... And the psychic space is a public one of course – Jung's collective unconsciousness couldn't be more shared! More to come – but I have 30 essays to mark!

...

338

From: Tim Parks
Sent: 11 November 2015
To: Amit Chaudhuri
Hi Amit,

Largely thanks to the conference I finally got round to
writing this piece on one's constant sense of scandal
about the books other people like. It might amuse.
      http://www.nybooks.com/blogs/nyrblog/2015/
nov/10/how-could-you-like-that-book/

...

From: Amit Chaudhuri
Sent: 17 November 2015
To: Tim Parks

Dear Tim,
I read this with much pleasure during my short sojourn
back in the UK. I'm back in Calcutta now. I think the
long quote from Ferrante is telling, as is your reading of
it. The passage is similar to ones I encountered in, and
was mystified by, in Days of Abandonment. Actually, it's
not Ferrante who's mystifying; it's the response to her...
      You end rather generously by saying that other
people's tastes at least add up to a kind of diversity. I like
this as an ironical concession on your part, though it's
precisely diversity that's lacking in global literature and
in these responses. Also, do you think that responses to
Coetzee and Sebald – who are, in many ways, interesting
writers – themselves lack diversity?
      By the way, do you know that NYRB Classics is
republishing several novels by Henry Green in 2016/17?
      Hope all's well.
      As ever,
      Amit

...

From: Tim Parks
Sent: 17 November 2015
To: Amit Chaudhuri

Thanks Amit. It's always good when you know that a piece has been read by someone who kind of knows what I'm talking about. Ferrante is a complete mystery to me. My only explanation is that deep down even literary folk want to read cheap melodrama, but like to feel that it is literature. Foreign writers are imagined as literary, I suppose...

In any event we should argue with our writers more. The pleasure is in the engagement, not in falling thrall to a plot.

Yep, I make concessions in these pieces because otherwise I'm just written off as a snob. Plenty of angry letters about the Ferrante comments, though no one seems able to excuse the melon...

Didn't know about the NYRB, no. Always hard to imagine Americans reading Green.

...

From: Kirsty Gunn
Sent: 23 November 2015
To: Tim Parks; Peter McDonald; Amit
Chaudhuri

Dear Tim,

I finished your 'survival guide' a while ago now and have been wanting to write – but have been so swamped with teaching and meetings, this is the first moment I've had to get on this email, even... When I am in Dundee, I never get the chance to turn this on, and all is rather old fashioned and lovely in that all is face-to-face and telephone calls...

Anyhow, back in London now so the email is turned on. How did your talk go here? I would like to hear about that.

And your book: yes, it's a stirring and necessary work, and I thoroughly enjoyed the whole set-up and premise: a timely reminder of the relationship of the author to his or her creative piece. 'A book is an event in the life of the author' indeed. You must have give a copy to John Carey, I am sure? As this idea is so utterly up his street... He and I, when I was his student, would have rousing debates around the subject – and we still do! For, as I suggested to you in an earlier email, I am not in full agreement with you about the finite expression of such a relationship.

Yes, there must be links and traces and hopes embedded in the work that line directly back to the author, of course... How could there not be, and it is always interesting that it is so, and might, for some more than others, enrich a reading, to bear such lines in mind...

However, to my mind, such an evaluation does not also take account of the mysteries of making art – a mystery that need not be akin to anything 'mysterious' like inspiration or automatism or dream state (though such approaches, old Jungian disciple that I am, are interesting to me, it is true) – but a mystery in the sense that enquiry is mysterious: the 'out there' for the scientist or mathematician the same as for the artist, in this way. he work as site of investigation, not confirmation. This approach would seek to uncouple the author from the output, to read the fiction as a kind of adventure, to make something (reader and writer both) that – while based on certain known conditions or autobiography, perhaps – nevertheless wants to explore and extend and imagine

341

way beyond those other versions, already established, of self.

So, in the same way, the reader may read into a text without needing to feel he or she has to 'gel' with it, to use your word, feel attachment to it the way one might feel attachment to an individual. For my part, I don't feel this personal connection is necessary to my evaluation of a fiction... In fact, the word 'like' may not be even part of it. I read and write to experience an idea of other that is not linked to psychological or social investigation – but, rather, is an 'other' that comes out of, emerges from, the text itself; an other that is created from the arrangement of words, and/or lyrical and other features that together may create a reading that has little to do with this character or that and my feelings about them and their circumstances.

In the same way, the linear reading – the idea of a story that builds, or concludes, or fades away... all of these things... The way we incline to talk about lives, histories, circumstances... I would be seeking to undo that notion also, and to think, rather, of fiction as a kind of plane – with key scenes and moments that flare up, that may change and influence me – containing moments, not complete narrative trajectories, that I remember and hold. This is why Lawrence gets special mention from you, I know... Everything about his long fiction resists the traditional idea of novel – which is why I love him too... So I am interested in fiction for it's providing a sort of psychic and emotional temperature, an atmosphere, a new kind of place in which, for a while, I may live.

None of which is to say I am not interested in character and circumstance, either – how could one not be? And of course I can understand why individuals (especially men, and especially people of our age) who are sensitive and clever, like you and Peter and so many others, adore Coetzee... In Peter's reading of the public

342

function of literature, someone like that fits the bill entirely. For my part, though, there aren't many writers who enlist me in their projects to that end. I have read and re-read *War and Peace* and will continue to do so for the rest of my life – for the reason that the characters contained there engage me more and more with every visit, and more and more I understand and love them. But it seems to me that they are rare in novels in the sense that they are people, not constructs. They're not 'characters' at all actually... And we love people, they are interesting and strange and familiar all at once. They are us.

It's just that not many writers, to my mind, really write about character in the end. (For my part, I would never dare to try. It seems to me to be a near impossible thing to pull off.) They write about ideas – with the characters attached. So Tess, with her mouth, red inside like a snake, is interesting to me for not being like a person that I might know at all, but as a set of attributes, as you suggest... So the challenge for me, in that book, say, and others by Hardy and Dickens and so on, is whether the sentences have enough jump and life and 'self' about them, to be more than simply freight trains carrying ideas of character and plot. For I never have the expectation, for the most part, that there is going to be enough of the latter on board... Do I need to go back and re-read these stories about this character and that, entrapped in this or another particular plot – even with your terrific guide of Valeria Ugazio illumining my reading? Probably not. Whereas I can take any amount of Andrei coming back into his father's house on a snowy night to discover the fate of his wife and to feel his father's arms around him...

With that kind of stuff going on, the sentences can go hang! For the most part, though, for me, the sentences are the mysterious content, the other, the all... Fiction,

343

this kind of novel, not a way to talk 'about' a thing, but the thing itself.

But in the end, all our views and readings are a gorgoeus muddle, aren't they, as you say?

As this email certainly is – and for sure I am certainly framing my own thoughts within a belief system that suits my own writing and hopes for fiction as much as your book serves yours. It's good of you to remind us of that, and of the ways media and other debates force binaries whereas muddles are so much more interesting for those of us who don't want to be journalists or in debating teams.

So your book gave me nothing but pleasure – and I thank you for it. If it's just out, the reviews will be coming in and I'll be looking out for the responses...

Back to my Dundee emails now – and alas – all questions about essays that I've already answered but that they are worried about. When did students become so... worried? That they were doing the right thing? That were following 'correct procedure' as one of them asked last week...?

Crikey. Bring on the novels!

Kirsty

...

From: Tim Parks
Sent: 24 November 2015
To: Kirsty Gunn; Peter McDonald; Amit Chaudhuri

Dear Kirsty,

Many thanks for this. I've read it a couple of times and really agree with most of what you say. I mean, I don't have any difficulty taking your points. Obviously in my book I'm underlying the continuity between writer

344

and work, but there are oceans unexplained, nor is there
any need to know anything about an author to establish
a relation with the work and the mood of the work.
Lawrence's 'Snake' offers us an encounter that is all about
fear and overcoming fear. Our reading of it will have to
do, in part, with who we are, our relation to fear, but also
our sensibility to a certain kind of poetry. There's no
need for character or plot here. I suppose what Ugazio's
framework does is offer some useful questions one can
ask so as to help identify the atmosphere we are moving
in. I just foolishly accepted to review Franzen's new book
for an Italian paper. I dislike it intensely. I realise that
every dialogue is a competition, a battle, and the whole
book is about winning and losing. But totally different
from Muriel Spark, who is also, in her way, all about
competition. This is indeed mysterious.

Good luck with your students. Sometimes I feel
exhausted with mine. It's never ending.

Have a great day and again thanks.

Tim

...

From:	Amit Chaudhuri
Sent:	24 November 2015
To:	Tim Parks; Kirsty Gunn; Peter McDonald

Dear Kirsty, Tim and Peter,

It's great to read this. Ever since 16 October,
there's been a fascinating exchange of thoughts among
a small group of people, and I feel privileged to be able
to read it and sometimes contribute to it. It makes me
almost think it should be a separate chapter or appendix
in a book. Appendices – and this conversation is an

appendix to the symposiums – can be as interesting as the
main body itself, and sometimes more. I feel there's much
of real interest here.

    Yours,
    Amit

...

From: Kirsty Gunn
Sent: 27 November 2015
To: Amit Chaudhuri;Tim Parks; Peter
McDonald

I love the idea of the appendices of conversation... It
reflects your use of the word 'desultory' again, Amit...
Liminal, without direct political purpose, porous and
shape shifting...

Appendix II
How Could You Like That Book?
TIM PARKS

I rarely spend much time wondering why others do not enjoy the books I like. Henry Green, an old favourite, almost a fetish, is never an easy read and never offers a plot that is immediate or direct. 'There's not much straight shootin,' he admitted, in the one interview he gave. Elsa Morante is so lush and fantastical, so extravagantly rhetorical, she must seem way over the top to some. Thomas Bernhard offers one nightmare after another in cascades of challenging rhetoric; it's natural to suspect he's overdoing it. Christina Stead is so wayward, so gloriously tangled and disorganised, it's inevitable that some readers will grow weary. And so on.

Perhaps it's easy for me to understand why so many are not on board with these writers because I occasionally feel the same way myself. In fact it may be that the most seductive novelists are also the ones most willing to risk irritating you. Faulkner comes to mind, so often on the edge between brilliant and garrulous. Italy's Carlo Emilio Gadda was another. Muriel Spark. Sometimes even Kafka. Resistance to these writers is never a surprise to me.

On the other hand, I do spend endless hours mulling over the mystery of what others like. Again and again the question arises: How *can* they?

I am not talking about genre fiction, where the pleasures are obvious enough. Reviewing duties over the last few years have had me reading Stieg Larsson, E.L. James, and a score of Georges Simenon's *Maigrets*. Once you accept the premise that you are reading for entertainment, their plots and brightly-drawn dramatis personae quickly pull you in. However 'adult' the material, one is reminded of the way one read as a child: to know what happens. You turn the pages quickly, even voraciously, and when something galls – the ugly exploitation of sexual violence in Larsson, the cartoon silliness of James, the monotonous presentation of

Maigret as the dour, long-suffering winner – you simply skip and hurry on, because the story has you on its hook. You can see why people love these books, and above all love reading lots of them. They encourage addiction, the repetition of a comforting process: identification, anxiety/ suspense, reassurance. Supposedly realistic, they actually take us far away from our own world and generally leave us feeling pleased that our lives are spared the sort of melodrama we love to read about.

But what are we to say of the likes of Haruki Murakami? Or Salman Rushdie? Or Jonathan Franzen? Or Jennifer Egan, or recent prize-winners like Andrés Neuman and Eleanor Catton, or, most monumentally, Karl Ove Knausgaard? They are all immensely successful writers. They are clearly very competent. Knausgaard is the great new thing, I am told. I pick up Knausgaard. I read a hundred pages or so and put it down. I cannot understand the attraction. No, that's not true, I do get a certain attraction, but cannot understand why one would commit to its extension over so many pages. It doesn't seem attractive *enough* for what it is asking of me.

Take Elena Ferrante. Again and again I pick up her novels and again and again I give up around page fifty. My impression is of something wearisomely concocted, determinedly melodramatic, forever playing on Neapolitan stereotype. Here, in *My Brilliant Friend*, the narrator is remembering a quarrel between neighbours:

> As their vindictiveness increased, the two women
> began to insult each other if they met on the street or
> the stairs: harsh, fierce sounds. It was then that they
> began to frighten me. One of the many terrible scenes
> of my childhood begins with the shouts of Melina and
> Lidia, with the insults they hurl from the windows
> and then on the stairs; it continues with my mother
> rushing to our door, opening it, and looking out,
> followed by us children; and ends with the image, for

350

me still unbearable, of the two neighbors rolling down
the stairs, entwined, and Melina's head hitting the
floor of the landing, a few inches from my shoes,
like a white melon that has slipped from your hand.

What can one say? Making no effort of the
imagination, Ferrante simply announces melodrama:
'Harsh, fierce sounds'; 'One of the many terrible scenes
of my childhood'; insults are 'hurled'. The memory is
'for me still unbearable' though in the following pages
the incident is entirely forgotten. Is 'entwined' really the
right word for two people locked in struggle on the stairs?
As in a B movie, a head hits the floor a few inches from
our hero's shoes. Then comes the half-hearted attempt to
transform cartoon reportage into literature: 'like a white
melon that has slipped from your hand.'

I can't recall dropping a melon myself, but if the
aim of a metaphor is to bring intensity and clarity to an
image, this one goes in quite a different direction. The
dull slap of the soft white melon hitting the ground and
rolling away from you would surely be a very different
thing from the hard crack of a skull and the sight of
a bloody face. I'm astonished that having tossed the
metaphor in, out of mechanical habit one presumes, the
author didn't pull it right out again. And even more I'm
astonished that other people are not irritated by this
lazy writing.

It's not only fiction that does this to me. I am told,
for example, that Stephen Grosz's book *The Examined
Life* – a psychoanalyst giving us his most interesting case
histories – is a work of genius and is selling like hotcakes.
I buy a copy, and halfway through I toss it away, literally,
at the wall, in intense irritation. How can people like
these stories, with their over-easy packaging of what are
no doubt extremely complex personal problems, their
evident and decidedly unexamined complacency about
the rightness of the analyst's intervention?

There. I live under the constant impression that other people, other readers, are allowing themselves to be hoodwinked. They are falling for charms they shouldn't fall for. Or imagining charms that aren't there. They should be making it a little harder for their authors. Reading Neuman's *The Traveler of the Century*, I appreciate that he is brilliant, that he effortlessly churns out page after page of complex prose, but I feel the whole thing is an ambition-driven exercise in literariness. Same with so many who flaunt their fancy prose. Even when I read an author I recognise as a very serious and accomplished artist – Alice Munro, Colm Tóibín – I begin to wonder how people can be so wholehearted in their enthusiasm. Both writers, it seems to me, equate fiction with the manufacture of a certain rather predictable pathos, an unspoken celebration of our capacity for compassion and the supposed redemption of suffering in the pleasure of fine prose and good storytelling. No doubt these things do have their worth; I acknowledge that; it is the growing impression that they are merely being rehearsed that is wearisome. Toni Morrison is another. The writer has learned how to concoct our sophisticated drug for us. How can readers feel at ease with that?

No sooner have I articulated my amazement, my sense of betrayal almost, than I begin to feel insecure. Is it really possible that so many people I respect have got it wrong? Close friends as well. Am I an inveterate elitist? A puritan? Or resentful of other people's success? Shouldn't I perhaps relax and enjoy my reading a little more rather than approaching books with constant suspicion?

On the other hand, there are those moments when a work overcomes my suspicion, and persuades me that what I'm reading really is something more than a carefully calculated literary operation. I remember my first encounters with W.G. Sebald, or J.M. Coetzee, or Natalia Ginzburg – and those moments give me great

352

pleasure and make me feel happy with how I read. Then
I'm glad
I didn't waste too much time with the white melons.

      Where to go with this uncertainty? Perhaps rather
than questioning other readers' credulity, or worrying
about my own presumption, what might really be worth
addressing here is the whole issue of incomprehension:
mutual and apparently insuperable incomprehension
between well-meaning and intelligent people, all brought
up in the same cultural tradition, more or less. It's
curious, for example, that the pious rhetoric gusting
around literature always promotes the writing and reading
habit as a powerful communication tool, an instrument
for breaking down barriers, promoting understanding –
and yet it is exactly over my reaction to books that I tend
to discover how completely out of synch with others I am.

      I have often argued not just over whether *Disgrace*
is a good novel, but over what it means. How can you
suppose (I grow heated) that Coetzee is too austere,
that he lacks a sense of humour? How can you imagine
that he is claiming a direct moral equivalence between a
professor sleeping with one of his students and a band of
young men raping a woman in her isolated farmhouse?
Yet people do suppose Coetzee has no humour and they
do imagine he means that equivalence. And perhaps he
does. Certainly I have no way of proving he doesn't.

      Could this be the function, then, or at least one
important function of fiction: to make us aware of our
differences? To have our contrasting positions emerge
in response to these highly complex cultural artifacts?
Not that superficial togetherness in celebration that
the publishing industry, the literary festivals, and the
interminable literary prizes are forever seeking to
generate, the happy conviction that we have found a
new literary hero and can all gloat together over his or
her achievement. But all the heated debate that actually

353

preceded the prize-giving; the shifting alliances as each book was discussed; the times you just couldn't believe that the fellow jurist who supported you over book A is now seriously proposing to ditch book B; and so on.

In this view, our reaction to literature becomes a repeated act of self-discovery. Our contrasting reactions to the books we read tell us who we are. We are our position in relation to each other as understood in the reaction to these books. Reading other peoples' takes on Primo Levi, or Murakami, or David Eggers, and comparing them to my own, I get some sense of who we all are and what we're up to. Sometimes this turns out to be far more interesting than reading the book itself.

If this is the case, then, the important thing would be, first, really to understand one's own reaction, to observe it with great care; and, second, to articulate it honestly, without any fudging for fear that others might disagree. Though even a fudge is a declaration of identity. And nothing could be more common among the community of book reviewers than fudging.

10 November 2015
From *The New York Review of Books Daily*

This piece was originally published online
by *The New York Review of Books Daily*
on 10 November 2015

Appendix III
A Novel Kind of Conformity
TIM PARKS

What happens when a multi-million dollar author gets things wrong? Not much. Take the case of Haruki Murakami and his recent novel *Colorless Tsukuru Tazaki and His Years of Pilgrimage*. The idea behind the story is fascinating: What do you do when your closest friends eject you from the group without the slightest explanation? But the narrative is dull throughout and muddied by a half-hearted injection of Murakami-style weirdness – people with six fingers and psychic powers – that eventually contributes nothing to the very simple explanation of what actually happened. The book received mixed to poor reviews from embarrassed admirers and vindictive critics. Nevertheless, millions of copies were quickly sold worldwide and Murakami's name remains on the list of likely Nobel winners.

How many times would Murakami have to get things wrong, badly wrong, before his fans and publishers stopped supporting him? Quite a few. Actually, no matter what Murakami writes, it's almost unimaginable that his sales would ever fall so low that he would be considered unprofitable. So the Japanese novelist finds himself in the envious position (for an artist) of being free to take risks without the danger of much loss of income, or even prestige.

This is not the case with less successful authors. Novelists seeking to make a living from their work will obviously be in trouble if a publisher is not confident enough in their success to offer a decent advance; and if, once published, a book does not earn out its advance, publishers will be more hesitant next time, whatever the quality of the work on offer. Authors in this situation will think twice before going out on some adventurous limb. They will tend to give publishers what they want. Or try to.

The difficulties of the writer who is not yet well established have been compounded in recent years by

357

the decision on the part of most large publishers to allow their sales staff a say in which novels get published and which don't. At a recent conference in Oxford – entitled Literary Activism – editor Philip Langeskov described how on hearing his pitch of a new novel, sales teams would invariably ask, 'But what other book is it like?' Only when a novel could be presented as having a reassuring resemblance to something already commercially successful was it likely to overcome the sales staff veto.

But even beyond financial questions I would argue that there is a growing resistance at every level to taking risks in novel writing, a tendency that is in line with the more general and ever-increasing anxious desire to receive positive feedback, or at least not negative feedback, about almost everything we do, constantly and instantly. It is a situation that leads to something I will describe, perhaps paradoxically, as an intensification of conformity, people falling over themselves to be approved of.

How can I flesh out this intuition? At some point it slipped into the conversation that high sales are synonymous with achievement in writing. Perhaps copyright was partly responsible. A novelist's work is to be paid for by a percentage of the sales achieved. This aligns the writer's and the publisher's interests and gets us used to thinking about books in terms of numbers sold. Add to that the now obligatory egalitarian view of society, which suggests that all reader responses are of equal worth, and you can easily fall into the habit of judging achievement in terms of the number of readers rather than their quality.

So, when praising a novel they like, critics will often give the impression, or perhaps seek to convince themselves, that the book is a huge commercial success, even when it isn't. Such has been the case with Karl

Ove Knausgaard. Apparently it isn't imaginable that one can pronounce a work a masterpiece and accept that it doesn't sell. Conversely, writer Kirsty Gunn recently spoke (again at the Literary Activism conference) of a revelatory moment when she, her husband, the editor David Graham, and others were celebrating another milestone in the extraordinary success of Yann Martel's *Life of Pi*, which Graham was responsible for publishing in the UK. 'Suddenly I had to leave the room,' Gunn said, describing a moment of intense dismay. 'I realized we had reached the point where we were judging books by their sales.'

Copyright has been with us two hundred years and more, but the consequent attention to sales numbers has been recently and dramatically intensified by electronic media and the immediate feedback it offers. Announce an article (like this one) on Facebook and you can count, as the hours go by, how many people have looked at it, clicked on it, liked it, etc. Publish a novel and you can see *at once* where it stands on the Amazon sales ratings (I remember a publisher mailing me the link when my own novel *Destiny* amazingly crept into Amazon UK's top twenty novels – for about an hour). Otherwise, you can track from day to day how many readers have reviewed it and how many stars they have given it. Everything conspires to have us obsessively attached to the world's response to whatever we do.

Franzen talks about this phenomenon in his recent novel *Purity*, suggesting that, simply by offering us the chance to check constantly whether people are talking about us, the internet heightens a fear of losing whatever popularity we may have achieved: 'the fear of unpopularity and uncoolness... the fear of being flamed or forgotten.' Hence the successful novelist is constantly encouraged to produce more of the same. 'It's incredible,' remarks Murakami in an interview, 'I write a novel every

three or four years, and people are waiting for it. I once
interviewed John Irving, and he told me that reading a
good book is a mainline. Once they are addicted, they're
always waiting.'

Well, is 'addiction' what a literary writer should
want in readers? And if a writer accepts such addiction,
or even rejoices in it, as Murakami seems to, doesn't it
put pressure on him, as pusher, to offer more of the same?
In fact it would be far more plausible to ascribe the
failure (aesthetic, but not commercial) of *Colorless Tsukuru
Tazaki* and indeed Franzen's *Purity*, not to the author's
willingness to take exciting risks with new material
(Ishiguro's bizarre *The Buried Giant*, for example), but
rather to a tired, lacklustre attempt to produce yet
another bestseller in the same vein. Both writers have
in the past taken intriguing distractions from their core
business – Franzen with his idiosyncratic *Kraus Project*,
Murakami with his engaging book on running – but when
it comes to the novel, it's back to the same old formula,
though without perhaps the original inspiration or energy.
Financial freedom is not psychological freedom.

Yet, to create anything, genuinely new writers need
to risk failure, indeed to court failure, aesthetically *and*
commercially, and to do it again and again throughout
their lives, something not easy to square with the growing
tendency to look on fiction writing as a regular career.
'How have you survived as a writer twenty years and
more?' a member of the public asked Kirsty Gunn after
she had spoken of her absolute refusal to adapt her work
to a publisher's sense of what was marketable. 'Day job,'
she briskly replied.

Is it really possible, then, to be free as a writer?
Free from an immediate need for money, free from the
need to be praised, free from the concern of how those
close to you will respond to what you write, free from
the political implications, free from your publisher's

eagerness for a book that looks like the last, or worse still, like whatever the latest fashion might be?

I doubt it, to be honest. Perhaps the best one can ever achieve is a measure of freedom, in line with your personal circumstances. Anyway, here, for what it's worth, are two reflections drawn from my own experience:

1. So long as it's compatible with regular writing, the day job is never to be disdained. A steady income allows you to take risks. Certainly I would never have written books like *Europa* or *Teach Us to Sit Still* without the stability of a university job. I knew the style of *Europa*, obsessive and unrelenting, and the content of *Teach Us to Sit Still*, detailed accounts of urinary nightmares, would turn many off. And they did; one prominent editor refused even to consider *Teach Us*, because 'the word prostate makes me queasy.' Yet both books found enthusiastic audiences who were excited to read something different.

2. When you're trying to write something seriously new, *don't show it to anybody until it's finished.* Don't talk about it, seek no feedback at all. Cultivate a quiet separateness. 'Anything great and bold,' observed Robert Walser, 'must be brought about in secrecy and silence, or it perishes and falls away, and the fire that was awakened dies.'

Oddly enough these are conditions that are most likely to hold at the beginning of your writing career when you're hardly expecting to make money and nobody is waiting for what you do. Which perhaps explains why the most adventurous novels – Günter Grass's *The Tin Drum*, Elsa Morante's *House of Liars*, Kingsley Amis's *Lucky Jim*, J.D. Salinger's *The Catcher in the Rye*, James Baldwin's *Go Tell It on the Mountain*, Nicholson Baker's *The Mezzanine*, Thomas Pynchon's *V*, Marilynne Robinson's *Housekeeping* – are very often early works. Celebrity, it would appear, breeds conformity.

From *The New York Review of Books Daily*

This piece was originally published online by *The New York Review of Books Daily* on 1 December 2015, and was written, in part, in response to the Literary Activism event held St. Hugh's College in Oxford in October 2015.

Notes on Contributors

DEREK ATTRIDGE's many books include studies of poetic form, South African literature (and J.M. Coetzee's fiction in particular), James Joyce, and literary theory (with a special interest in the thought of Jacques Derrida). Work in progress includes a study of poetry in performance from Homer to Shakespeare and an edited collection of essays on Zoë Wicomb. Having taught in the UK and the USA, as well as holding Visiting Professorships in several other countries, he is now Emeritus Professor in the Department of English and Related Literature at the University of York.

SWAPAN CHAKRAVORTY is Rabindranath Tagore Distinguished Chair in the Humanities at Presidency University, Kolkata. He has been Professor of English, Jadavpur University, and Director General, National Library, Kolkata. His books in English and Bengali include *Society and Politics in the Plays of Thomas Middleton* (Clarendon Press, 1996), *Conversations with Gayatri Chakravorty Spivak* (Seagull, 2007), *Bangalir Ingreji Sahityacharcha* (Anustup, 2006), and *Shakespeare* (Papyrus, 1999). His edited book *Mudraner Sanskriti o Bangla Boi* (Ababhas, 2007) won the Narasingh Das Award of Delhi University in 2009. He was a contributory editor to Gary Taylor and John Lavagnino (gen. ed.), *The Collected Works of Thomas Middleton* (Clarendon Press, 2008), and *Thomas Middleton and Early Modern Textual Culture* (Clarendon Press, 2008). He has co-edited three volumes on book history in India.

AMIT CHAUDHURI is the author of six novels, the latest of which is *Odysseus Abroad*. He is also a critic and a musician and composer. He is a Fellow of the Royal Society of Literature. Awards for his fiction include the Commonwealth Writers Prize, the Betty Trask Prize, the Encore Prize, the Los Angeles Times Book Prize for Fiction, and the Indian government's Sahitya Akademi Award. In 2013, he was awarded the first Infosys Prize in the Humanities for outstanding contribution to literary studies. He is Professor of Contemporary Literature at the University of East Anglia.

ROSINKA CHAUDHURI is Professor of Cultural Studies and Dean (Academic Affairs) at the Centre for Studies in Social Sciences, Calcutta (CSSSC). Her most recent publication is *A History of Indian Poetry in English* (New York: Cambridge University Press, 2016). Her books include *The Literary Thing: History, Poetry and the Making of a Modern Literary Culture* (Oxford University Press: 2013, Peter Lang: 2014); *Freedom and Beef-Steaks: Colonial Calcutta Culture* (Orient Blackswan: 2012) and *Gentlemen Poets in Colonial Bengal: Emergent Nationalism and the Orientalist Project* (Seagull: 2002). She has edited *Derozio, Poet of India: A Definitive Edition* (Oxford University Press, 2008), and, with Elleke Boehmer, *The Indian Postcolonial* (Routledge UK, 2010). She has also translated and introduced Rabindranath Tagore in *Letters from a Young Poet (1887-94)* (Penguin Modern Classics, 2014). Currently, she is working on 'An Acre of Green Grass: English Writings of Buddhadeva Bose' for Oxford University Press, New Delhi. Her next research project is tentatively titled 'Young Bengal and the Empire of the Middle Classes'.

JON COOK is a Professor of Literature and Director of the Centre for Creative and Performing Arts at the University of East Anglia (UEA). He has worked closely with Amit Chaudhuri on the development of UEA's programme of creative writing workshops and symposia in India. His recent publications include *Poetry in Theory* and a biographical study, *Hazlitt in Love*. He has taught at universities in India, Europe, and the United States.

DAVID GRAHAM has worked in publishing for over 25 years. He was Managing Director of Canongate Books from 2000 to 2006, followed by similar leadership roles at the literary magazine and book publisher Granta and Portobello Books, and also at The Aurum Publishing Group where he launched the non-fiction imprint Union Books. He is currently the managing director of the award-winning illustrated publisher Pavilion Books. He lives in London with his wife, writer Kirsty Gunn, and their two children.

PETER D. MCDONALD is Professor of English and Related Literature at the University of Oxford and a Fellow of St. Hugh's College. He writes on literature, the modern state, and the freedom of expression; the history of writing systems, cultural institutions, and publishing; multilingualism, translation, and interculturality; and on the limits of literary criticism. His main publications include *British Literary Culture and Publishing Practice, 1888-1914* (Cambridge University Press, 1997), *The Literature Police: Apartheid Censorship and its Cultural Consequences* (Oxford University Press, 2009), and *Artefacts of Writing: Ideas of the State and Communities of Letters from Matthew Arnold to Xu Bing* (Oxford University Press, forthcoming 2017).

JAMIE MCKENDRICK has published six collections of poetry and two Selected Poems. He edited *The Faber Book of 20th-Century Italian Poems* (2004) and has translated the novels and short stories of Giorgio Bassani. The final two novels of Bassani's Romanzo di Ferrara are forthcoming with Penguin Modern Classics. He has translated Valerio Magrelli's poems, *The Embrace* (Faber and Faber, 2009), and Antonella Anedda's poems, *Archipelago* (Bloodaxe, 2015), as well as Pier Paolo Pasolini's verse play *Affabulazione*, which was performed at the London Print Room.

SAIKAT MAJUMDAR is the author, most recently, of the novel *The Firebird*, one of *The Telegraph*'s (Calcutta) Best Books of 2015, and a finalist for the Bangalore Literature Festival Fiction Prize. The novel is forthcoming in the US in 2017 as *Play House*. He is also the author of *Prose of the World* (2013), which received Honourable Mention in the Modernist Studies Association's Annual Book Prize, 2014, and an earlier novel, *Silverfish* (2007). He is currently at work on new book titled 'The Amateur', along with a new novel. He is Professor of English and Creative Writing at Ashoka University, Haryana, India.

TIM PARKS is a novelist, essayist, travel writer, and translator based in Italy. Author of fifteen novels, including *Europa, Destiny, Cleaver*, and, more recently, *Thomas & Mary: A Love Story*; he has translated works by Moravia, Calvino, Calasso, Machiavelli, and Leopardi. While running a postgraduate degree course in translation in Milan, he writes regularly for the *London Review of Books* and *The New York Review of Books*. His many non-fiction works include *Italian Neighbours, An Italian Education, A Season with Verona and Italian Ways*, as well as a memoir on chronic pain and meditation, *Teach Us to Sit Still*. His critical work includes the essay collection *Where I'm Reading From*, and most recently, *The Novel: A Survival Skill*, a reflection on the relationship between novelists, their writing, and their readers.

DUBRAVKA UGREŠIĆ is a writer based in Amsterdam. She is the author of several novels (*Baba Yaga Laid an Egg, The Ministry of Pain, The Museum of Unconditional Surrender*), short story collections (*Lend Me Your Character*) and essays (*Europe in Sepia, Karaoke Culture, Nobody's Home*). Ugrešić is a recipient of several literary awards (Neustadt Literary Prize). For more detailed information visit Ugrešić's website: www.dubravkaugresic. com

LAETITIA ZECCHINI is a research fellow at the CNRS in Paris, France. Her research interests and publications focus on contemporary Indian poetry, the politics of literature, postcolonial criticism as a field of debate, and issues of modernism and cosmopolitanism. She is the author of *Arun Kolatkar and Literary Modernism in India: Moving Lines* (Bloomsbury, 2014), and has recently co-edited two journal issues ('Problèmes d'histoire littéraire indienne' for the *Revue de Littérature comparée*, 2015, and 'Penser à partir de l'Inde' for the journal *Littérature*, 2016). She is currently working on questions of censorship and cultural regulation in India and on a special issue of the *Journal of Postcolonial Writing* called 'The Worlds of Bombay Poetry'.